Spelling

for Christian Schools® 6

Home Teacher's Edition

Bob Jones University Press, Greenville, SC 29614

Consultants
from the administration, faculty, and staff of Bob Jones University

Philip D. Smith, Ed.D., *Provost*
Grace C. Collins, Ph.D., Chairman, *Department of Linguistics*
Kenneth H. Frederick, Ph.D., Chairman, *Division of Practical Studies,*
    School of Religion
Walter G. Fremont, Ed.D., *Dean of the School of Education*
Melva M. Heintz, M.A., *Elementary Principal*
Janice A. Joss, M.A.T., *Graduate School of Education*
James Davis, M.A., *Project Director, Bob Jones University Press*

NOTE:
The fact that materials produced by other publishers are referred to in this volume does not constitute an endorsement by Bob Jones University Press of the content or theological position of these materials or any other materials produced by such publishers. The position of Bob Jones University Press, and the University itself, is well known. Any references and ancillary materials are listed as an aid to the student or the teacher in an attempt to maintain accepted academic standards of the publishing industry.

Photo Credits
The following agencies and individuals have furnished materials to meet the photographic needs of this textbook. We wish to express our gratitude to them for their important contribution.

Suzanne Altizer 21
Chicago Department of Aviation 109
George R. Collins 49
Digital Stock 53
Dave Fisher 25
Greenville County Library 101
Brian D. Johnson 41, 89, 93, 121
Sam Laterza 69
PhotoDisc, Inc. cover photo
George Rogier 117
Unusual Films 5, 9, 13, 17, 29, 33, 37, 45, 57, 61, 65, 70, 77, 81, 85, 97, 125, 129, 133, 137, 141, 145
Georgi P. Vins 113
John Wolseiffer 105

SPELLING 6 for Christian Schools® Home Teacher's Edition

Authors
Joanne Hall and Ann Greenleaf
    With Jan Joss and Arlene Orton

Other Contributors
Gloria Repp, Connie Collins, Tim Davis, Billy Howard, and Grace Suh

Project Editor
Suzette Jordan

Produced in cooperation with the Bob Jones University School of Education, Bob Jones Elementary School, and selected home educators.

for Christian Schools is a registered trademark of Bob Jones University Press.

©1990, 2000 Bob Jones University Press
Greenville, South Carolina 29614

Printed in the United States of America
All rights reserved

ISBN 1-57924-412-2

15 14 13 12 11 10 9 8 7 6 5 4

Contents

especially written for a home-setting

a program designed to teach the skill of spelling by:

1 Focusing on phonics principles.
The lessons take advantage of the many regularities of English spelling, building on the same phonics principles that are used in teaching reading.

2 Emphasizing the understanding of patterns and generalizations, rather than memorizing lists of words.
Instead of memorizing each word, the student is led to understand a spelling pattern so that he can use the knowledge of that pattern to spell other words with the same pattern.

3 Supporting interactive teaching that draws on a student's knowledge and reasoning.
The student is actively involved in the teaching-learning process through the teacher's use of questions and discussion.

4 Applying spelling skills through original composition activities.
By writing weekly in a journal, the student has an opportunity to apply his spelling skill in a meaningful and enjoyable setting. During this time he is using words from his own vocabulary, is aware of how he spells, and is receiving help so that he can correctly spell all the words he uses.

5 Teaching a study cycle that makes use of visual, auditory, and kinesthetic approaches to learning.
The study method endorsed enables the student to see, hear, and write the word each time he studies it.

6 Teaching graded dictionary skills.
Since the dictionary is a spelling and writing tool, the student should learn not only to use it but also to think of it in connection with spelling and writing.

7 Making use of a pretest, a midweek test, and a final test.
Tests, which are planned to fall on the *recall* part of the learning cycle, *recall–study–recall–study–recall,* are used as teaching tools and not simply as a means of evaluating the student's progress. The week begins with a *pretest,* the first *recall* of the cycle, and is a significant factor in the fostering of permanent learning.

8 Including activities to instill an interest in and a love for the English language.
Each weekly unit contains a study of how to interpret a modern word that is used in the Bible.

Suggested Daily Schedule
for Home Education

Grade 1

First Grade English Skills . . . . 60-70 min.
    Listening . . . . 5-10 min.
    Phonics and Structural Analysis . . . . 15-20 min.
    Handwriting . . . . 5-10 min.
    Word Work . . . . 10-15 min.
    Grammar and Composition . . . . 10-15 min.
Spelling . . . . 15-20 min.
Bible . . . . 20-30 min.
Reading . . . . 20-30 min.
Heritage/Science . . . . 15-25 min.
Math . . . . 15-25 min.
Music/Art . . . . 15-25 min.

Grades 2-6

Bible . . . . 20-25 min.
Writing and Grammar . . . . 15-30 min.
Reading . . . . 20-30 min.
Math . . . . 20-30 min.
Spelling . . . . 15-25 min.
Handwriting . . . . 5-10 min.
Heritage/Science . . . . 15-25 min.
Music/Art . . . . 15-25 min.

Table of Daily Lesson Content

Week Unit	Day	Student Page	Lesson Emphasis
1	1	2	Pretest Skills: adding a suffix beginning with a vowel to a word ending in *ss* adding a suffix that forms a different part of speech division of words with VC/CV Guided research activity: *Where in the World?*
	2	3 3-4	Word for Word: *impression* Worktext activity: word meaning and spelling practice
	3	146-47 148	Study time and trial test Introduce dictionary section of worktext Dictionary skill: estimation of place of words in a dictionary Worktext activity: dictionary skill reinforcement
	4	5	Journal writing: how I've changed
	5	5	Study time and final test The King's English: *profession*
2	1	6 6	Pretest Word bank selections Skills: adding a suffix beginning with a vowel to a consonant ending with a consonant letter using morphophonemics as an aid to spelling Guided research activity: *Where in the World?*
	2	7 7-8	Word for Word: *hospital* Worktext activity: word meaning and spelling practice Guided activity: *Connect a Word*
	3	149	Study time and trial test Dictionary skills: guide words Worktext activity: dictionary skill reinforcement
	4	9	Journal writing: making this a good year
	5	9	Study time and final test The King's English: *evangelist*
3	1	10 10	Pretest Word bank selections Skills: adding a suffix beginning with a vowel to a word ending with a consonant adding an extra letter before adding an ending using morphophonemics as an aid to spelling Guided research activity: *Where in the World?*
	2	11 11-12	Word for Word: *exhibit* Worktext activity: word meaning and spelling practice Guided activity: *If and Might*
	3	150 150	Study time and trial test Dictionary skill: entry words Worktext activity: dictionary skill reinforcement
	4	13	Journal writing: choosing friends
	5	13	Study time and final test The King's English: *habitation*

Week Unit	Day	Student Page	Lesson Emphasis

4	1	14
		14
			Pretest
			Word bank selections
			Skills: adding a suffix beginning with a vowel letter to a
			    word ending with a consonant letter
			    adding a suffix beginning with *o* to a word that ends
			    with *ge*
			    using morphophonemics to aid in spelling
			Guided research activity: *Where in the World?*

	2	15 15-16	Word for Word: *humor* Worktext activity: word meaning and spelling practice
	3	151 151	Study time and trial test Dictionary skill: proper noun entries Worktext activity: dictionary skill reinforcement
	4	17	Journal writing: my reaction to punishment
	5	17	Study time and final test The King's English: *seraphim*
5	1	18 18	Pretest Word bank selections Skills: adding the suffix *-or* suffixes and parts of speech Guided research activity: *Where in the World?*
	2	19 19-20	Word for Word: *detect* Worktext activity: word meaning and spelling practice
	3	152	Study time and trial test Dictionary skill: location of words in a dictionary Worktext activity: dictionary skill reinforcement
	4	21	Journal writing: being responsible
	5	21	Study time and final test The King's English: *direct*
6	1	22 22	Skills: review skills of Units 1-5 Worktext activity: phonics review
	2	23-24	Worktext activity: word meaning and spelling practice Guided activity: *Analogies Anonymous*
	3		Study time and trial test
	4	25	Journal writing: serving others
	5	25	Study time and final test The King's English: *transgression*

Week Unit	Day	Student Page	Lesson Emphasis
7	1	26 26	Pretest Word bank selections Skills: /yo͞on/ spelled *un*, meaning related to "one" /bī/ or /bə/ spelled *bi*, meaning related to "two" /trī/ spelled *tri*, meaning related to "three" Guided research activity: *Where in the World?*
	2	27 27-28	Word for Word: *union* Worktext activity: word meaning and spelling practice Guided activity: *Test Your Tongue*
	3	153 153	Study time and trial test Dictionary skill: word forms Worktext activity: dictionary skill reinforcement
	4	29	Journal writing: on winning
	5	29	Study time and final test The King's English: *jealous*
8	1	30 30	Pretest Word bank selections Skills: /tĕl/ spelled *tel*, meaning related to "far" /skōp/ or /skŏp/ spelled *scope* or *scop*, meaning related to "view" /mī•krō/ spelled *micro*, meaning related to "small" Guided research activity: *Where in the World?*
	2	31 31-32	Word for Word: *microbe* Worktext activity: word meaning and spelling practice Guided word meaning activity: *Fit the Clue*
	3	154	Study time and trial test Dictionary skill: sample sentences Worktext activity: dictionary skills reinforcement
	4	33	Journal writing: on losing
	5	33	Study time and final test The King's English: *scapegoat*
9	1	34 34	Pretest Word bank selections Skills: /jē•ŏ/ spelled *geo*, meaning related to "earth" /mŏn′ə/ or /mə•nŏ′/ spelled *mono*, meaning related to "single" /grăf/ spelled *graph*, meaning related to "written" /ô′tə/ or /ô′tō/ spelled *auto*, meaning related to "self" Guided research activity: *Where in the World?*
	2	35 35-36	Word for Word: *autograph* Worktext activity: word meaning and spelling practice Guided activity: *All About Me*
	3	155 155	Study time and trial test Dictionary skills: pronunciation key Worktext activity: dictionary skills reinforcement
	4	37	Journal writing: what I collect
	5	37	Study time and final test The King's English: *paradise*

Week / Unit	Day	Student Page	Lesson Emphasis
10	1	38 38	Pretest Word bank selections Skills: /dīn/ spelled *dyn* at the beginning of a word, meaning related to "power" /hīd/ or /hīd•rō/ spelled *hyd* and *hydro*, meaning related to "water" /bī•ŏ/ or /bī•ə/ spelled *bio* at the beginning of a word, meaning related to "life" /âr/ spelled *aer* at the beginning of a word, meaning related to "air" Guided research activity: *Where in the World?*
	2	39 39-40	Word for Word: *hydrophobia* Worktext activity: word meaning and spelling skill Guided activity: *Who-What?*
	3	 156	Study time and trial test Dictionary skill: identifying primary and secondary syllable stress Worktext activity: dictionary skills reinforcement
	4	41	Journal writing: I love my country
	5	41	Study time and final test The King's English: *conscience*
11	1	42 42	Pretest Word bank selections Skills: /dī•ə/ or /dī•ă′/ spelled *dia*, meaning related to "across" or "through" /mē•tər/ or /mə•tər/ spelled *meter*, meaning related to "measure" Guided research activity: *Where in the World?*
	2	43 43-44	Word for Word: *diamond* Worktext activity: word meaning and spelling practice Guided activity: *Concentration*
	3	 157	Study time and trial test Dictionary skill: understanding the definition in a dictionary entry Worktext activity: dictionary skills reinforcement
	4	45	Journal writing: being thankful
	5	45	Study time and final test The King's English: *surety*
12	1	46	Skills: review skills of Units 7-11
	2	47-48	Worktext activity: word meaning Guided activity: *Sense and Nonsense*
	3		Study time and trial test Guided activity: *SETtle It!*
	4	49	Journal writing: a time capsule
	5	49	Study time and final test The King's English: *hallelujah*

Week Unit	Day	Student Page	Lesson Emphasis

13	1	50
		50
		50
			Pretest
			Word bank selections
			Skills: adding a suffix beginning with a vowel letter to a word
			      ending with a consonant letter
			      syllable rule: VC/CV *(an•noy)*
			      syllable rule: V/CV *(ma•jor)*
			      syllable rule: VC/V *(legal•ity)*
			      syllable rule: VV (one sound) *(an•noy•ance)*
			Guided research activity: *Where in the World?*

	2	51 51-52	Word for Word: *annoy* Worktext activity: word meaning and spelling practice
	3	 158 158	Study time and trial test Dictionary skill: choosing the best definition Worktext activity: dictionary skill reinforcement
	4	53	Journal writing: after graduation
	5	 53	Study time and final test The King's English: *adorn*

14	1	54
		54
		54
			Pretest
			Word bank selections
			Skills: adding a suffix beginning with a vowel letter to a word
			      ending in *e*
			      changing *-le* to *-ility*
			Guided research activity: *Where in the World?*

	2	55 55-56	Word for Word: *appreciate* Worktext activity: spelling practice, word meaning Guided activity: *Content Conclusion*
	3	 159 159	Study time and trial test Dictionary skill: choosing the correct entry word Worktext activity: dictionary skill reinforcement
	4	57	Journal writing: reading at home
	5	 57	Study time and final test The King's English: *promote*

15	1	58
		58
			Pretest
			Word bank selections
			Skills: adding a suffix beginning with *i* to a word ending with
			      a hard *c*
			      adding a suffix beginning with *i* to a word ending
			      with /k/ spelled *c*
			      dropping the *y* before adding a suffix beginning with a
			      vowel letter
			Guided research activity: *Where in the World?*

	2	59 59-60	Word for Word: *optical* Worktext activity: word meaning and suffix spellings Guided activity: *Concentration*
	3	 160 160	Study time and trial test Dictionary skill: recognizing synonyms Worktext activity: suffix spellings
	4	61	Journal writing: Christmas
	5	 61	Study time and final test The King's English: *melody*

Week Unit	Day	Student Page	Lesson Emphasis

16	1	62 62	Pretest
			Word bank selections
			Skills: adding a two-syllable ending
			    adding a suffix beginning with a vowel letter to a word
			    ending in *e*
			Guided research activity: *Where in the World?*

	2	63 63-64	Word for Word: *execute* Worktext activity: word meaning and spelling practice
	3	161 161	Study time and trial test Dictionary skill: recognizing homonyms and choosing the correct one Worktext activity: dictionary skill reinforcement
	4	65	Journal writing: why I don't get everything I want
	5	65	Study time and final test The King's English: *guide*

17	1	66 66	Pretest
			Word bank selections
			Skills: using morphophonemics to aid in spelling
			    adding the suffix *-ity* to words ending in *ile*
			    adding the suffix *-ity* to words ending in *ble*
			Guided research activity: *Learning About the States*

	2	67 67-68	Word for Word: *futile* Worktext activity: word meaning Guided activity: *Thinkalogies*
	3	162 162	Study time and trial test Dictionary skill: recognizing slang, idioms, and informal language Worktext activity: dictionary skill reinforcement
	4	69	Journal writing: why I like Sunday
	5	69	Study time and final test The King's English: *present*
18	1	70	Skills: review skills of Units 13-17
	2	71-72	Worktext activity: word meaning and spelling practice
	3		Study time and trial test Guided activity: *Words in the News*
	4	73	Journal writing: elderly people
	5	73	Study time and final test The King's English: *congregation*

Week Unit	Day	Student Page	Lesson Emphasis
19	1	74 74	Pretest Word bank selections Skills: /ăst/ or /əst/ spelled *ast*, meaning related to "star" /sĕn/ or /sĕnt/ spelled *cen* or *cent* at the beginning of a word, meaning related to "hundred" /mĭl/ or /məl/ spelled *mill* at the beginning of a word, meaning related to "thousand" Guided research activity: *Where in the World?*
	2	75 75-76	Word for Word: *astronaut* Worktext activity: word meaning and spelling practice Guided activity: *Say It in a Word*
	3	163 163	Study time and trial test Dictionary skill: using patterns and rules to divide words into syllables Worktext activity: dictionary skill reinforcement
	4	77	Journal writing: when my friend got something I wanted
	5	77	Study time and final test The King's English: *cherubim*
20	1	78 78	Pretest Word bank selections Skills: /tĕr•ə/ or /tər/ spelled *terri* or *ter*, meaning related to "earth" /mŭl•tə/ spelled *multi* at the beginning of a word, meaning related to "many" /krĕd/ or /krĭd/ spelled *cred*, meaning related to "believe" Guided research activity: *Where in the World?*
	2	79 79-80	Word for Word: *credible* Worktext activity: word meaning and spelling skill
	3	164 164	Study time and trial test Dictionary skill: using accent mark rules Dictionary activity: dictionary skill reinforcement
	4	81	Journal writing: I got something my friend wanted
	5	81	Study time and final test The King's English: *convert*
21	1	82 82	Pretest Word bank selections Skills: /ô•də/, /ô•dē/, or /ô•dĭ/ spelled *audi* at the beginning of a word, meaning related to "to hear" /kôr/ or /kôrp/ spelled *corp*, meaning related to "body" /vĭ/ spelled *vi* at the beginning of a word, meaning related to "to see" Guided research activity: *Where in the World?*
	2	83 83-84	Word for Word: *audition* Worktext activity: word meaning and spelling practice Guided activity: *Remember, Remember*
	3	165 165	Study time and trial test Dictionary skill: identifying words that have more than one spelling Worktext activity: dictionary skill reinforcement
	4	85	Journal writing: going out to eat
	5	85	Study time and final test The King's English: *audience*

Week Unit	Day	Student Page	Lesson Emphasis
22	1	86 86	Pretest Word bank selections Skills: /pŏp•yə/ spelled *popu* at the beginning of a word, meaning related to "people" /sōl/ or /sŏl/ spelled *sol* at the beginning of a word, meaning related to "alone" /vĕr/ or /vûr/ spelled *ver* at the beginning of a word, meaning related to "true" Guided research activity: *Where in the World?*
	2	87 87-88	Word for Word: *sole* Worktext activity: word meaning and spelling practice
	3	166	Study time and trial test Worktext activity: dictionary skill review
	4	89	Journal writing: something that seemed bad turned out to be something good
	5	89	Study time and final test The King's English: *manager*
23	1	90 90	Pretest Word bank selections Skills: /ĕv•ə/ spelled *evi* at the beginning of a word, meaning related to "to see" /grăj/ spelled *grad* at the beginning of a word, meaning related to "step" or "degree" /kûr/ or /kər/ spelled *cur* at the beginning of a word, meaning related to "to run" /lĭb/ spelled *lib* at the beginning of a word, meaning related to "free" Guided research activity: *Where in the World?*
	2	91 91-92	Word for Word: *currency* Worktext activity: word meaning and spelling practice puzzle, suffixes, word meaning Guided activity: *Tongue Twisters*
	3	167	Study time and trial test Dictionary skill: pronunciation key Worktext activity: dictionary skill reinforcement
	4	93	Journal writing: something that seemed good turned out to be bad
	5	93	Study time and final test The King's English: *liberty*
24	1	94 94	Skills: review skills of Units 19-23 Worktext activity: spelling practice
	2	95-96	Worktext activity: word meaning and spelling practice
	3		Guided activity: *Context Clues* Study time and trial test Guided activity: *Letter by Letter*
	4	97	Journal writing: I was ridiculed for my beliefs
	5	97	Study time and final test The King's English: *manifest*

Week Unit	Day	Student Page	Lesson Emphasis
25	1	98 98	Pretest Word bank selections Skills: adding a suffix beginning with a vowel letter to a word ending in silent *e* closed syllables open syllables Guided research activity: *Where in the World?*
	2	99 99-100	Word for Word: *perspire* Worktext activity: word meaning and spelling practice Guided activity: *Rhymealong*
	3	168 168	Study time and trial test Dictionary skill: part of speech Worktext activity: dictionary skill reinforcement
	4	101	Journal writing: if I could live anywhere
	5	101	Study time and final test The King's English: *sanctification*
26	1	102 102	Pretest Word bank selections Skills: adding a suffix beginning with a vowel letter to a word ending with *e* adding a suffix beginning with a consonant letter to a word ending with *e* Guided research activity: *Where in the World?*
	2	103 103-4	Word for Word: *statistics* Worktext activity: word meaning and spelling practice Guided activity: *Think and Replace*
	3	169 169	Study time and trial test Dictionary skill: etymologies Worktext activity: dictionary skill reinforcement
	4	105	Journal writing: lost in a foreign country
	5	105	Study time and final test The King's English: *virtuous*
27	1	106 106	Pretest Word bank selections Skills: difficult spellings and pronunciations Guided research activity: *Where in the World?*
	2	107 107-8	Word for Word: *kindergarten* Worktext activity: word meaning and spelling practice Guided activity: *Alpha and Omega*
	3	170	Study time and trial test Worktext activity: dictionary skill review of etymologies
	4	109	Journal writing: alone in a big city
	5	109	Study time and final test The King's English: *sepulcher*

Week Unit	Day	Student Page	Lesson Emphasis
28	1	110 110	Pretest Word bank selections Skills: difficult pairs of words reviewing rules for syllabication Guided research activity: *Where in the World?*
	2	111 111-12	Word for Word: *solution* Worktext activity: word meaning and spelling practice Guided activity: *Latin Relatives*
	3	171 171	Study time and trial test Dictionary skill: choice of correct definition Worktext activity: dictionary skill reinforcement
	4	113	Journal writing: living in the Soviet Union
	5	113	Study time and final test The King's English: *intercession*
29	1	114 114	Pretest Word bank selections Skills: adding a suffix that causes an internal change Guided research activity: *Where in the World?*
	2	115 115-16	Word for Word: *mischief* Worktext activity: word meaning and spelling practice Guided activity: *Best Choice*
	3	172 172	Study time and trial test Dictionary skill: definitions Worktext activity: dictionary skill reinforcement
	4	117	Journal writing: my country
	5	117	Study time and final test The King's English: *revelation*
30	1	118 118	Skills: review skills of Units 25-29 Worktext activity: spelling practice
	2	119-20	Worktext activity: word meaning and spelling practice Guided activity: *Just the Same*
	3		Study time and trial test Guided activity: *Alike or Not*
	4	121	Journal writing: describing myself to a pen pal
	5	121	Study time and final test The King's English: *abundance*

Week Unit	Day	Student Page	Lesson Emphasis
31	1	122 122	Pretest Word bank selection Skills: /nā/ or /nə/ spelled *na* at the beginning of a word, meaning related to ''to be born'' /nā/ or /năt/ spelled *na* or *nat* at the beginning of a word, meaning related to ''nature'' /grā/ or /grăt/ spelled *gra* or *grat* at the beginning of a word, meaning related to ''pleasing'' /sûr/ or /sər/ spelled *cir* at the beginning of a word, meaning related to ''around'' Guided research activity: *Where in the World?*
	2	123 123-24	Word for Word: *circus* Worktext activity: word meaning and spelling practice Guided activity: *Which Word?*
	3	 173	Study time and trial test Dictionary skills: etymologies Worktext activity: dictionary skill reinforcement
	4	125	Journal writing: my grandparents
	5	 125	Study time and final test The King's English: *regeneration*
32	1	126 126	Pretest Word bank selections Skills: /dĭk/ spelled *dict* at the beginning of a word, meaning related to ''to say'' /pôrt/ spelled *port*, meaning related to ''to carry'' /spēsh/, /spəsh/, and /spĕsh/ spelled *spec*, meaning related to ''kind'' or ''appearance'' Guided research activity: *Where in the World?*
	2	127 127-28	Word for Word: *species* Worktext activity: word meaning and spelling practice Guided activity: *Definition Delight*
	3	 174 174	Study time and trial test Dictionary skill: checking the spelling of words with suffixes Worktext activity: dictionary skill reinforcement
	4	129	Journal writing: an unforgettable experience
	5	 129	Study time and final test The King's English: *sabbath*
33	1	130	Pretest Word bank selection Skills: /trăns/ spelled *trans* at the beginning of a word, meaning related to ''across'' or ''through'' Guided research activity: *Where in the World?*
	2	131 131-32	Word for Word: *translate* Worktext activity: word meaning and spelling practice Guided activity: *Words Within*
	3	 175 175	Study time and trial test Dictionary skill: checking the spelling of a word Worktext activity: dictionary skill reinforcement
	4	133	Journal writing: looking forward to being a teen-ager
	5	 133	Study time and final test The King's English: *husbandman*

Week Unit	Day	Student Page	Lesson Emphasis
34	1	134 134	Pretest Word bank selection Skills: /sĭm/ or /sĭn/ spelled *sym* or *syn* at the beginning of a word, meaning related to "together" /krŏn/ spelled *chron,* meaning related to "time" /ĕks/ spelled *ex* at the beginning of a word, meaning related to "to reach" or "outward" Guided research activity: *Where in the World?*
	2	135 135-36	Word for Word: *symptom* Worktext activity: word meaning and spelling practice Guided activity: *Fillerup*
	3	176	Study time and trial test Worktext activity: using the dictionary to check spellings
	4	137	Journal writing: an answer to prayer
	5	137	Study time and final test The King's English: *synagogue*
35	1	138 138	Pretest Word bank selection Skill: French word origins Guided research activity: *Where in the World?*
	2	139 139-40	Word for Word: *bouquet* Worktext activity: word meaning and spelling practice Guided activity: *Match-Up*
	3	177 177	Study time and trial test Dictionary skill: proofreading Worktext activity: dictionary skill reinforcement
	4	141	Journal writing: a job I had
	5	141	Study time and final test The King's English: *endure*
36	1	142 142	Skills: review skills of Units 31-35 Worktext activity: word meaning
	2	143-44	Worktext activity: word meaning and spelling practice Guided activity: *The Clue Review*
	3		Study time and trial test Guided activity: *Country Haiku*
	4	145	Journal writing: sixth grade
	5	145	Study time and final test The King's English: *transfiguration*

Instructional Materials

Teacher's Materials

Teacher Manual This manual includes all of the daily lesson plans for teaching spelling generalizations, dictionary skills, journal writing, study skills, guided activities, and vocabulary building. Along with the lesson plans, this volume features miniature reproductions (with answers) of the student's *Spelling Worktext*. This manual also includes a section entitled *General Lesson Plans,* which provides the teacher with information and special help in teaching each segment of the lesson plans in *SPELLING for Christian Schools® 6 Home Teacher's Edition.*

Home Student's Materials

Student Worktext This worktext provides lists of words that are chosen because of their frequent use in the writing and speech of a sixth grader. The words are drawn from word families that are taught in phonics and are found on researched lists of words and from the content areas.

As in phonics, words are grouped according to generalizations that teach spelling patterns. Interesting activities that center on word meanings help the student enjoy using the listed words with each lesson. A new dictionary skill is taught and then practiced in an enjoyable, theme-oriented activity. The book features a journal-writing activity that promotes the application of spelling through creative, written language.

General Lesson Plans

Dear Home Educator,

The formation of this spelling program is based on research into how children learn. If the teaching methodology suggested is followed closely, your student will eventually have success in spelling. The worktext is of great value only if it is used as part of the total program. Detailed instructions for teaching each part of the spelling program are given in the information that follows.

Much time can be saved by reading this section in total before teaching the first unit of spelling. When you complete the reading, you will have an understanding of the philosophy behind the program.

The Spelling Authors

General Information

- **Understanding the nature of spelling**

  Learning to spell does not usually come as easily for students as learning to read. The reason for this is that a student cannot develop all the skills he needs to spell as quickly as he can learn to decode (in reading) or use context clues. The majority of students when trying to spell words, rely totally on their visual memories. For most students, this is not enough. If a student can develop other skills to use in spelling, he will be more successful. He cannot develop all the skills he needs to spell as quickly as he can learn to decode (in reading) or use context clues. Achievement-test spelling scores, therefore, should not be compared to reading scores. A student's spelling success can be seen if scores progress from one year to another.

- **Learning to spell**

  We need to teach spelling first through the eye-gate (the visual sense) by grouping words together that have a certain spelling pattern. Using these groupings, we can then teach the generalizations that determined how the words were grouped. The teaching of a generalization draws a student's attention to certain spelling patterns. Only a certain number of these patterns, however, can be included in a given spelling lesson. Because there are 250 spellings for the forty-four sounds, spelling instruction should not stop with the primary grades but should be taught throughout the upper elementary grades also. We try to involve three approaches to learning when we teach spelling: visual, auditory, and kinesthetic. Your student sees the word on the page, he hears the sounds in the word each time it is read orally or repeated, and he writes the word.

It is through the actual application of spelling in the writing experience that a student has the opportunity to remember and use what he saw in the pattern groupings, and also what he has seen before in his reading experience. Since spelling is a *writing* skill, the emphasis of the teacher should always be on writing (composition).

- **Reading the symbol for a sound**

  In a generalization there will often be a symbol that is a representation for a sound heard in some of the list words. There will be slashes around the symbol, and these slashes should be read "the sound."

  > The symbol /ā/ is read "the long a sound."

- **Understanding the relationship between sounds and spellings**

  When a word is dictated, the student hears the sound and must write the spelling.

  > /l/ is sometimes spelled *ll* at the end of a word. Your student hears the sound /l/ at the end of a word and writes the letters *ll.*

- **Teaching by asking questions (inductive teaching)**

  This type of teaching is the process by which you, the teacher, ask questions that encourage your student to make observations about the information presented. In using this method to teach spelling, you not only involve your student in really looking at the words, but you also encourage him to think about the spellings. At the same time, you help him discover what he *already* knows about the words and their spellings.

First Day

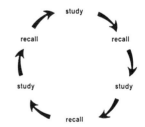

- **Giving the pretest**

  The pretest is an important part of your student's learning process. It represents the *first recall* in the cycle *recall-study-recall-study-recall,* which, if followed, should lead to successful spelling. The pretest serves as the initial contact with the unit's words. It introduces the spelling patterns and generates the thought processes that will aid in understanding the information taught that week. As you give each pretest, use the following procedure:

1. Help your student relax by letting him know that he may make mistakes on this test, but that you want him to try to write the words as he thinks they are spelled.
2. Instruct him to keep his worktext closed until *after* the pretest.
3. Begin the pretest by telling your student to look for spelling patterns as he writes the words. You may also ask him to make observations during the pretest. Remember, you are teaching him, not testing him.
4. Pronounce the word, use it in a sentence, repeat it, and then instruct your student to write it.
5. After all the words have been dictated and after the student has written his responses, ask him to to open his book and check his own pretest.

• **Checking the pretest**

Your student checks his own spelling against the correct spelling. In doing this, he is taking another step toward permanent learning. As he checks his spelling, he rewrites any incorrect words.

• **Choosing the week's *Word Bank* words**

Your student chooses his weekly *Word Bank* words from a section located in the back of the spelling worktext called *My Word Bank*. Further explanation about where these words come from is found under the instructions for the *Fourth Day*.

After your student corrects his pretest, he chooses two words from his *Word Bank* and writes them on lines 19 and 20 of the spelling list. Each one is a *Word Bank Entry*.

When he takes his third- and fifth-day spelling tests, he should be ready to spell these two words correctly. You will be told how to handle correctly spelled *Word Bank* words under the instructions for the *Fifth Day*.

• **Introducing the generalization words (words 1-14)**

As you teach the generalizations, show your student how the words relate to each other, and help him discover common spelling patterns by asking questions. The generalizations are not memorized; instead, they are recognized and applied to the list words as well as other encountered words.

• **Introducing the nongeneralization words (words 15-18)**

Because these words do not necessarily fit into common spelling patterns, they are more difficult to remember. Read each of the words to your student, and give any visual associations that might aid the spelling of these words.

In sixth grade your student will be spelling various countries. You will be discussing facts already known about each country along with doing research with encyclopedias, newspapers, and magazines to discover new information.

• **Completing the handwritten list**

After teaching the generalizations and after introducing the nongeneralization words, your student writes each of the words in the list on the lines provided in the spelling worktext. The lines appear on the first page of each unit, except for the review units. (You will need to remind your student often to use his most legible handwriting and to spell each word correctly.) After he writes each word completely, check his handwriting and his spelling, so that he will see and read only a correctly spelled word.

• **Placing the accent marks**

After spelling the word correctly with clear handwriting in the handwritten list, your student must correctly *place the accent mark* where it belongs in each word in the printed list. This will help him learn how the stress in each word affects its pronunciation and also how the pronunciation of a word helps in spelling it.

Second Day

- **Using the Bible-verse activity**

  After reading the verse (which is located at the top of the second page of each lesson) discuss what it means and how it can be applied. Ask your student to point out the spelling word in the verse.

- **Using the *Word for Word* activity**

  This section is meant to be read and enjoyed. Begin by asking your student to share what he knows about the meaning of the word. This will increase his reading comprehension (understanding) as he then reads information he has just recalled. He will add new facts to his knowledge, building upon concepts he had prior to reading this section. You may need to read it to him at first as he reads it silently beside you. Point out the drawing and other interesting things written about the word. Give your student time to practice reading this section on his own. He may wish to read it to you or to another family member.

- **Using the reinforcement activities**

  Allow your student to complete the reinforcement activities (located on the second and third pages of each lesson), giving help only when it is needed. These activities are designed to strengthen word meaning and the skills of the unit.

- **Developing word meaning**

  Included in this manual are word meaning activities. Each activity is designed to develop and reinforce the meaning of spelling words from the list. The teacher is encouraged to create similar word challenges in units where this activity is not found.

A. Read the verse.
   1. Underline the three verbs that describe what the writer is asking God to do.
   2. Circle the word in the verse that has the Bible meaning "to test, to try, to prove," but today means "to look at fully; to inspect."

> *Examine* me, O Lord, and *prove* me; *try my reins and my heart.*"
> *Psalm 26:2*

B. The incorrect word part in each of these nonsense words contains a clue to help you change it to a correct spelling word.

   1. allicipate
   2. termoutate
   3. potama
   4. exayours
   5. narmousion
   6. examicountry
   7. fascoutate
   8. persteeple
   9. narreat
   10. pakaretan

   1. participate
   2. terminate
   3. Panama
   4. examine
   5. narration
   6. examination
   7. fascinate
   8. perspire
   9. narrate
   10. Pakistan

C. Find and write a spelling word that is an antonym (the opposite) of each word in italics.

   1. My dad told us only yesterday of the *beginning* of his job at the space center.
   2. I sat down to *ignore* my new book.
   3. My teacher always wants complete *withdrawal* from her class.

   1. termination
   2. examine
   3. participation

D. Arrange the countries in this unit in order according to population size, beginning with the highest population. Use your Spelling Dictionary.

   1. Pakistan
   2. Nigeria
   3. Norway
   4. Panama

WORD FOR WORD

perspire

Did you know that your skin is full of holes? The next time you perspire after a game of basketball, look at the droplets of moisture on your arm or your face.

The word *perspire* comes from two Latin words: *per*, meaning "through," and *spirare*, meaning "to breathe." The process of perspiration provides your body with a superb cooling system that seems to breathe through the tiny openings, or pores, of your skin.

99

E. Several spelling words are hidden in the design below. Find them by connecting only the lines that are given. (The letters may be used more than once.)

   1. participate
   2. fascination
   3. Nigeria
   4. participation
   5. Panama
   6. termination
   7. starvation
   8. Pakistan
   9. terminate
   10. fascinate
   11. examine
   12. starve
   13. examination

F. Write the spelling word that best completes each newspaper advertisement.

Free eye ___1___ Visit Operation Eye at 290 Reservation Road.

Help fight ___2___ in Africa. Give to the "Fight for Life" fund.

Come to the All-American Auction and ___3___ in the fun by bringing things to sell.

Does your deodorant defeat your ___4___? Try "Whip It"—the deodorant for doers!

   1. examination
   2. starvation
   3. participate
   4. perspiration

Words to Master

examine	termination	starve	Norway
examination	participate	starvation	Pakistan
fascinate	participation	narrate	Panama
fascination	perspire	narration	_____
terminate	perspiration	Nigeria	_____

100

Third Day

- **Guiding the study time**

  Direct your student in using the procedure given on the back cover of his spelling worktext called *Learning to Spell a Word*:

  1. **Look** at the word and say it aloud.
  2. **Hear** each sound as you close your eyes; and say the word again.
  3. **Spell** the word as you look at each letter.
  4. **Write** the word and say it again.
  5. **Close** your eyes and **think** of how the word is spelled.
  6. **Write** the word again and **check** your spelling.

- **Giving the trial test**

  Pronounce each word, use it in a sentence, and then pronounce it again.

  > Your student needs to take all three tests: the pretest, the trial test, and the final test.

  Testing is part of the *recall-study-recall* cycle and is important to the learning process. The correct spelling of a word on a test does not indicate mastery. Each time your student writes the word it will benefit him in achieving permanent learning.

- **Giving the dictation sentence(s)**

  To help your student visualize the dictation sentence and improve concentration skills, follow these steps:

  1. Instruct your student to put his pencil down.
  2. Say the sentence twice, slowly.
  3. Lead your student in saying it with you once.
  4. Tell him to write the sentence.

     Note: Do not repeat the sentence. Soon, your student will learn to concentrate on the sentence as it is said twice. If the requirement seems to frustrate your student, give him a shortened form of the sentence. In time he will be able to work up to the full-length sentence.

- **Teaching the dictionary skill(s)**

  Beginning on page 146, the worktext has a special section for teaching dictionary skills. One of these pages is assigned in each unit. Introduce the dictionary skills as stated in the boxes or on the page, and then ask questions to get your student involved in the skill. On some dictionary pages, you will need to guide your student as he uses the skill. Do whatever teaching is needed, because your purpose is for your student to develop a knowledgeable use of the dictionary.

Learning to Spell a Word

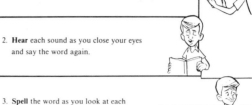

1. **Look** at the word and say it aloud.

2. **Hear** each sound as you close your eyes and say the word again.

3. **Spell** the word as you look at each letter.

4. **Write** the word and say it again.

5. **Close** your eyes and **think** of how the word is spelled.

6. **Write** the word again and **check** your spelling.

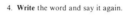

The part of speech is given in the dictionary entry in italics. In some dictionaries, the parts of speech are abbreviated. If a word can be used as more than one part of speech, that part of speech is also named in italics.

au·to·graph /ô′ tə graf/ or /ô′ tə graf/ *noun, plural* **autographs** A written name or signature of a famous person. Autographs are saved by fans or collectors. *verb* **autographed, autographing, autographs** To write one's own name or signature on: *The actor autographed the program of the play for me.*

Look at the excerpt from the dictionary. Find the first part of speech: *noun;* now find the second part of speech: *verb.* For the following exercise, locate each underlined word below in your Spelling Dictionary. Notice the parts of speech that are listed and decide which one applies to the underlined word. Write that part of speech on the blank. The first one is completed for you.

1. Tom's classmates <u>autographed</u> his cast. ___*verb*___
2. The <u>moral</u> of the story was "honesty pays." **noun**
3. That college <u>graduate</u> is a potential teacher. **adjective**
4. My brother <u>courted</u> his girl for a long time. **verb**
5. We have a <u>direct</u> line to my dad's phone. **adjective**
6. They <u>named</u> their baby for his grandfather. **verb**
7. Our car has an <u>automatic</u> transmission. **adjective**
8. Uncle George holds a <u>minor</u> office in the state government. **adjective**
9. Mary's grandfather was a <u>major</u> in the Army. **noun**
10. One <u>characteristic</u> of our church is friendliness. **noun**
11. Susan and her family attended an <u>aerial</u> show. **adjective**
12. We could <u>sense</u> the Christmas spirit in our whole family. **verb**
13. The young boy offered to be Candy's <u>guide</u>. **noun**

168

Use with Unit 25.
Skill: identifying parts of speech

Fourth Day

- **Making a journal**

  Direct your student to prepare a journal, a folder with ample notebook paper secured inside. Ask him to personalize his journal with a special cover: a drawing, a design, or a picture cut from a card or magazine.

- **Introducing the *Journal Entry Idea***

  Look at the picture first and discuss the mood, ideas, and activities depicted there. Generate some thoughts as to what your student might want to write about. Read the paragraph to confirm or change the direction of the writing assignment. Expand on the feelings and questions presented. Your student should be excited and primed with ideas when he begins writing.

> Your student should always use a **pencil** when writing in his journal that so he can make corrections easily.

- **Guiding the journal activity**

  In writing a journal, your student has an opportunity to express his ideas using his own vocabulary words. The journal will help him be more aware of how he spells words as he develops a spelling consciousness.

  1. Instruct your student to place a pencil, his spelling worktext, his journal, and a piece of scrap paper on his desk.
  2. Ask him to write a note to you in his journal about the ideas generated from the paragraph and the picture, using his own words and his own personal experience.
  3. Direct him to address you in the salutation (''Dear Mother'').
  4. Be available so that your student can ask you for help and instruction in spelling. If he does not know how to spell a word, he should do the following:
     a. Write the word to the best of his ability on the piece of scrap paper.
     b. Ask you to check his spelling attempt(s).
  5. Praise him for any part of the word that is correctly spelled, and help him correct his mistakes.
  6. Instruct him to copy the word correctly in his journal. Do all this as quickly as possible to keep his focus on the content of his journal writing. When he has completed his writing, direct him to copy the correctly spelled word into the section entitled *My Word Bank* at the back of each spelling worktext.

Journal Entry Idea

I live in a little town called Crockleford Heath in southeastern England. My father is a farmer, and we also keep some sheep. The climate here is a lot like it is in some parts of the United States. I find many things to do for fun along the coast, which is not far from where I live. I don't go to school in my town because it is too small; I go to school in Colchester, leaving early Monday morning and staying till school is over on Friday afternoon.

Does this sound interesting to you? Think of a place in another country where you would like to live. Describe life there.

The King's English
sanctification

The Latin word *sanctus*, which means "holy" or "sacred," led to our English word **sanctification**. The Hebrew and Greek terms translated *sanctification* mean "a setting apart" or "separation." Therefore, something that is sanctified is set apart from the world, separated unto God.

In the beginning, when God finished creating the world, He blessed the seventh day and sanctified it, setting it apart for His use.

Every believer belongs to God. Hebrews 10 tells us we are saints, that we are sanctified because we have been saved from the judgment of our sins. When Christ paid the price of our redemption with His own blood, He paid it once and for all. We are His.

Because we are His, we have an obligation to Christ. We continue the process of our sanctification by growing in our Christian life. As we read God's Word, pray, and worship Him, we grow to be more Christ-like. When Christ returns for us, our sanctification will be complete, for we will become like Him.

Exodus 13:2
Hebrews 10:10-14
1 Peter 3:15

101

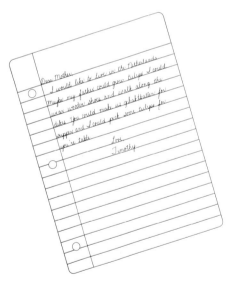

7. After no longer than ten minutes of writing, give a five-minute warning and then tell him to write a closing (''Sincerely,'' or ''Yours truly,'') and to sign his name.
8. Collect the journal.

- **Reading the journal**

  Before another journal time, the person to whom your student has addressed his letter (which will be the same person each time, usually the mother) does the following:

  1. Reads the journal entry.
  2. Writes a brief reply, using the same style as the student.
  3. Writes correctly any words that the student has misspelled (up to four) on a piece of scrap paper and attaches it to the journal page. (The student will later correct the misspelled words in his journal.)

> If more than four words are misspelled, you can make spelling corrections in your student's journal, using an eraser and pencil. The purpose for this is to encourage him to continue writing.

The reader **DOES NOT:**

  - Mark the journal entry with red pencil or ink.
  - Look for errors other than spelling.

- **Returning the journal**

  Instruct your student to do the following after you have returned his journal entry from the previous week:

  1. Erase each of the misspelled words indicated and write them correctly in the journal entry.
  2. Record alphabetically each of the misspelled words in the section of the spelling worktext called *Word Bank.* Two words will be chosen weekly from this section and added to the list of words. Your student will write the words on the blanks provided on the first page of each unit.

> The spelling unit becomes more personalized when it includes the words individually recognized and chosen by your student from his writing vocabulary.

WORD BANK

The following pages make up your Word Bank. This is a section where you can record the words that you especially need to learn to spell. Whenever you misspell a word in your journal or other written work, find the correct spelling and write that problem word here in the proper alphabetical section.

Each week choose two or more words from your Word Bank and write them on the Word Bank entry lines on the first page of that unit. Study these words as part of your spelling list and write them from memory on the trial and final tests.

After you have written a word correctly on the final test, mark the small box in front of that word to indicate your success.

A

198

Fifth Day

- **Guiding the study time**

  Spend a few minutes helping your student review his spelling words, demonstrating how to use the *recall-study-recall-study-recall* method. The student tests himself at this point in the *recall* phases of this cycle in preparation for the final written test, using the study method given on the back of the student worktext.

- **Giving the final test**

  The procedure for the final test is the same as that for the trial test given on the *Third Day*.

> Remember, in order to complete the learning cycle from the pretest to the final test, it is important that your student take all three tests.

- **Recording correct spellings in *Word Bank***

  After a student has correctly spelled a *Word Bank* word on the final test, he shades in the square that precedes that word in his *Word Bank*.

> The principal purpose of the spelling test is not to secure a grade. The test is a teaching procedure designed to develop permanent internalization of common spelling patterns. The outcome should be the transfer of the spelling patterns to other words with the same patterns.

- **Using *The King's English* section**

  Call attention to *The King's English* section found on the final page of each lesson in the worktext. This section explains in greater depth the meaning and origin of an interesting word used in the Bible. Use this lesson to foster an awareness of and an appreciation for the words that present God's message to us.

  Talk with your student about the picture and the featured word, determining what he already knows prior to reading the selection. Ask him to read the paragraph silently and then to read it aloud to you. He may wish to read it later to a family member.

  Ask the questions that are given as a way to discuss the information with your student. Use the Bible verses, the Bible Action Truths, and the Bible Promises listed to make the section more meaningful and applicable to your student's life. (See the Supplement for a total list of Bible Action Truths and Bible Promises.)

Journal Entry Idea

I live in a little town called Crockleford Heath in southeastern England. My father is a farmer, and we also keep some sheep. The climate here is a lot like it is in some parts of the United States. I find many things to do for fun along the coast, which is not far from where I live. I don't go to school in my town because it is too small; I go to school in Colchester, leaving early Monday morning and staying till school is over on Friday afternoon.

Does this sound interesting to you? Think of a place in another country where you would like to live. Describe life there.

The King's English

sanctification

The Latin word *sanctus*, which means "holy" or "sacred," led to our English word **sanctification.** The Hebrew and Greek terms translated *sanctification* mean "a setting apart" or "separation." Therefore, something that is sanctified is set apart from the world, separated unto God.

In the beginning, when God finished creating the world, He blessed the seventh day and sanctified it, setting it apart for His use.

Every believer belongs to God. Hebrews 10 tells us we are saints, that we are sanctified because we have been saved from the judgment of our sins. When Christ paid the price of our redemption with His own blood, He paid it once and for all. We are His.

Because we are His, we have an obligation to Christ. We continue the process of our sanctification by growing in our Christian life. As we read God's Word, pray, and worship Him, we grow to be more Christ-like. When Christ returns for us, our sanctification will be complete, for we will become like Him.
Exodus 13:2
Hebrews 10:10-14
I Peter 3:15

101

Spelling Progress Chart

Description: The chart is located at www.bjup.com resources/products under Spelling 1-6. This is an optional chart. You may print a copy of the chart for each student. It is useful for a student to record individual progress on final tests.

Directions: Guide the students in recording their scores on the Spelling Progress Chart. Each week identify the total number of words spelled correctly on the final test. Direct each child to record this information on the bar graph by coloring one square for each correct word beginning at the bottom of the column. The numbers across the bottom of the two graphs are the weekly unit numbers and review unit numbers.

Notes: The number of spelling words for the final test varies depending on the grade level. These graphs may be used at any level as long as the number of words does not exceed 20 for unit tests and 32 for review tests.

Dear Home Educator,

The formation of this spelling program is based on research into how children learn. If the teaching methodology suggested is followed closely, your student will eventually have success in spelling. The worktext is of value only if it is used as part of the total program. Detailed instructions for teaching each part of the spelling program are given in a section called General Lesson Plans, found in the front of this manual. Much time can be saved by reading each section in total before teaching the first unit of spelling.

The Spelling Authors

Unit 1

Worktext pages 2-5
Dictionary pages 146-48

―――――― **Generalization emphasis** ――――――

1. **Adding a suffix beginning with a vowel letter to a word ending in *ss***–When adding a suffix beginning with a vowel letter to a word ending in *ss*, do not change the spelling of the base word. *process, procession*

2. **Dividing words with the pattern VC/CV**–Divide a word with the VCCV spelling pattern between the two consonant letters. *VC/CV, suc • ces • sion*

―――――――――― **Materials** ――――――――――

- A world map or an atlas
- The *A* volume of an encyclopedia
- Drawing paper
- A folder for keeping loose papers

Read each spelling word and place the accent mark over the correct syllable. Then write the words on the blanks, connecting the syllables.

1. pro·cess´ **or proc´ess**   1. _____
2. pro·ces´sion   2. _____
3. pro·fess´   3. _____
4. pro·fes´sion   4. _____
5. im·press´   5. _____
6. im·pres´sion   6. _____
7. de·press´   7. _____
8. de·pres´sion   8. _____
9. op·press´   9. _____
10. op·pres´sion   10. _____
11. suc·cess´   11. _____
12. suc·ces´sion   12. _____
13. trans·gress´   13. _____
14. trans·gres´sion   14. _____
15. Af·ghan·i·stan   15. _____
16. Al·ba·ni·a   16. _____
17. Al·ge·ri·a   17. _____
18. An·dor·ra   18. _____
19. Word Bank entry   19. _____
20. Word Bank entry   20. _____

2

First Day

Give the pretest. Give the pretest and ask your student to check and correct his own work.

> A suffix added to a word usually forms a new word. *big, biggest; clap, claps*

After reading words 1-14 on page 2 to your student, apply generalization number one, using the suggested questions:

- What spelling do the words *process, profess, impress, depress, oppress, success,* and *transgress* have in common? *(They all end in ss.)*
- What suffix has been added to each of these words in this list? *(-ion)*
- What happens to the spelling of each base word when the suffix *-ion* is added? *(The spelling of the base word does not change.)*

Note: Apply the questions asked or statements made only to the words that fit the pattern being taught. We suggest a way to present the generalization and follow it with questions to ask and statements to make. After all the other observations have been made regarding a generalization, you might ask your student to make a statement that sums up what he now knows about the words in the list that fit a generalization presented. Example: What can you say about a word ending in two consonant letters that has a suffix beginning with a vowel letter added to it: *The spelling of the base word does not change.*

Apply generalization number two to words 1-14, using the suggested questions and statement:

- Write the pattern VCCV where your student can see it and ask him if he can remember or figure out what those letters represent in a word. *(vowel letter-consonant letter-consonant letter-vowel letter)*
- Where would you usually divide such a word into syllables? *(between the two consonant letters: VC • CV)*
- Look at the words that have the suffix *-ion* added to them. What do you notice about the way they are divided into syllables? *(They are divided with the VC/CV pattern and in the case with the last two consonant letters, the second goes with the suffix.)*

Introduce words 15-18 on page 2.
The last four words in each unit of the sixth grade spelling text will be the names of countries. Since these words do not fit comfortably with a generalization, their spellings are not taught that way. You will need to give your student any helps you can for remembering them.

- Point out that *Afghanistan* has one silent *h* and three /ă/'s.
- There are three different pronunciations for *a* in *Albania.*
- *Algeria* has /ĭr/ spelled *er.*
- There are two *r*'s in *Andorra.*

Following the *Spelling Dictionary* in the student worktext is a section called *Geographic Entries.* It provides information about the capitals and the population of each country.

Guide a research activity: *Where in the World?* Using a world map, help your student locate the four countries from the spelling list and mark them with a pin or small colored dot. Take note of each country's geographic relationship to the United States: N, S, E, W, NE, etc. Help your student determine the *continent* where each country is located. Also help him recognize neighboring countries, mountains, oceans, and any other distinctive features of each country. Use the designated volume of an encyclopedia to encourage your student to discover other interesting facts about each country.

Use any of the following suggestions to guide further study of each country as it appears in a spelling list.

1. Mount your world map on the wall to be used each day for this activity and for related subjects.
2. Ask your student to look in newspapers and magazines for articles about the countries, cut them out, and put them in a scrapbook or folder entitled *Our World.*
3. Allow your student to choose one of the countries and draw its flag as depicted in an encyclopedia. Keep the maps drawn for each unit in a file or folder, later to be made into a personal flag book.
4. Instruct your student to use an encyclopedia to discover information about the countries. He could create a folder in which is recorded or charted facts about a country's location, population, and capital city as explained in the *Geographic Entries* section.
5. Relate your research to the mission field, finding out if your local church is supporting missionaries in a country you have chosen to investigate. Ask your student to write a letter to them encouraging the work they are doing and sharing the things he has learned about their country.

It is recommended that at least one *optional activity* be done each week. Certainly more than one could be done if your student is especially interested in finding out more about the world. The activities can be varied, one week devoted to map drawing and another to using the newspapers and magazines, etc.

Use the handwritten list on page 2. After your student has written each word on the appropriate line, check his work for spelling and legibility. Instruct him then to place an accent mark in each multi-syllable word in the printed list.

4. pro‑fes‑sion	4. *profession*

Second Day

Use the Bible verse activity on page 3. Ask the following questions to encourage your student to think about the meanings of the words in the verse and of the verse.

1. What is the *book of the law?*
2. How could you keep it from *departing out of your mouth?*
3. What does it mean to *meditate?*
4. What does it mean to *observe to do according to all that is written therein?*
5. What do you think the word *prosperous* means in this context?
6. What do you suppose the Lord calls *success?*
7. What do you think God is trying to tell us in this verse? (BAT: 6a Bible study)
8. How can you begin to do what the verse says to do?

> Any answer your student gives that shows that he is thinking is better than a memorized or "parroted" statement that he does not understand. Accept any answer, not by saying it is correct, but by using it to lead him to the correct one. He knows more than he realizes he knows, but he must be made to **think,** if what he has learned is to be permanent.

Have fun with the *Word for Word* section on page 3. Draw from your student other meanings for the word *impression.* Talk with him about someone who has made an *impression* on him and what kind of *impression* he is making on others.

Use worktext pages 3 and 4 to reinforce word meaning and the skills of the unit. Read the directions and give help, if needed, as your student completes the pages.

Third Day

Give your student time to study the words, using the study method printed on the back cover of the spelling worktext.

Dictate the word list for the trial test.

Give the following dictation sentences:

1. I have the **impression** that Dr. Hanson is proud of the **success** he's had in his **profession.**
2. The people in **Afghanistan** were under **oppression** for many years.
3. A **succession** of illnesses had kept Tom from having **success** with his science project.

---

name _____

A. Read the verse.
  1. Underline the words that tell what Christians should think about continually.
  2. Circle the word in this verse that has the Biblical meaning "something done with prudence, insight, and common sense," but today means "the carrying out of some desired goal."

> "*This book of the law* shall not depart out of thy mouth; but thou shalt meditate therein day and night, that thou mayest observe to do according to all that is written therein: for then thou shalt make thy way prosperous, and then thou shalt have good success." *Joshua 1:8*

Look at *impress* and *impression.* Could you put *impress* in the same place in a sentence that you put *impression?* Try it! Of course it doesn't work. Adding a suffix to a word usually changes the way that word is used in a sentence.

B. Choose the correct word for each sentence from the word pairs given below. Notice how the word is used in the sentence.

impress, impression
  1. My teacher was trying to ____ me with the idea that I needed to learn calligraphy.   1. *impress*
  2. I got the ____ that she wanted us to enter the contest.   2. *impression*

profess, profession
  3. If you ____ to be a Christian, you should act like one.   3. *profess*
  4. Nursing is a good ____ for those who like to help people.   4. *profession*

oppress, oppression
  5. It is wrong for powerful men to ____ poor people.   5. *oppress*
  6. My grandparents left Poland because of the ____ of the government.   6. *oppression*

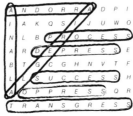

After taking a nap, have you ever found strange marks on your face or arms? You probably realized that whatever you were lying on while you slept had made an *impression* on you. The word *impression* comes from a Latin word meaning "to press on." If you have had your teeth straightened, you may remember that before the dentist began his work, he pressed on your teeth with a thick substance that hardened into an *impression* of your teeth. Can you think of other ways impressions are made?

impression

3

C. Eight words from your spelling list are hidden in the word search below. Circle them and then write each word in the blanks.

A	N	D	O	R	R	A	D	P	I
I	A	K	Q	S	J	U	W	O	
N	L	B	P	R	O	C	E	S	S
A	R	D	E	P	R	E	S	S	E
B	T	G	C	G	H	N	V	T	F
L	I	S	U	C	C	E	S	S	H
A	O	P	P	R	E	S	S	Q	R
T	R	A	N	S	G	R	E	S	S

1. *Andorra*
2. *process*
3. *depress*
4. *success*
5. *oppress*
6. *transgress*
7. *Albania*
8. *Algeria*

D. Add the suffix -*ion* to the following words.

| 1. transgress | 2. impress | 3. process | 4. success | 5. profess | 6. depress |

1. *transgression*
2. *impression*
3. *procession*
4. *succession*
5. *profession*
6. *depression*

E. Think about it!
  1. Which two-syllable words have two sets of double consonants?
  2. Which spelling word has second and fourth syllables that rhyme?
  3. Which three countries have names ending with the same letter?

1. *oppress, success*
2. *Afghanistan*
3. *Albania, Andorra, Algeria*

Words to Master

process	impression	success	Albania
procession	depress	succession	Algeria
profess	depression	transgress	Andorra
profession	oppress	transgression	_____
impress	oppression	Afghanistan	_____

4

Use pages 146 and 147 to introduce the dictionary section of the worktext. Ask your student to open to these pages, read the title of the dictionary section to you, and tell you its significance. Ask him to leaf through the pages, noting that there is a cartoon strip at the top of each. Tell him that Dick Shanary will be using the same skills to catch the criminal *Lefty Werds* that he will be using to work these pages. Ask him to decide who Dick is and who Lefty is as they appear on these two pages. Ask him whom he thinks the dog running beside the man in blue belongs to. Go over with him all the different parts of the dictionary entry and page that are in bold print on page 147, asking him to tell you how each is used or what each does.

 Dictionary skill: In order to use a dictionary more effectively, *estimate in what fourth of the dictionary a word is located: A-F, G-L, M-R, or S-Z.*

Use a dictionary to introduce the dictionary skill. Write where your student can see it: *A-F, G-L, M-R, S-Z.* Tell him that these are the four parts of the dictionary. Show him how to hold the dictionary so that four fingers are on the front cover, four on the back cover, and his thumbs meeting in the middle of the stack of pages. Inform him that you will say a word and then he is to look at these divisions and decide which fourth the word is in and open the dictionary to that part. The following are some words you can use: *chaldron, theorem, pieplant, dialect, hypnosis, roaster, xenia, emphasize, shingles, kinetic, forlorn, migrant.*

Use page 148 to teach this week's dictionary skill. After you are certain that your student understands the skill, guide him as he completes the exercise.

You can use a dictionary more effectively if, when looking for a word, you first estimate in what fourth of the dictionary the word is located.

In the paragraph below are certain underlined words. Write either 1, 2, 3, or 4 on each blank according to what section of the dictionary the word would be in: Section 1 is made up of letters A through F; Section 2 is letters G through L; Section 3 is M through R; and Section 4 is S through Z.

This year you will be receiving instruction on the various ways you can use a dictionary. A dictionary has special sections that you may not have noticed before.

One section you may not be familiar with is the information given on the history of the English language. English is made up of many languages, such as German, Latin, Greek, French, and Anglo-Saxon. The Scandinavians also contributed to the English spoken in England. We all know that American English is almost a language of its own.

When a word has a foreign origin, that origin is given after the definition of the word in the dictionary entry.

1. receiving **3**	10. before **1**	19. French **1**
2. instruction **2**	11. familiar **1**	20. Anglo-Saxon **1**
3. various **4**	12. information **2**	21. Scandinavians **4**
4. ways **4**	13. history **2**	22. contributed **1**
5. use **4**	14. English **1**	23. spoken **4**
6. dictionary **1**	15. language **2**	24. American **1**
7. special **4**	16. German **2**	25. almost **1**
8. sections **4**	17. Latin **2**	26. foreign **1**
9. noticed **3**	18. Greek **2**	27. origin **3**

148

Use with Unit 1
Skill: estimating the place of words in the dictionary

Fourth Day

If you do not want to use the journal idea given in the student text for this lesson, an alternate idea is given following the one which refers to page 5.

Guide the journal time, using the *Journal Entry Idea* on page 5 (optional) and the information given in the front of this manual. Motivate your student by letting him tell ways in which he has changed since he was in kindergarten. Encourage him to see that he has changed not only physically but also emotionally and mentally. Ask whether his ideas, fears, and goals have changed over the years. Ask if he has changed spiritually. (BAT: 3a Self-concept)

Use an alternate journal entry idea. Talk with your student about a special visit that your family made to some friend or relative this summer. Get his reactions to how different the home of this person was from his own home. Get him to compare such things as the food, the rules, the surroundings, the talk, etc. Then ask him to write his ideas for his first journal entry.

A lively discussion always needs to precede your student's writing of his journal entry. The more he verbalizes his ideas, the easier it will be for him to write about them.

Fifth Day

Guide the study time.

Dictate the word list for the final test.

Give the following dictation sentences.
1. Do not **transgress** the law in **Andorra**.
2. The man from **Albania** tried to **impress** me with his jokes.
3. He watched a **procession** of camels in **Algeria**.

Journal Entry Idea

The first day of school! Getting-new-books-day and getting-to-choose-your-desk day and getting-reacquainted-with-your-friends day. How do you feel about it? Do you remember how you felt when you started kindergarten or first grade? How frightened were you, or how excited? Think about how different you feel now, compared to how you felt then. How different do you *look*? Look around you. How do you think your school friends and surroundings are different from those first-year surroundings? This year, it's a we're-now-the-big-shots look. Compare your first year of school to now.

The King's English

profession

The Latin word *professio* means "declaration" and comes from the word *profiteri,* which means "to declare." Our Declaration of Independence officially stated, or declared, the position of the colonies.

In the Bible, *homologen* is used to mean "confessing, or saying publicly." When a person makes a **profession** of faith in Christ, he officially states that he has accepted Christ as his Saviour. He is openly and publicly declaring his faith. Jesus anointed the eyes of the blind man with clay and told him to wash in the pool of Siloam. When challenged by the Pharisees, the man spoke out boldly, professing that Jesus was a Prophet. Later, he told Jesus, "Lord, I believe."

After declaring our faith in Christ, we must live in faith. Paul tells us to "fight the good fight of faith, lay hold on eternal life, whereunto thou art also called, and hast professed a good profession before many witnesses."

I Timothy 6:12
Hebrews 4:14
John 9

Use *The King's English* on page 5. After your student has read this section silently, read it with him orally, discussing it as you read. Use the Bible verses and good comprehension questions to make certain he understands it completely. The questions below may be used.
1. What does the word *profession* mean?
2. What is a person doing when he makes a *profession* of faith in Christ?
3. Do you make a profession to yourself or to others?
4. Why is it important to make an open, public declaration of faith?
5. What should you be careful to do after you have declared your faith in Christ? (BAT: 1c Separation from the world)

Unit 2

Worktext pages 6-9
Dictionary page 149

Generalization emphasis

---

1. **Adding a suffix beginning with a vowel letter to a word ending with a consonant letter**—When adding a suffix that begins with a vowel letter to a word ending with a consonant letter, do not change the spelling of the base word. *mental, mentality*

2. **Using morphophonemics as an aid in spelling**—The spelling of a word is made more obvious by the pronunciation (due to the stress) of a related word. *men'tal, men • tal' i • ty*

> The word *morphophonemics* means a "change in the sound of a word caused by the shifting of the stress." While you don't use this word with your student, you can teach him to be aware of these changes in stress.

Materials

- A world map or an atlas
- The *A* volume of an encyclopedia
- Graph paper

First Day

Give the pretest. After you have given the pretest and your student has checked and corrected it, give him time to select two of the words from his Word Bank to use as this week's *Word Bank Entries*.

> Each syllable in a word contains a vowel. The number of syllables in a word is the number of vowels. In words of two or more syllables, one syllable, referred to as the *stressed syllable,* always receives more voice stress (emphasis) than the others. *formality /fôr • măl' ĭ • tē/*

After reading words 1-14 on page 6 to your student, apply generalization number one in the following way, using the suggested statements and questions:

- What do the words *mental, moral, formal, technical, hospital, punctual,* and *individual* have in common? *(They all end in al.)*

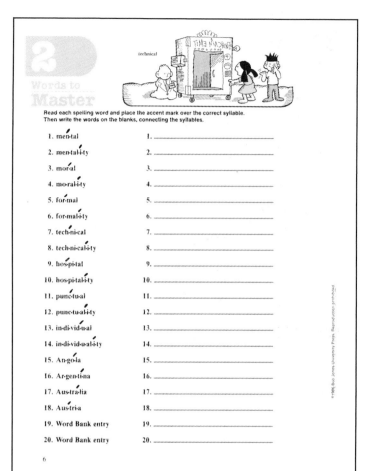

2 Words to Master

Read each spelling word and place the accent mark over the correct syllable. Then write the words on the blanks, connecting the syllables.

1. men·tal	1. _____
2. men·tal·i·ty	2. _____
3. mor·al	3. _____
4. mo·ral·i·ty	4. _____
5. for·mal	5. _____
6. for·mal·i·ty	6. _____
7. tech·ni·cal	7. _____
8. tech·ni·cal·i·ty	8. _____
9. hos·pi·tal	9. _____
10. hos·pi·tal·i·ty	10. _____
11. punc·tu·al	11. _____
12. punc·tu·al·i·ty	12. _____
13. in·di·vid·u·al	13. _____
14. in·di·vid·u·al·i·ty	14. _____
15. An·go·la	15. _____
16. Ar·gen·ti·na	16. _____
17. Aus·tra·lia	17. _____
18. Aus·tri·a	18. _____
19. Word Bank entry	19. _____
20. Word Bank entry	20. _____

6

- Notice the words formed from these base words. How did the spelling of each base word change when the suffix *-ity* was added? *(The spelling of the base words did not change.)*
- What usually happens when a suffix beginning with a vowel letter is added to a word ending in a consonant letter? *(The spelling of the base word is not changed.)*

> The schwa (sound) is pronounced like *uh* and always stands for a vowel letter found in an unstressed syllable. It is represented by the symbol ə. *technical /těk' nĭ • kəl/*

Apply generalization number two to words 1-14 in the following way, using the suggested questions and statements:

- Listen as I say the following two words: *mental, mentality.* On which syllable of *mental* do you hear the schwa (uh sound)? *(the second)*
- In *mentality,* what do you hear on that second syllable? *(/ă/)*
- How does *mentality* help you spell *mental?* *(You know that the schwa in the second syllable of* mental *is spelled with an* a.*)*

- In a similar way, deal with the other word pairs: *moral, morality; formal, formality; technical, technicality; hospital, hospitality; punctual, punctuality;* and *individual, individuality.*

> Remind your student that the schwa (/ə/) can be spelled with any vowel letter, so it helps to think of a related word in which that vowel letter does not have the schwa (sound).

Introduce words 15-18 on page 6.

- All four countries end in *a*.
- *Austria* and *Australia* both begin with *Austr* and both end with *ia*.

Guide a research activity: *Where in the World?* Help your student locate the countries with names in the spelling list on a world atlas or map. Ask him to use the *A* volume of an encyclopedia to expand his geographic and general country knowledge according to the ideas and optional activities presented in Unit 1. This activity can be done the first day or later in the week. It can be ongoing, begun on Monday and completed on Friday. Use flexibility and creativity to keep this activity fresh and appealing.

Use the handwritten list. After your student has written each word on the appropriate line, check his list for spelling and legibility. Instruct him to place an accent mark in each multi-syllable word of the printed list.

Second Day

> Any answer your student gives that shows that he is thinking is better than a memorized or "parroted" statement that he does not understand. Accept any answer, not by saying it is correct, but by using it to lead him to the correct one. He knows more than he realizes he knows, but he must be made to **think,** if what he has learned is to be permanent.

Use the Bible verse activity on page 7. Ask the following questions to encourage your student to think about the meanings of the words in the verse and of the verse:
1. What does the word *hospitality* mean in this verse? (BAT: 5e Friendliness)
2. What does *without grudging* mean? (BAT: 5b Giving)
3. What is God telling us in this verse?
4. What can we learn from this verse? (BAT: 5a Love)

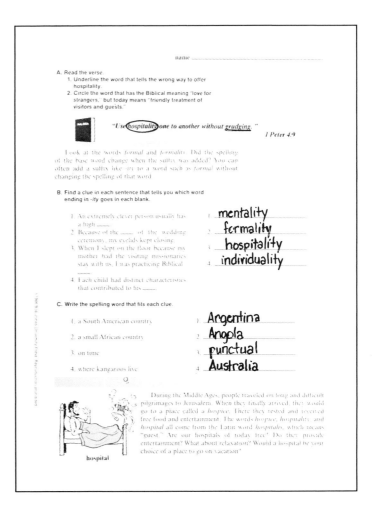

Have fun with the *Word for Word* section on page 7. Talk with your student about some of the new kinds of hospitals that we have today. Some are actually called *hospices.* Ask him to describe any hospital that he has been a patient in or has visited.

Use worktext pages 7 and 8 to reinforce word meaning and the skills of the unit. Read the directions and give help, if needed, as your student completes the pages.

Guide a spelling activity: *Connect a Word.* Ask your student to write a long spelling word on a piece of graph paper. Let him connect another spelling word to the first word, crossword puzzle fashion. Continue until no more words can be added. The challenge is to see how many words can be used. This activity can be done with any unit and with a variety of combinations. Later you may want to take this activity one step further and have your student make a crossword puzzle.

Third Day

Give your student time to study the words, using the study method printed on the back cover of the spelling worktext.

Dictate the word list for the trial test.

Give the following dictation sentences:

1. The country of **Argentina** has twice as many people as the continent of **Australia**.
2. Those who work in a hospital should be both **moral** and **punctual**.
3. Three traits a Christian should try to develop are **morality, punctuality,** and **hospitality.**

Dictionary skill: The *guide words* on a given page of a dictionary tell what words are on that page. The guide word on the left is the first word on the page; the guide word on the right is the last word on the page.

Use page 149 to teach this week's dictionary skill. Teach the skill of using guide words by showing your student again the opening two pages of the dictionary section, "The Adventures of Dick Shanary." Ask him to read the title of the dictionary section and explain to you its significance. After you are certain that your student understands the skill, guide him as he completes the exercise.

Say *mental* and *mentality* to yourself. Did the stress in this word pair change when you added the suffix? In *mental,* the second syllable has the schwa sound, which can be spelled several different ways. In the word *mentality,* the stress comes on the second syllable, changing the schwa sound to a short *a* sound. If you listen for the second syllable in *mentality,* it will help you remember how to spell the indistinct schwa sound in the second syllable in *mental.* This clue will help you remember how to spell other words with the schwa sound.

D. Add the suffix *-ity* to each of the following base words, writing them in syllables and putting in the accents. Be sure to notice the change in stress and pronunciation.

1. mental	1. men tal′ i ty
2. moral	2. mor al′ i ty
3. formal	3. for mal′ i ty
4. technical	4. tech ni cal′ i ty
5. hospital	5. hos pi tal′ i ty
6. punctual	6. punc tu al′ i ty

E. Proofread this want ad, find the misspellings, and write the corrected words on the lines.

Wanted: indevidual to help with cooking in hospitle in Ostria. Must have some mentil ability and no morol problems. Formul training or teknikil experience not necessary. Apply at 160 Columbia St. at 9:00 A.M.— punctuality is important.

1. individual
2. hospital
3. Austria
4. mental
5. moral
6. formal
7. technical
8. punctuality

Words to Master

mental	formality	punctual	Argentina
mentality	technical	punctuality	Australia
moral	technicality	individual	Austria
morality	hospital	individuality	_____
formal	hospitality	Angola	_____

8

---

name _____

CASE #001 "FINDING WORDS" *(continued)*

The guide words, which appear at the top of each page in a dictionary, are the first and last entry words on the page. Every word on a given page will be alphabetically listed between the guide words.

A. If the guide words on a page were the two words given below, underline the entry words that would appear on that page.

1. patient/punctual	2. hospital/individuality	3. formality/furthermore
<u>pedestrian</u>	handicap	<u>formula</u>
<u>pessimistic</u>	<u>humid</u>	<u>foul</u>
<u>postage</u>	<u>hypnotize</u>	<u>foundation</u>
puncture	<u>ideal</u>	fuss
puppet	involve	feminine
<u>pearl</u>	irregular	<u>frankfurter</u>
<u>politician</u>	investigate	<u>freshman</u>
<u>predominant</u>	<u>ignorance</u>	<u>fumes</u>
<u>pavement</u>	<u>illustrate</u>	<u>fringe</u>
philosophy	issue	

B. Look in your Spelling Dictionary and write the guide words that you find on the pages that list the following words.

1. mentality	manuscript	and	mortgage
2. technical	state	and	telescopic
3. individual	hard	and	join
4. formality	fan²	and	ham

Use with Unit 2
Skill: using guide words   149

Fourth Day

Return last week's journal. Give your student time to correct the misspelled words in his previous journal entry and record them in his Word Bank.

Guide the journal time, using the *Journal Entry Idea* on page 9 and the information given in the front of this manual. After your student has read the paragraph, ask him to tell you what it said. Discuss with him how you and he can make this sixth grade year of home schooling really special. Let him tell you of times when he may have started something with a negative attitude and how that attitude affected what he did. Discuss the concept that a person's outward attitude is a reflection of his heart attitude. (BATs: 2f Enthusiasm, 6c Spirit-filled, 7d Contentment)

Fifth Day

Guide the study time.

Dictate the word list for the final test.

Give the following dictation sentences.

1. The lawyer went through the **formality** of explaining each **technicality**.
2. The missionary received a bill from a **hospital** in **Argentina**.
3. Dr. Fisher has studied the **mentality** and **individuality** of six gorillas.

Use *The King's English* on page 9. After your student has read the text silently, read it with him orally. Guide him to a thorough understanding, using the Bible verses, discussion, and questions. The following questions could be used:

1. The word *evangelist* comes from the Greek word *angelos* and the Greek prefix *eu*. What is the meaning of these Greek words?
2. What does an evangelist do?
3. Why are all Christians considered evangelists? (BAT: 5c Evangelism and missions)

Journal Entry Idea
"Oh, I dread sixth grade!" "Oh, I'm going to love sixth grade!" Which one of these quotations sounds like you? Do you have a this-year-will-be-the-best-year attitude or a this-will-be-an-awful-year attitude? Can you make this an exceptional, exciting, enthusiastic, enthralling, enormously excellent year? Do you think the Lord wants you to be *discouraged* or *delighted* with being in sixth grade? Do you think you will have a better year if you look *faint* or *forward*? Decide what kind of an outlook you are going to take about this year and then describe it.

The King's English
evangelist
In the Greek word *angelos,* which means "messenger," you can see our word *angel.* We think of **angels** as messengers of God. It is interesting that the Greek word for **evangelist** uses *angelos* with a prefix *eu* that means "good." So we have *eu* + *angelos,* or "messenger of good." An evangelist is a messenger who brings good news.

God has given certain people the special ministry of being evangelists, of going abroad and spreading the good news that Christ has paid the penalty for sin. In the Bible, Philip, who led the Ethiopian eunuch to the Lord, is described as an evangelist. The Apostle Paul also did the work of an evangelist, traveling many miles by land and sea on his missionary trips to spread the gospel. In a larger sense, all Christians are evangelists, because we all have the responsibility of sharing the good news about Jesus Christ.
II Timothy 4:5
Acts 21:8
Ephesians 4:11

Unit 3

Worktext pages 10-13
Dictionary page 150

―――――― Generalization emphasis ――――――

1. **Adding a suffix beginning with a vowel letter to a word ending with a consonant letter**–When a suffix beginning with a vowel letter is added to a word ending with a consonant letter, the spelling of the base word does not change. *patriot, patriotic*

2. **Adding an extra letter before adding an ending**–Sometimes it is necessary to add an extra letter before adding an ending to a word. *horizon, horizontal*

3. **Using morphophonemics as an aid in spelling**–The spelling of a word is made more obvious by the pronunciation (stress) of a related word. *drama, dramatic*

―――――――――― Materials ――――――――――

• A world map or an atlas
• The *B* volume of an encyclopedia
• Prepare the following activity for Day 2.

If and Might

1. If I gave my life for my country, I might be considered a ___*patriot*___.
2. If I were good at public speaking, I might give a ___*dramatic*___ reading.
3. If I were told to draw a line from one side of the paper to the other, I might draw a ___*horizontal*___ line.
4. If I were naming just forty-eight states, I might be naming all the states in the ___*continental*___ United States.
5. If I were always biting my fingernails, I might be acquiring a bad ___*habit*___.
6. If I were driving along an interstate highway, I might see a sign that would ___*prohibit*___ hitchhiking.
7. If I saw people standing in line at the art museum, I might decide to visit the ___*exhibition or exhibit*___ too.
8. If I were a good artist, someone might want to ___*exhibit*___ my drawings.
9. If I fly our country's flag on holidays, that might mean that I am ___*patriotic*___.
10. If I lived on a prairie, I might be able to see the ___*horizon*___ in every direction.

First Day

Give the pretest. After you have given the pretest and your student has checked and corrected it, give him time to choose two of the words from his Word Bank and write them as this week's *Word Bank Entries*.

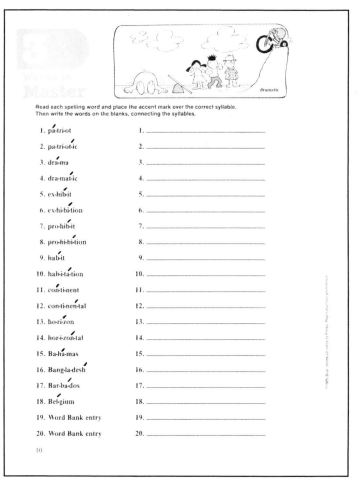

Read each spelling word and place the accent mark over the correct syllable. Then write the words on the blanks, connecting the syllables.

1. pa·tri·ot	1. _____
2. pa·tri·ot·ic	2. _____
3. dra·ma	3. _____
4. dra·mat·ic	4. _____
5. ex·hib·it	5. _____
6. ex·hi·bi·tion	6. _____
7. pro·hib·it	7. _____
8. pro·hi·bi·tion	8. _____
9. hab·it	9. _____
10. hab·i·ta·tion	10. _____
11. con·ti·nent	11. _____
12. con·ti·nen·tal	12. _____
13. ho·ri·zon	13. _____
14. hor·i·zon·tal	14. _____
15. Ba·ha·mas	15. _____
16. Bang·la·desh	16. _____
17. Bar·ba·dos	17. _____
18. Bel·gium	18. _____
19. Word Bank entry	19. _____
20. Word Bank entry	20. _____

10

After reading words 1-14 on page 10 to your student, apply generalization number one in the following way, using the suggested statements and questions:

• Look at the words *patriot, exhibit, prohibit, habit,* and *continent.* What do you notice about the last letter in each of these words? *(The last letter is a* t, *a consonant letter.)*
• What happens to the spelling of each of these base words when a suffix beginning with a vowel letter is added? *(The spelling of each base word is not changed.)*
• Write the following words where your student can see them and ask him to read them with you. Ask what happened to the spelling of each of these words when its suffix was added: *magnet, magnetic; atom, atomic; artist, artistic. (When the suffix beginning with a vowel letter was added, the spelling of the base word did not change.)*

Apply generalization number two to words 3-4 and 13-14, using the following statement and question:

• Look at the two pairs of words: *drama, dramatic* and *horizon, horizontal.* What happened to base words when the endings *-ic* and *-al* were added? *(An extra letter was added to each base word before the suffix.)*

Apply generalization number three to words 1-14 in the following way, using the suggested statements and questions:

- Review the principle of morphophonemics by looking at the word pair *patriot, patriotic.* Ask your student to look away from his list and say the word *patriot.* Ask him what he can say about the spelling of the third syllable. *(The spelling is unclear because the syllable has the schwa "uh.")*
- Do the same with *patriotic* and ask about the third syllable. *(It makes the /ŏ/.)*
- How does the pronunciation of *patriotic* help the spelling of *patriot*? *(The /ŏ/ in* patriotic *identifies that the schwa in* patriot *is spelled with an o.)*
- Go over the pairs of words listed below and show how the shift in stress in the second word can clarify the spelling in the unstressed last syllable of the first word: *drama, dramatic; exhibit, exhibition; prohibit, prohibition; continent, continental; horizon, horizontal.*

Introduce words 15-18 on page 10.

- The four countries in this week's list sound very much like the way they are spelled.
- *Bangladesh* has a hard *g* while *Belgium* has a soft *g.*
- It is the *iu* spelling in Belgium that makes the *g* soft.

Guide a research activity: *Where in the World?*
Help your student locate the countries with names in the spelling list on a world atlas or map. Ask him to use the *B* volume of an encyclopedia to expand his geographic and general country knowledge according to the ideas and optional activities presented in Unit 1.

Use the handwritten list. After your student has written each word on the appropriate line, check his list for spelling and legibility. Instruct him to place an accent mark correctly in each multi-syllable word in the printed list.

Second Day

Use the Bible verse activity on page 11. Discuss the verse with your student, using the following questions:

1. What kind of house would a *house of the wicked* be?
2. What does it mean to be *just?*
3. What is a *habitation?*
4. What is God telling us in this verse? (BAT: 4a Sowing and reaping)
5. What can we learn from this verse? (Bible Promise A. Liberty from Sin)

Have fun with the *Word for Word* section on page 11. Read the paragraph with your student and discuss all the different exhibits that you and he have seen. Discuss the real meaning of the word and what meaning he has given the word up to now.

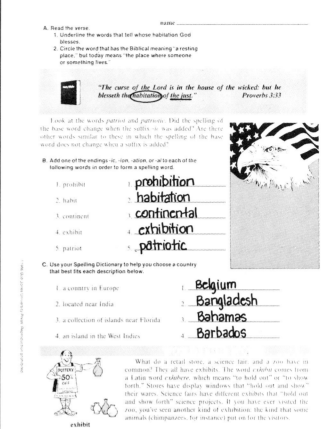

Use worktext pages **11** and **12** to reinforce word meaning and the skills of the unit. Read the directions and give help, if needed, as your student completes the pages.

Guide a word meaning activity: *If and Might.* Your student is to read each sentence and choose the spelling word that best completes the idea, using the prepared activity. (This should be done orally.)

Provide a copy of the activity found in the *Materials* section.

Third Day

Give your student time to study the words, using the study method printed on the back cover of the spelling worktext.

Dictate the word list for the trial test.

Give the following dictation sentences:
1. Last summer we saw a **patriotic drama** about the Great Smoky Mountains.
2. Far beyond the **horizon** lies the **continent** of Europe.
3. My friend from **Bangladesh** took me to an art **exhibition** from his country.

> Dictionary skill: *Entry words* in the dictionary are listed in alphabetical order.

Use page **150** to teach this week's dictionary skill. After you are certain that your student understands the skill, guide him as he completes the exercise.

Look at the words *drama* and *dramatic.* Notice that an extra letter had to be added to the base word before the suffix *-ic* could be used. What was that extra letter?

D. Keeping in mind that a base word is often changed before the suffix is added; give the information called for below.

1. Give the extra letter that is added to *drama* before the ending *-ic;* then write the word the way it looks before and after the ending is added.

t, drama, dramatic

2. Give the extra letter that is added to *horizon* before the ending *-al* is added; then write the word the way it looks before and after the ending is added.

t, horizon, horizontal

E. Fill in the blanks below with the correct spelling word.

Last week we watched a __1__ about the __2__ men and women who helped to win freedom for our country. The __3__ I liked best was George Washington. He sounded __4__ when he encouraged the men in the __5__ Army to keep on fighting. At an __6__ in the auditorium, we examined the different kinds of weapons that his men used. I especially liked the guns and was glad our teacher didn't __7__ us from touching them.

1. **drama**
2. **patriotic**
3. **patriot**
4. **dramatic**
5. **Continental**
6. **exhibit**
7. **prohibit**

F. Write the spelling words from your list that have the stress on the first syllable.

1. **patriot**
2. **drama**
3. **habit**
4. **continent**

Words to Master

patriot	exhibition	continent	Bangladesh
patriotic	prohibit	continental	Barbados
drama	prohibition	horizon	Belgium
dramatic	habit	horizontal	_____
exhibit	habitation	Bahamas	_____

12

Entry words are listed alphabetically between guide words. (Guide words are the first and last entry words on a dictionary page.)

Follow the instructions given below, using the entry words given.

1. Write the entry word with the respelling /chĕr´ ish/.
2. Write the entry word that is defined first as an adjective and then as a noun.
3. Write the entry word that has the following word as its plural: *chefs.*
4. Write the entry word that has three definitions.
5. Write the two entry words that represent people.
6. Write the entry word that has as one definition "to keep or think of fondly."
7. Write the entry word that has as a respelling /chĕr´ ē/.
8. Write the entry word that is defined as a game.

1. **cherish**
2. **chemical**
3. **chef**
4. **cherry**
5. **chef, chemist**
6. **cherish**
7. **cherry**
8. **chess**

150

Use with Unit 3.
Skill: finding entry words

Fourth Day

Return last week's journal. Give your student time to correct the misspelled words in his previous journal entry and record them in his Word Bank.

Guide the journal time, using the *Journal Entry Idea* on page 13 and the information given in the front of this manual. Ask your student to give his opinion concerning the influence that a friend can have upon a person's life. Talk about his experiences with friends and how to make friends. Discuss the importance of choosing the right kinds of friends. (BATs: 1c Separation from the world, 3d Body as a temple, 5a Love, 5e Friendliness)

Fifth Day

Guide the study time.

Dictate the word list for the final test.

Give the following dictation sentences.

1. The American **patriot** took his letters to the history **exhibit.**
2. My sister has a **habit** of being too **dramatic** when she is excited.
3. Both **Barbados** and the **Bahamas** are beautiful vacation spots.

Use *The King's English* on page 13. After your student reads this section silently, read it aloud with him. Use discussion, the Bible verses, and questions to make certain he understands the material completely. Discuss with him the picture and how it must have been for the Israelites to live in tents and travel every day. Especially stress to him that when he believes on the Lord Jesus Christ, God comes into his body in the person of the Holy Spirit. The questions below may also be used:

1. What is a home and what purpose does it serve?
2. Why does God refer to Himself as our habitation?
3. Where did God abide when He was with the Israelites as they traveled to the Promised Land?
4. How does God abide in a Christian today? (BAT: 3d Body as a temple)

Journal Entry Idea

"But, Mom, if I'm not a friend of his, I won't be popular at all! I'll just be a miserable *nothing* if I'm not at least semi-popular!"

How do *you* pick *your* friends? Is this your attitude toward choosing your friends? Maybe you would never *say* that, but do you feel that way? Do you like that well-dressed, well-coordinated, full-of-talent, "cool" person, or do you look for the person who has good inner qualities? Write about how you choose your friends. If you have had an interesting experience with a friend, write about it.

The King's English
habitation

Have you ever compared your home to those of other people? Are they alike or different? What purpose does a house serve? The word **habitation** comes from the Latin word *habitare*, which means "to dwell." Your home is your dwelling place. It protects you from the elements and provides a place to work and relax.

In Psalm 71:3, the Hebrew word *maon* refers to God as the psalmist's "habitation," for he continually turns to the Lord for strength and safety. By the same token, God is the habitation, or place of rest and safety, for us too.

When the children of Israel traveled to the Promised Land, they built the tabernacle as a dwelling place for God. Later, Solomon built the temple of God in Jerusalem. Today, God abides (or dwells) in a Christian through the Holy Spirit.

Isaiah 57:15 tells us that God lives in a high and holy place. There He has prepared a place for us and will return to receive us unto Himself.

Psalm 71:3
Isaiah 57:15
Isaiah 32:18

13

Unit 4

Worktext pages 14-17
Dictionary page 151

——————— Generalization emphasis ———————

1. **Adding a suffix beginning with a vowel letter to a word ending with a consonant letter**–When a suffix beginning with a vowel letter is added to a word ending with a consonant letter, the spelling of the base word does not change. *humor, humorous*

2. **Adding a suffix beginning with *o* to a word that ends in *ge*–**When a suffix that begins with *o* is added to a word that ends with *ge*, the spelling of the base word does not change. *courage, courageous*

3. **Using morphophonemics as an aid in spelling**–The spelling of a word is made more obvious by the pronunciation (stress) of a related word. *potent, potential*

——————————— Materials ———————————

- A world map or an atlas
- The *B* volume of an encyclopedia

4 Words to Master

Read each spelling word and place the accent mark over the correct syllable. Then write the words on the blanks, connecting the syllables.

1. hu·mor
2. hu·mor·ous
3. dan·ger
4. dan·ger·ous
5. cour·age
6. cou·ra·geous
7. ad·van·tage
8. ad·van·ta·geous
9. court
10. cour·te·ous
11. po·tent
12. po·ten·tial
13. pro·vide
14. prov·i·dence
15. Be·lize
16. Bo·liv·i·a
17. Bra·zil
18. Bul·gar·i·a
19. Word Bank entry
20. Word Bank entry

14

First Day

Give the pretest. After you have given the pretest and your student has checked and corrected it, give him time to choose two of the words from his Word Bank and write them as this week's *Word Bank Entries.*

After reading words 1-14 on page 14 to your student, apply generalization number one in the following way, using the suggested questions and statements:

- Look at the words *humor, danger, potent,* and *court.* What do you notice about the last letter in these words? *(They all end with a consonant letter.)*
- Look at the related words in the spelling list: *humorous, dangerous, potential, courteous.* What suffixes were added to these words? *(-ous, -ial, -eous)*
- What do the suffixes have in common? *(They all begin with vowel letters.)*
- Was the spelling of the base words changed when the suffixes were added? *(no)*

Apply generalization number two to the words *courage* and *advantage,* using the following statement and questions:

- What sound comes at the end of the words *courage* and *advantage?* *(/j/)*

- Look at the words *courageous* and *advantageous.* Was the spelling of the base word changed when the suffix *-ous* was added? *(no)*
- Why was the *e* kept when the suffix was added? *(The sound of the consonant letter* g *is /j/ if it precedes an* e.*)*

Apply generalization number three to words 5-8 and 11-14 in the following way, using the suggested questions:

- Go over the following word pairs slowly, asking which word in each pair helps to clarify the pronunciation and spelling of a syllable in the other word. *(This happens because the schwa is changed to a short or long vowel.)*
- How does the word *courageous* help spell the word *courage? (The second syllable in* courageous *is clearly heard as /ā/ which helps spell the schwa in the second syllable of* courage.*)*
- Ask this same question of the words *advantage, advantageous; potent, potential; provide, providence. (The word* provide *helps spell the word* providence.*)*

Introduce words 15-18 on page 14.

- *Belize* has a schwa spelled with an *e.*
- *Bolivia* and *Bulgaria* both have an ending syllable with /ēə/ spelled *ia.*

Guide a research activity: *Where in the World?* Help your student locate the countries with names in the spelling list on a world atlas or map. Ask him to use the *B* volume of an encyclopedia to expand his geographic and general country knowledge according to the ideas and optional activities presented in Unit 1.

Use the handwritten list. After your student has written each word on the appropriate line, check his list for spelling and legibility. Instruct him to place an accent mark in each word in the printed list.

Second Day

> Any answer your student gives that shows that he is thinking is better than a memorized or "parroted" statement that he does not understand. Accept any answer, not by saying it is correct, but by using it to lead him to the correct one. He knows more than he realizes he knows, but he must be made to **think,** if what he has learned is to be permanent.

Use the Bible verse activity on page 15. Discuss the verse with your student, using the following questions:

1. What does it mean to *wait on the Lord?*
2. What does it mean to *be of good courage?*
3. How do you think God strengthens our hearts?
4. What is God telling us in this verse? (BAT: 6b Prayer)
5. Why can you be safe waiting on the Lord? (Bible Promise: H. God as Father)

Have fun with the *Word for Word* section on page 15. Read the paragraph with your student, especially noting the meaning for the Latin word that *humor* comes from. Talk with him about how God can help him to have a good humor instead of complaining and being grouchy. God speaks of this when He addresses the fruit of the Spirit.

Use worktext pages 15 and 16 to reinforce word meaning and the skills of the unit. Read the directions and give help, if needed, as your student completes the pages.

Third Day

Give your student time to study the words, using the study method printed on the back cover of the spelling worktext.

Dictate the word list for the trial test.

Give the following dictation sentences:

1. Missionaries to **Brazil** often take **dangerous** trips.
2. It's good to have a sense of **humor,** but you must also be **courteous.**
3. God's **providence** protects us in times of **danger.**

> Dictionary skill: Sometimes *proper nouns* are listed in alphabetical order along with the other entry words. Most dictionaries have special sections for biographical and geographical entries.

Use page 151 to teach this week's dictionary skill. Before your student gets started on the dictionary exercise, help him find the section in the geographical section of his Spelling 6 dictionary. You might also guide him as he finds the biographical and geographical sections of a college dictionary. After you are certain that your student understands the skill, guide him as he completes the exercise.

Fourth Day

Return last week's journal. Give your student time to correct the misspelled words in his previous journal entry and record them in his Word Bank.

Guide the journal time, using the *Journal Entry Idea* on page 17 and the information given in the front of this manual. After your student has read this material, ask him to explain to you what he read. Elicit his remembrances of times when he has been in fights with his sisters or brothers and how he felt at the time. Draw out his feelings on being punished. The more you get him to talk about this subject, the easier it will be for him to write about it. You might want to end your prewriting time by discussing how God wants Christians to respond to punishment. (BATs: 2a Authority, 4a Sowing and reaping, 4d Victory)

---

name _____

Some proper nouns (names) can be found among the alphabetically listed words. Some are listed in a separate section following the regular listing of words.

New-found-land |nōō´fən land| or |nōō´fən länd´| or |nyōō´fən land| or |nyōō´fən länd´| or |nōō found´land| or |nyōō´ found´land| **1.** An island off the southeastern coast of Canada. **2.** A province of Canada, consisting of this island and nearby territories. The capital of Newfoundland is St. John's.
New Hamp-shire |hămp´shər| or |hăm´shər| or |hămp´shir´| or |hăm´shir´| A state in the northeastern United States. The capital of New Hampshire is Concord.
New Jer-sey |jûr´zē| A state in the eastern United States. The capital of New Jersey is Trenton.
new-ly |nōō´lē| or |nyōō´lē| —*adverb* Recently; lately; just: *a newly discovered chemical product; a newly mown lawn.*
New Mex-i-co |měk´sĭ kō´| A state in the southwestern United States. The capital of New Mexico is Santa Fe.
news |nōōz| or |nyōōz| —*noun* (Used with a singular verb.) Information about one or more events that have recently happened. News may be passed on from person to person or reported by newspapers, news magazines, radio, or television.

Using the dictionary entry words above, answer the questions given below.

1. Which proper noun entry has six different respellings?
2. Which two entries are not proper nouns?
3. Which entry is a place that is not part of the United States?
4. Which proper noun entry mentions the city of Trenton?
5. Which entry is defined as an adverb?
6. Which entry is the name of a southwestern state?
7. Which entry is a noun that is used with a singular verb?
8. Which entry is the name of a northeastern state?

1. Newfoundland
2. newly, news
3. Newfoundland
4. New Jersey
5. newly
6. New Mexico
7. news
8. New Hampshire

Use with Unit 4
Skill: finding proper noun entries   151

Journal Entry Idea

"Oh, oh! Now you've done it!" you say to your brother. The small, insignificant, minuscule thing the two of you were fighting about is forgotten, because on the floor, shattered at your feet, is your mother's favorite lamp. How did it happen? Well, you see it drastically differently from how your brother sees it. In his version, *you* pushed him. Which one will Mom believe? You have the sinking, sad sensation that she'll take neither version. You will both be punished.

Have you ever had a similar situation at your house? How did you take it when you were punished? Tell about it.

The King's English
seraphim

Seraphim are among the most exalted of God's angels. In Isaiah's wonderful vision of God's throne, he saw these six-winged beings. Two wings covered the face, two covered the feet, and two enabled the beings to fly as they praised God, crying "Holy, holy, holy."

The meaning of the Hebrew word *seraph,* or *seraphim,* is doubtful. It may mean "to burn." Because of this, some think the seraphim are "burning" or brilliant ones. Others connect *seraph* with the Arabic *sharafa,* which means "high" or "exalted," and think of them simply as noble angelic beings.

In any case, their function seems clear. Besides glorifying God, the seraphim act as a medium of communication between heaven and earth. As the cherubim are agents of God's judgment, the seraphim are agents of cleansing. In Isaiah 6, a seraphim removed the prophet's sin by touching a burning coal to his lips.
Isaiah 6:2, 6-7

17

Use *The King's English* on page 17. After your student has read this section silently, read it with him orally. Use discussion, the Bible verses, and questions to make certain he understands the material given. The following questions can be used:

1. What are *seraphim?* Describe them.
2. Besides glorifying God, what else do seraphim do?
3. God allows us to sin, but how does He provide a means of cleansing from our sins? (BATs: 1b Repentance and faith, 6e Forgiveness, 7a Grace)

Fifth Day

Guide the study time.

Dictate the word list for the final test.

Give the following dictation sentences.

1. Being **courageous** gives you an **advantage** over those who oppose you.
2. The king tried to **provide** safety for those in his **court.**
3. My brother has great **potential** for writing **humorous** fiction.

Unit 5

Worktext pages 18-21
Dictionary page 152

--- **Generalization emphasis** ---

Adding the suffix *-or* — When the suffix *-or* is added to a word that ends with a consonant letter, the spelling of the base word does not change. *inspect, inspector*

--- **Materials** ---

* A world map or an atlas
* The *G* volume of an encyclopedia

First Day

Give the pretest. After you have given the pretest and your student has checked and corrected it, give him time to choose two of the words from his Word Bank and write them as this week's *Word Bank Entries.*

After reading words 1-14 on page 18 to your student, apply the generalization, using the following questions and statements:

* Look at the words *inspect, direct, conduct, detect, collect, edit,* and *instruct.* What do you notice about the last letter in these words? *(The last letter is the consonant letter* t.*)*
* What suffix was added to each of these words? *(The suffix* -or.*)*
* What happens to the spelling of a base word when the suffix *-or* is added to a word ending with a consonant letter? *(The spelling does not change.)*

Introduce words 15-18 on page 18.

* Draw attention to the silent *h* in *Ghana.*
* Point out that *Grenada* has a schwa in the first and last syllables.

Guide a research activity: *Where in the World?* Help your student locate the countries with names in the spelling list on a world atlas or map. Ask him to use the *G* volume of an encyclopedia to expand his geographic and general country knowledge according to the ideas and optional activities presented in Unit 1. Be sure to check the *Geographic Entries* section for valuable information about the countries. Use this lesson for trying a different "optional activity" not tried before.

5 Words to Master

Read each spelling word and place the accent mark over the correct syllable. Then write the words on the blanks, connecting the syllables.

1. in‑spect´	1. _____
2. in‑spec´‑tor	2. _____
3. di‑rect´	3. _____
4. di‑rec´‑tor	4. _____
5. con‑duct´	5. _____
6. con‑duc´‑tor	6. _____
7. de‑tect´	7. _____
8. de‑tec´‑tor	8. _____
9. col‑lect´	9. _____
10. col‑lec´‑tor	10. _____
11. ed´‑it	11. _____
12. ed´‑i‑tor	12. _____
13. in‑struct´	13. _____
14. in‑struc´‑tor	14. _____
15. East and West Ger´‑ma‑ny	15. _____
16. Gha´‑na	16. _____
17. Greece	17. _____
18. Gre‑na´‑da	18. _____
19. Word Bank entry	19. _____
20. Word Bank entry	20. _____

18

Use the handwritten list. After your student has written each word on the line provided, check his work for spelling and legibility. Instruct him to place the accent mark correctly in each multi-syllable word in the printed list.

Second Day

Use the Bible verse activity on page 19. Make certain your student understands the sentence *I will guide thee with mine eye.* You might start with the following question: *How does God lead and what does He mean by His eye?*

Have fun with the *Word for Word* section on page 19. Discuss with your student the meaning of the word *detect* and how it applies to modern medicine. The many tests that doctors and hospitals give now are good at *detecting* problems and diseases. Early *detection* of cancer, for example, is something he has probably heard discussed. Ask him to think of *detecting* in other areas of life.

Use worktext pages 19 and 20 to reinforce word meaning and the skills of the unit. Read the directions and give help, if needed, as your student completes the pages.

Third Day

Give your student time to study the words, using the study method printed on the back cover of the spelling worktext.

Dictate the word list for the trial test.

Give the following dictation sentences:

1. Are you prepared for the art **instructor** to **inspect** your work?
2. A good band **conductor** can **detect** the sound of each instrument.
3. A magazine **editor** tries to **collect** interesting stories and articles.

Dictionary skill: When looking for a word in a dictionary, use the following steps:
  Decide which fourth of the dictionary the word is in.
  Using the guide words, locate the page the word is on.
  Find the word on the page.

A. Read the verse.
1. Underline the word that tells what God says He will use to guide us.
2. Circle the two-syllable word that means "to cause to act wisely; to teach."

"I will instruct *thee and teach thee in the way which thou shalt go: I will guide thee with mine eye."*　　　*Psalm 32:8*

Compare the two words *inspect* and *inspector* and think about how they would be used in a sentence. Besides the *-or* ending, how are they different? Notice that *inspect* is a verb and *inspector* is a noun. You will find that in several of your spelling words, the *-or* ending can change a verb to a noun.

B. Write each of the first fourteen spelling words in one of the two columns below. Each word will go under either the nouns *(persons or things)* or the verbs *(actions).*

verbs *(actions)*	nouns *(persons or things)*
inspect	inspector
direct	director
conduct	conductor
detect	detector
collect	collector
edit	editor
instruct	instructor

C. From the first fourteen words, write the two in which the stress comes on the first syllable.

1. edit　　　2. editor

He wears dark sunglasses, a black fedora, and a big tan raincoat with the collar turned up. He rids the streets of lurking lawbreakers. Who is he? He's a detective, of course! Our word *detect* comes from two Latin words: *de*, which means "from," and *tect*, which means "cover." Therefore, to detect is to uncover, or to take the cover from something. Detectives uncover clues in order to track down criminals. What do a lie detector and a metal detector uncover?

detect

19

D. Who Am I?

1. I keep my eyes open for detective products.
2. My job involves teaching.
3. I check written material before it is printed.
4. I transmit heat, light, sound, and electric charges.
5. My possessions may range from bottle caps to stamps.
6. I take charge of whatever is going on.

1. inspector
2. instructor
3. editor
4. conductor
5. collector
6. director

E. Use spelling words to complete the Bible verses.

1. "I will ____ thee and teach thee in the way which thou shalt go." Psalm 32:8a
2. "So the king returned, and came to Jordan. And Judah came to Gilgal, to go to meet the king, to ____ the king over Jordan." II Samuel 19:15
3. "In all thy ways acknowledge him, and he shall ____ thy paths." Proverbs 3:6
4. "For though ye have ten thousand ____ in Christ, yet have ye not many fathers." I Corinthians 4:15a

1. instruct
2. conduct
3. direct
4. instructors

F. Unscramble the names of countries given below. Remember to capitalize the first letter of each name.

1. adgnear
2. hnaag
3. ates gyamren
4. egecre
5. sewt erangmy

1. Grenada
2. Ghana
3. East Germany
4. Greece
5. West Germany

Words to Master

inspect	conductor	edit	Ghana
inspector	detect	editor	Greece
direct	detector	instruct	Grenada
director	collect	instructor	_____
conduct	collector	East and	_____
		West Germany	

20

Use page 152 to teach this week's dictionary skill. After you are certain that your student understands the skill, guide him as he completes the exercise.

Fourth Day

Return last week's journal. Give your student time to correct the misspelled words in his previous journal entry and record them in his Word Bank.

Guide the journal time using the *Journal Entry Idea* on page 21 and the information given in the front of this manual. Hold a discussion about having responsibilities and how they enable a person to grow mentally and spiritually. Discuss experiences your student has had doing jobs and duties that called for him to be responsible.

Fifth Day

Guide the study time.

Dictate the word list for the final test.

Give the following dictation sentences.
1. That metal **detector** belongs to a coin **collector**.
2. The police **inspector** will **conduct** the search.
3. The **director** of the play will **instruct** the stage crew.

Use *The King's English* on page 21. After your student has read this section silently, read it with him orally. Use the Bible verses, discussion, and good comprehension questions to make certain your student understands the material completely. The following questions can be used:

1. What are some temptations that you face as a Christian?
2. How can you receive God's guidance? (BATs: 6a Bible study, 6b Prayer)
3. What are the results of allowing God to direct your life?

To find a word in the dictionary, first decide in which fourth of the dictionary you should look. Then, using the guide words (at the top of each page), locate the page the word is on. Use your knowledge of the alphabet to locate the word on that page.

Write the information specified in each statement below. Use your Spelling Dictionary.

1. Write the respelling for *Greece*.
2. Write the two words that *momentous* comes between.
3. Find *Argentina* in the Spelling Dictionary and give its capital.
4. Write the first definition for *individual*.
5. Write the plural of *drama*.
6. Write the guide words for the page on which you find *formality*.
7. Find *courageous* and write what part of speech it is.
8. In what section of the dictionary (*A-F, G-L, M-R, S-Z*) would *impression* fall?
9. Give an entry word found on page 186 of your Spelling Dictionary.
10. Write the second definition for the word *profession*.
11. Give the population of the country of *Bangladesh*.
12. Write the guide words for the page that *success* is on.
13. Write all the respellings for the word *director*.
14. Write the plural of *advantage*.

1. /grēs/
2. momentary and monogram
3. Buenos Aires
4. single; separate
5. dramas
6. fan² and ham
7. adjective
8. G-L
9. any word between hard and join
10. the group of persons doing some work
11. 88,700,000
12. state and telescopic
13. /dĭ rĕk′tər/, /dī rĕk′tər/
14. advantages

152

Use with Unit 5.
Skill: locating words in the dictionary

Journal Entry Idea

More than anything else in the world, you wanted to get a parakeet, so your parents let you have one. Their only condition was that *you* had to take care of him. He was beautiful, and it was fun to clean his cage once a day.

After about two weeks, a bad case of responsibility rheumatism began to develop—not in the bird, but in you! The parakeet chirped constantly and made all kinds of noise as it swished its beak over the floor of its cage. The crazy bird kept throwing stuff out of its cage, and you had to clean it up. Whose idea was this parakeet, anyway?

Have you ever had an experience like this? Tell about it.

The King's English
direct

In *Pilgrim's Progress* by John Bunyan, the character named Christian faced many difficulties in staying on the King's Highway. So it is with us. As Christians, we face many temptations that would turn us from the right way. Sometimes the temptations of the world pull us backward, or another direction looks easier than the one we should take. How can we be sure we are doing what is right?

Proverbs 3:6 tells us to acknowledge the Lord, and He will **direct** our paths. The Hebrew word *yashar* means to "make straight." As the Lord guided the children of Israel through the wilderness, He will guide us if we allow Him to do so. When we read His Word and communicate with Him through prayer, we receive the guidance we need.

In the New Testament Paul tells the Thessalonians that the Lord can direct their hearts into the love of God. Under His direction, we will not only know His will for our lives but also know Him more perfectly.

Proverbs 3:6
II Thessalonians 3:5
Proverbs 21:29

21

Unit 6

Worktext pages 22-25

—— Generalization emphasis ——
Generalization statements can be found in Units 1-5.

—— Materials ——
- Prepare the following activity for Day 2.

Analogies Anonymous
1. foolishness : wisdom :: tardiness : _punctuality_
2. frown : serious :: smile : _humorous_
3. tidy : messy :: safe : _dangerous_
4. untruth : lie :: sin : _transgression_
5. open : closed :: freedom : _oppression_
6. job : employment :: career : _profession_
7. attorney : advocate :: teacher : _instructor_
8. up and down : back and forth :: vertical : _horizontal_
9. hate : selfishness :: love : _hospitality_
10. giver : distributor :: keeper : _collector_

First Day

For review, apply the generalizations found in Lessons 1-5 to the word list on page 22.

Use worktext page 22 to reinforce word meaning and the skills of the unit. Read the directions and give help, if needed, as your student completes the page.

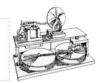

1. profession	9. inspector	17. humorous	25. Bangladesh
2. oppression	10. conductor	18. dangerous	26. Belgium
3. succession	11. collector	19. courageous	27. Ghana
4. transgression	12. instructor	20. advantageous	28. Grenada
5. exhibition	13. technicality	21. potential	29. Argentina
6. prohibition	14. hospitality	22. providence	30. Australia
7. continental	15. punctuality	23. Afghanistan	31. Bolivia
8. horizontal	16. individuality	24. Algeria	32. Brazil

A. Use the Morse code to decode these words; then write the message on the lines below.

A ·—	H ····	O —— —	V ···—
B —···	I ··	P ·——·	W ·——
C —·—·	J ·———	Q ——·—	X —··—
D —··	K —·—	R ·—·	Y —·——
E ·	L ·—··	S ···	Z ——··
F ··—·	M ——	T —	
G ——·	N —·	U ··—	

Humorous instructors are considered dangerous by Communists in Afghanistan; beware this oppression of your individuality.

22

Second Day

Use the Bible verse activity on page 23. Ask the following questions to determine whether your student knows what the verse means.

1. What do you think it means to *hold fast?*
2. What is your *profession of faith?*
3. Who is *faithful as promised?* (Bible Promise: D. Identified in Christ)

Use worktext pages 23 and 24 to reinforce word meaning and the skills of the unit. Read the directions and give help, if needed, as your student completes the pages.

Guide an activity to develop word meaning: *Analogies Anonymous.* An *analogy* is a comparison between things otherwise dissimilar. Examples: *Glove* is to *hand* as *sock* is to *foot.* An analogy can be written as a formula–*glove : hand :: sock : foot.* Provide a copy of the activity found in the *Materials* section. Explain that in order to determine the answer, one must look at how the first pair of words relates to each other. That same relationship is required of the second pair of words. Guide your child's thinking with appropriate questions and comments.

Third Day

Give your student time to study the words, using the study method printed on the back cover of the spelling worktext.

Dictate the word list for the trial test.

Give the following dictation sentences:

1. **Punctuality** is important for someone in the legal **profession.**
2. Many countries such as **Argentina** have had a **succession** of military leaders.
3. The **collector** had an **exhibition** of **humorous** cartoons from newspapers twenty years old.

---

name _____

B. Read the verse.
1. Underline the five words that tell what Christians should hold fast.
2. Circle the word that has the Biblical meaning "a statement that says the same thing," but today means "an occupation that calls for special study."

> *"Let us hold fast the profession of our faith without wavering; (for he is faithful that promised.)*   *Hebrews 10:23*

C. Write the spelling word that each respelling represents.

1. /pō tĕn′ shəl/   **potential**
2. /ĭn də vij ōō ál′ ĭ tē/ **individuality**
3. /kŏn tə nĕn′ tal/   **continental**
4. /tech nǐ kál′ ǐ tē/   **technicality**

D. Write a spelling word to complete each tongue twister.

1. The ___ carries contracts in his carrying case that could completely cancel his concert.   **conductor**
2. The indignant ___ identified Ivan's inchworms.   **inspector**
3. Dreadful Dan denied destroying the dentist's drill with his ___ dagger.   **dangerous**

E. Find a spelling word that is the antonym (opposite) of the word that is incorrect in each of the following sentences. Draw a line through the incorrect word and write the spelling word on the blank.

1. The teacher told us to draw a ~~vertical~~ line that began at the right side of the figure and ended at the left side.   **horizontal**
2. My dad had to talk to the ~~distributor~~ of the silver coins to see which years he wanted.   **collector**
3. The gracious lady was well known for her ~~unfriendliness.~~   **hospitality**
4. My mother's ~~permission~~ kept me from joining the team.   **prohibition**
5. Aunt Mary put her beautiful red roses in the ~~closet.~~   **exhibition**
6. My sister was given an award for her ~~tardiness~~ during the year.   **punctuality**

23

How did the word *advantage* change before its suffix *-ous* was added? *(It didn't.)* You may be able to think of other pairs of words that are similar, such as *live, lively* and *genuine, genuinely.* With these examples in mind, can you make a statement about adding suffixes to words that end in *e? (Sometimes the final e is not dropped when a suffix is added.)*

F. Now you can place a review word in each blank below by adding a suffix to the underlined word.

1. We thought it would be <u>advantage</u> to arrive early.   1. **advantageous**
2. Protecting the boy's body by covering it with his own was a <u>courage</u> act.   2. **courageous**
3. The sunshine our crops needed came to us by the <u>provide</u> of God.   3. **providence**

G. Write the four review words that ended in s before the suffix *-ion* was added.

1. **profession**   3. **succession**
2. **oppression**   4. **transgression**

H. Write the names of the countries on your review list in alphabetical order.

1. **Afghanistan**   6. **Belgium**
2. **Algeria**   7. **Bolivia**
3. **Argentina**   8. **Brazil**
4. **Australia**   9. **Ghana**
5. **Bangladesh**   10. **Grenada**

Words to Master

profession	inspector	humorous	Bangladesh
oppression	conductor	dangerous	Belgium
succession	collector	courageous	Ghana
transgression	instructor	advantageous	Grenada
exhibition	technicality	potential	Argentina
prohibition	hospitality	providence	Australia
continental	punctuality	Afghanistan	Bolivia
horizontal	individuality	Algeria	Brazil

24

Fourth Day

Return last week's journal. Give your student time to correct the misspelled words in his previous journal entry and record them in his Word Bank.

Guide the journal time using the *Journal Entry Idea* on page 25 and the information given in the front of this manual. After your student reads the paragraph, ask him to give you a short review of the content. Ask him to describe any kind of giving that he has done. Has he ever given something, expecting nothing in return? How does God bless that kind of giving? Discuss with him how giving is something Jesus taught much about when He was on earth. When we give, we have the satisfaction of knowing that we have obeyed the Lord Jesus. Ask your student to suggest some things he can do for others. (BATs: 5a Love, 5b Giving, 5e Friendliness)

Fifth Day

Guide the study time.

Dictate the word list for the final test.

Give the following dictation sentences:

1. The **instructor** told a **humorous** story.
2. The people from **Australia** are known for their **hospitality.**
3. The **courageous** soldier was on a **dangerous** mission in **Bolivia.**

> Any answer your student gives that shows that he is thinking is better than a memorized or "parroted" statement that he does not understand. Accept any answer, not by saying it is correct, but by using it to lead him to the correct one. He knows more than he realizes he knows, but he must be made to **think** if what he has learned is to be permanent.

Use *The King's English* on page 25. After your student reads this section silently, read it with him orally using discussion, the Bible verses, and questions. Make certain that he knows that *sin* is anything that God does not approve. Every person has a different idea of what is and what is not *sin*. What really matters, however, is what *God* thinks of what we do. The following are some questions you might use:

1. What is a *transgression?*
2. What was the transgression that Saul committed against the Lord?
3. How can you have your transgressions blotted out before God? (BATs: 1a Understanding Jesus Christ, 1b Repentance and faith)

Journal Entry Idea

You have that I-never-wanted-anything-else-so-much-in-my-life feeling about the varsity tournament, but your parents have said that they simply can't afford it. You bravely go on with your life, and then one week before the tournament, you get an envelope delivered to your desk and inside . . . a ticket to the tournament! Who could have done such a wonderful thing for you?

That kind of a deed is "pure religion" according to James 1:27. Jesus also said to do things for others who could not repay you. Tell about something that was done for you by someone who wanted nothing in return or tell how you could do something like that for someone else.

The King's English

transgression

Our word **transgression** comes from a Greek word that means "overstepping." It is often used as a synonym for the word *sin* but refers particularly to the breaking of the law.

In 1 Chronicles 10, we read about the death of King Saul. Saul had been anointed by God to lead His people as their king, but as Saul gained power and popularity, he began to trust in himself and his kingdom instead of in the Lord. Verse 13 of 1 Chronicles, chapter 10, says, "Saul died for his transgression which he committed against the Lord." Saul disobeyed God by going to someone other than God to find out what he should do. Do we ever take advice from someone who doesn't worship God? Saul died for his transgressions. The Bible says, "For the wages of sin is death."

We also transgress against God, but the Bible tells us that the Lord Jesus Christ, God's perfect Son, was called a transgressor because He took the penalty for our sins and died in our place. As a result of Christ's death on the cross, God has promised to blot out our transgressions.

I John 3:4
Mark 15:28
I Chronicles 10:1-14

25

Unit 7

Worktext pages 26-29
Dictionary page 153

Generalization emphasis

1. /yo͞on/ spelled *un* at the beginning of a word–/yo͞on/ at the beginning of a word is spelled *un*, if the meaning of the word is related to "one." *union*

2. /bī/ or /bə/ spelled *bi* at the beginning of a word–/bī/ or /bə/ at the beginning of a word is spelled *bi*, if the meaning of the word is related to "two." *bisect, binoculars*

3. /trī/ spelled *tri* at the beginning of a word–/trī/ at the beginning of a word is spelled *tri*, if the meaning of the word is related to "three." *triune*

Materials

- A world map or an atlas
- The *C* and *T* volumes of an encyclopedia
- Prepare the following activity for Day 2.

Test Your Tongue

1. How can the ___union___ be ___unanimous___ in urging me to use an ugly ___unicycle___ ?
2. While Bob was busy building beefy ___biceps___ , Bill borrowed his ___binoculars___ for bird watching.
3. Ursula urges Udele to wear the most ___unique___ uniform in the ___universe___ .

First Day

Give the pretest. After you have given the pretest and your student has checked and corrected it, give him time to choose two of the words from his Word Bank and write them as this week's *Word Bank Entries.*

> Knowing the spelling of Greek or Latin word parts can be a help in spelling. For example, your student wants to use the word *tripod.* As he begins to write it, he remembers the Greek prefix *tri* and how it is spelled. He knows a tripod has three legs and therefore assumes that the beginning of the word is spelled *tri* instead of *try.*

Guide a discussion about the English language. Ask your student if he knows why some words (like *colonel,* /ker • nal/) are so difficult to spell. Bring out the fact that the English language was influenced by many languages, including Greek, Latin, French, German, and Italian. The words that we use today are words that have come from

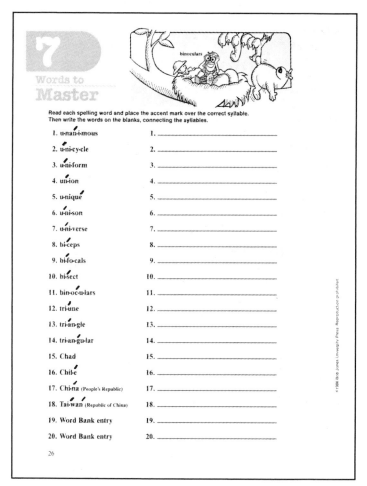

all these languages. The result of combining these languages makes for a language that sounds beautiful when we speak it; but it also makes for words that are difficult to spell.

After reading words 1-7 on page 26 to your student, apply generalization number one in the following way, using the suggested statements and questions:

- What do words 1-7 have in common? *(They all begin with the letters* un.*)*
- Do you know what any of these words mean? *(Your student may know that a* union *is an organization in which all the people agree to do one thing; he may know that* unison *is everyone's singing the same notes or saying the same thing; he may know that a person's* uniform *looks like everyone else's who does that job.)*
- Whatever definition your student gives for a word, use his definition to lead him to the correct definition that will involve the meaning of "one." Before discussing the meaning of each word, give your student a chance to tell what he thinks the word means or how he has heard it used. The following definitions will help:

      unanimous: "sharing the same opinion"
      unicycle: "a vehicle with one wheel"
      uniform: "always the same"

union: "an alliance for mutual interest"
unique: "being the only one of its kind"
unison: "in complete agreement" or "singing the same part"
universe: "all existing things"

- Ask your student how /yo͞o/ is spelled if it comes at the beginning of a word that has a meaning related to "one." *(un)*

After reading words 8-11 to your student, apply generalization number two to the words, following the same steps that you did in applying generalization number one. The following definitions will be helpful:

biceps: "a muscle with two points of origin"
bifocals: "having two different focal lengths"
bisect: "to cut or divide into two equal parts"
binoculars: "a pair of magnifying glasses, designed for use with both eyes"

- Ask your student how /bī/ or /bə/ is spelled if it comes at the beginning of a word that has a meaning related to "two." *(bi)*

After reading words 12-14 to your student, apply generalization number three, following exactly the same steps that you did in applying generalization number one. The following definitions will help:

triune: "being three in one"
triangle, triangular: "of or pertaining to a figure with three sides"

- Ask your student how /trī/ is spelled if it comes at the beginning of a word that has a meaning related to "three." *(tri)*

Introduce words 15-18 on page 26.

- Ask your student to give two homonyms (words that sound alike but have different spellings and meanings) for *Chile. (chilly, chili)*
- In *Taiwan,* /ī/ is spelled *ai.*

Guide a research activity: *Where in the World?* Help your student locate the countries with names in the spelling list on a world atlas or map. Ask him to use the *C* and *T* volumes of an encyclopedia to expand his geographic and general country knowledge according to the ideas and optional activities presented in Unit 1.

Since the countries *China (the People's Republic)* and *Taiwan (Republic of China)* have unusual backgrounds, you might ask your student to do reports on these two nations.

Use the handwritten list. After your student has written each word on the appropriate line, check his list for spelling and legibility. Instruct him to place an accent mark in each multi-syllable word in the printed list.

Second Day

Use the Bible verse activity on page 27. Use the following question to get your student to think about the meaning of the verse:

What does *for brethren to dwell together in unity* mean? (BAT: 5a Love)

Have fun with the *Word for Word* section on page 27. Read the paragraph with your student and discuss the origin of the word *union*. He may want to investigate an onion by pealing off the layers to see the different levels. Point out to him the similarity between the spelling of *onion* and *one*. You might ask him to do this demonstration for the family as he explains the word *union*.

Use worktext pages 27 and 28 to reinforce word meaning and the skills of the unit. Read the directions and give help, if needed, as your student completes the pages.

Guide an activity to develop word meaning: *Test Your Tongue.* Direct your student to fill in the blanks in the tongue-twister activity found in the *Materials* section of the lesson. He is to use spelling words that have the same beginning letters as most of the words in the sentence. He may use no word more than once. Then have your student try the tongue twisters he has created. Ask him to read them aloud as fast as he can.

---

name _____

A. Read the verse.
1. Underline the two words that describe what it is like when Christians have unity.
2. Circle the three-syllable word that means "the condition of being together in agreement."

"Behold, how good and how pleasant it is for brethren to dwell together in unity"
                                                    Psalm 133:1

If you look carefully at some of our English words, you will find parts of them that come from Greek or Latin words. In this unit, you will notice several words beginning with *uni-*, from the Latin word for "one." Knowing this helps you understand that *unicycle*, for example, refers to something with one wheel. It also gives you a hint for spelling the word correctly.
   Now compare *unicycle* with *bicycle*. What does *bicycle* mean? ("two wheels") What about *tricycle*? ("three wheels") Can you see the difference that *uni-*, *bi-*, and *tri-* make when they are added to the word *cycle*? Think about how these prefixes are related to the meaning of this week's spelling words.

B. Finish the spelling words below, using the definitions to help you.

1. the state of being united   1. **u n ion**
2. being the same as one another   2. **u n iform**
3. having the same pitch   3. **u n ison**
4. all existing things regarded as a whole   4. **u n iverse**
5. being the only one of its kind   5. **u n ique**
6. a vehicle having only one wheel   6. **u n icycle**
7. sharing the same opinion   7. **un animous**

WORD FOR WORD

union

Have you ever heard the expression, "In union there is strength"? Some people jokingly say, "In onion there is strength." If you've ever peeled an onion, you'll agree that onions are strong enough to make you cry, but did you know that *union* and *onion* really do have something in common? Both words come from the same Latin word, *unio*, which means "one." An onion is made up of many layers, and yet it is one vegetable; a union, like the United States, is made up of many sections that form one thing. Now you can ask someone, "How is the United States like an onion?"

27

C. Write the spelling word that means the same as the underlined phrase.

1. My teacher told me to draw a figure that has three sides.   1. **triangle**
2. The shape of the tent was like a triangle.   2. **triangular**
3. Our God is a three in one God.   3. **triune**

D. Fill in the missing vowels to find the correct spelling word for each set of consonants. Don't forget to capitalize the names of the countries.

| 1. chd | 3. chn | 5. bnclrs | 7. twn | 9. bfcls |
| 2. nnms | 4. nn | 6. nfrm | 8. chl | 10. nvrs |

1. **Chad**   6. **uniform**
2. **unanimous**   7. **Taiwan**
3. **China**   8. **Chile**
4. **union**   9. **bifocals**
5. **binoculars**   10. **universe**

E. Cross out the word that does not belong in each sentence below and write the correct substitute on the blank.

1. My mother's eyeglasses are ~~visuals~~.   1. **bifocals**
2. Ted worked on increasing the size of his ~~protons~~.   2. **biceps**
3. In math class, we learned to ~~insect~~ a right angle. 3. **bisect**

Words to Master

unanimous	unison	binoculars	Chile
unicycle	universe	triune	China
uniform	biceps	triangle	Taiwan
union	bifocals	triangular	
unique	bisect	Chad	

28

Third Day

Give your student time to study the words, using the study method printed on the back cover of the spelling worktext.

Dictate the word list for the trial test.

Give the following dictation sentences:

1. Mary wore a **unique** costume for the **China** skit at the missions service.
2. Never carry **binoculars** when you ride a **unicycle**.
3. The children from **Taiwan** sang in **unison**.

Dictionary skill: A *word form* in a dictionary entry is made up of the entry word plus one of the suffixes that can be added to it. Word forms are usually located after the main part of the entry and are printed in boldface type.

Use page 153 to teach this week's dictionary skill. After you are certain that your student understands the skill, guide him as he completes the exercise.

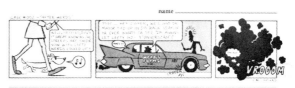

name _____

Following the entry word and the part of speech in the dictionary entry, the word forms (the word with different suffixes added) are given in darker print.

A. Decide which word from Unit 7 goes in each blank, find the word in your Spelling Dictionary, and write either the entry word or one of the word forms.

1. Toward the end of the Civil War, it became evident that the _____ would win.

2. The scouts were to appear in their _____ for the flag ceremony.

3. The weight lifter flexed his right arm to show off his _____.

4. My favorite exercise in geometry was _____ right angles.

5. God is a _____ God; He is three in one.

6. The _____ entertained the crowd on a bright blue unicycle.

7. The teacher told us to construct three equilateral _____.

8. The choir director told everyone to sing in _____.

9. That picture you have drawn is _____; no one else would think to draw that.

10. There were fifty bird watchers at our meeting, and they all carried _____.

1. Union
2. uniforms
3. biceps
4. bisecting
5. triune
6. unicyclist
7. triangles
8. unison
9. unique
10. binoculars

B. Find each of the following words in your Spelling Dictionary and write the number of the page on which you found it.

1. Afghanistan **195**	6. Brazil **195**	11. Argentina **195**
2. isthmus **186**	7. collector **182**	12. habit **185**
3. patriotic **189**	8. triangular **193**	13. profession **190**
4. prohibition **190**	9. Chad **195**	14. depression **183**
5. technical **192**	10. success **192**	15. exhibition **184**

Use with Unit 7
Skill: recognizing word forms and locating entry words

153

Fourth Day

Return last week's journal. Give your student time to correct the misspelled words in his previous journal entry and record them in his Word Bank.

Guide the journal time using the *Journal Entry Idea* on page 29 and the information given in the front of this manual. Ask your student to tell about times when he has won prizes and times when he has lost to others. If he feels he has never won anything before, ask him to describe how he would feel if he won a contest tomorrow. Ask him to explain the statement "*Everything* is the same, and yet *nothing* is the same." The more you can get him to talk about the journal idea, the easier it will be for him to write about it.

Fifth Day

Guide the study time.

Dictate the word list for the final test.

Give the following dictation sentences.

1. The vote to send a gift to **Chile** was **unanimous**.
2. Can you **bisect** each angle of a **triangle**?
3. Our **universe** is the creation of a **triune** God.

Use *The King's English* on page 29. After your student has read this section silently, read it with him orally. Use discussion, the Bible verses, and questions to make certain he understands the material. Get his ideas about what the word *jealous* means today. The following questions can be used:

1. What does it mean to be *jealous?*
2. Why do the Old Testament writers tell us that God is a jealous God?
3. What are some of the gods that we, as His children, might put before the true God?
4. Because we are Christians, what are we assured of? (Bible Promise: G. Christ as Friend)

Journal Entry Idea

You won! You sit there by the telephone, as still as a statue. It seems that time has stopped and the whole room is frozen forever in your memory. The goose bumps slowly spread over your body, and chills engulf you. You won! You weren't even going to enter the contest, and you won! After your body seems normal again, you look at yourself in the mirror. Yup! Same old you! You begin to feel as if it hadn't happened at all. Everything is the same; same you, same room, same day. *Everything* is the same, and yet *nothing* is the same. But you keep telling yourself . . . you won.

Tell about a time when you won and how you felt about it.

The King's English
jealous

What does the word **jealous** mean to you? The Bible says that our God is a jealous God. To be jealous means to want someone or something for yourself. You might think of jealousy as a bad trait, but when we speak of the jealousy of God, we must remember that a human's emotions are not the same as God's. Knowing what jealousy means to us helps us understand the Old Testament writers who tell us that God is a jealous God. The first commandment God gave Moses was that we are to have no other gods. We are His, and He will not share us with other gods.

Like a father, God watches over us, giving both the love and the discipline needed to guide and direct growing children. Unfaithful believers experience His chastening anger; persecuted believers experience His protective care. Because of His jealousy, we know that nothing and no one can separate us from His love. How blessed we are in having a "jealous" God.

Exodus 20:5
Deuteronomy 4:24
Zechariah 1:14

29

Unit 8

Worktext pages 30-33
Dictionary page 154

———— Generalization emphasis ————

1. **/tĕl/ spelled *tel* at the beginning of a word–**/tĕl/ at the beginning of a word is spelled *tel*, if the meaning of the word is related to "far." *televise*

2. **/skōp/ or /skŏp/ spelled *scope* or *scop* at the beginning or end of a word–**/skōp/ or /skŏp/ at the beginning or end of a word is spelled *scope* or *scop*, if the meaning of the word is related to "view." *telescope*

3. **/mī • krō/ spelled *micro* at the beginning of a word–**/mī • krō/ at the beginning of a word is often spelled *micro*, if the meaning of the word is related to "small." *microbe*

———— Materials ————

- A world map or an atlas
- The *C* volume of an encyclopedia
- Prepare the following activity for Day 2.

Fit the Clue

1. <u>periscope</u> : an object used in a submarine to look above the water
2. <u>microbe</u> : a small life form
3. <u>microphone</u> : a small instrument for transmitting sound
4. <u>microscopic</u> : a word that is used to describe something very small
5. <u>television</u> : a system for sending and receiving pictures and sounds
6. <u>microfilm</u> : a film that holds material reduced in size
7. <u>microwave</u> : an electromagnetic wave that is used for cooking
8. <u>microscope</u> : an instrument for looking at very small objects

First Day

Give the pretest. After you have given the pretest and your student has checked and corrected it, give him time to choose two of the words from his Word Bank and write them as this week's *Word Bank Entries*.

After reading words 1-6 on page 30 to your student, apply generalization one in the following way, using the questions and statements given below.

- What do the first six words have in common? *(They all begin with the spelling* tele.*)*
- What does the word *telescope* mean? *(Elicit the idea that it is an instrument that allows one to see faraway objects.)*

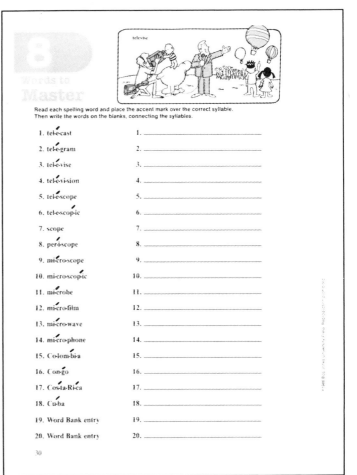

Read each spelling word and place the accent mark over the correct syllable. Then write the words on the blanks, connecting the syllables.

1. tel-e-cast   1. _____
2. tel-e-gram   2. _____
3. tel-e-vise   3. _____
4. tel-e-vi-sion   4. _____
5. tel-e-scope   5. _____
6. tel-e-scop-ic   6. _____
7. scope   7. _____
8. per-i-scope   8. _____
9. mi-cro-scope   9. _____
10. mi-cro-scop-ic   10. _____
11. mi-crobe   11. _____
12. mi-cro-film   12. _____
13. mi-cro-wave   13. _____
14. mi-cro-phone   14. _____
15. Co-lom-bi-a   15. _____
16. Con-go   16. _____
17. Cos-ta-Ri-ca   17. _____
18. Cu-ba   18. _____
19. Word Bank entry   19. _____
20. Word Bank entry   20. _____

30

- What does the word *television* mean? *(Elicit the idea that a television is bringing pictures from faraway into the home.)*
- What do you think these two meanings have in common? *(Elicit the fact that both meanings have to do with "far.")*
- Go over each word (1-6) discussing the meaning and showing how the word relates to "far." The following definitions will be helpful:

  telecast: "a broadcast that transmits visual images with accompanying sound"

  telegram: "a communication system that transmits and receives electrical impulses by wire"

  televise: "to broadcast the transmission of visual images with the accompanying sound"

  television: "the transmission of visual images with accompanying sound"

  telescope: "an instrument used to observe distant objects"

  telescopic: "of or pertaining to seeing distant objects by means of a telescope"

- Ask your student how /tĕ • lə/ is spelled if it comes at the beginning of a word that has a meaning related to "far." *(tele)*

After reading words **5-10** to your student, apply generalization number two to those words, following the same steps you used to apply generalization number one. The following definitions will be helpful:

> scope: "the range of one's thoughts and sights"
> periscope: "an instrument for observing a position displaced from a direct line of sight"

- Ask your student how /skōp/ is spelled when it comes at the end of a word that has a meaning related to "view" or "perception." *(scope)*
- Ask your student how /skŏp/ is spelled in *telescopic* and *microscopic*. Elicit the idea that *scop* is a closed syllable with a short vowel, so it is spelled without the *e*.

After reading words **9-14** to your student, apply generalization number two to those words, following the same steps that you used to apply generalization number one. The following definitions will help:

> microscope: "an instrument that produces magnified images of small objects"
> microscopic: "too small to be seen by the unaided eye"
> microbe: "a minute life form"
> microfilm: "a film on which materials are photographed greatly reduced in size"
> microwave: "an electromagnetic wave that ranges in length from one millimeter to one meter"
> microphone: "a small instrument that converts soundwaves into electrical currents"

- Ask your student how /mī • crō/ is spelled if it comes at the beginning of a word that has a meaning related to "small." *(micro)*

Introduce words 15-18 on page 30.
- The name *Colombia* has schwas in the first and last syllables.
- The *i* in *Rica* is pronounced /ē/.

Guide a research activity: *Where in the World?* Help your student locate the countries with names in the spelling list on a world atlas or map. Ask him to use the *C* volume of an encyclopedia to expand his geographic and general country knowledge according to the ideas and optional activities presented in Unit 1.

Use the handwritten list. After your student has written each word on the appropriate line, check spelling and legibility. Instruct him to place an accent mark in each multisyllable word in the printed list.

Second Day

Use the Bible verse activity on page 31. Discuss the verse with your student, using the following questions:

What is *wisdom* and where do you get it?
What is *folly?*
What does *excelleth* mean?
What is God telling us in this verse? (Bible Promise: I. God as Master)
What can you do to begin to get God's wisdom? (BAT: 6a Bible study)

Have fun with the *Word for Word* section on page 31. You might want to follow up the discussion on *microbes* with a discussion about how God arms a person's body with some very strong "small life" of its own called *antibodies*. These antibodies go after bacteria the minute they enter the person's body. The good "small life" attempts to consume the bad "small life." The good small life is usually successful; if it isn't, the person gets sick.

Use worktext pages 31 and 32 to reinforce word meaning and the skills of the unit. Read the directions and give help, if needed, as your student completes the pages.

Developing word meaning: *Fit the Clue.* Provide a copy of the activity found in the *Materials* section. Write a spelling word that goes with each of the clues.

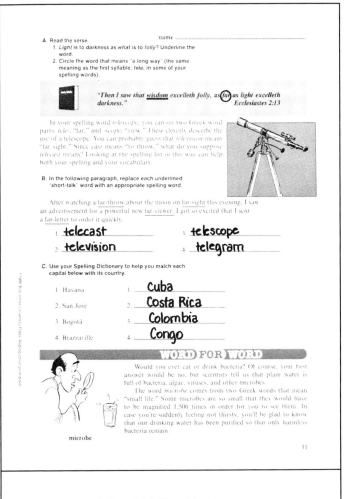

Third Day

Give your student time to study the words, using the study method printed on the back cover of the spelling worktext.

Dictate the word list for the trial test.

Give the following dictation sentences:

1. The **television** reporter gave his **microphone** to the man from **Cuba**.
2. The information on the **microfilm** showed the **scope** of Dr. Paul's book on **microwave** ovens.
3. A fishing boat near **Costa Rica** caught sight of a submarine's **periscope**.

> Dictionary skill: A *sample sentence or phrase* is usually given after each entry word or form of an entry word to illustrate how the word is used in a sentence.

Use page 154 to teach this week's dictionary skill. After you are certain that your student understands the skill, guide him as he completes the exercise.

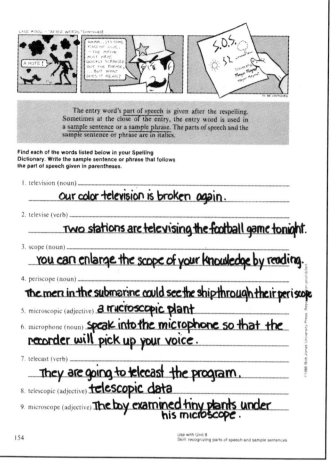

The entry word's part of speech is given after the respelling. Sometimes at the close of the entry, the entry word is used in a sample sentence or a sample phrase. The parts of speech and the sample sentence or phrase are in italics.

Find each of the words listed below in your Spelling Dictionary. Write the sample sentence or phrase that follows the part of speech given in parentheses.

1. television (noun) _____
   Our color television is broken again.

2. televise (verb) _____
   Two stations are televising the football game tonight.

3. scope (noun) _____
   You can enlarge the scope of your knowledge by reading.

4. periscope (noun) _____
   The men in the submarine could see the ship through their periscope

5. microscopic (adjective) a microscopic plant

6. microphone (noun) speak into the microphone so that the recorder will pick up your voice.

7. telecast (verb) _____
   They are going to telecast the program.

8. telescopic (adjective) telescopic data

9. microscope (adjective) The boy examined tiny plants under his microscope.

154

Use with Unit 8
Skill: recognizing parts of speech and sample sentences

Fourth Day

Return last week's journal. Give your student time to correct the misspelled words in his previous journal entry and record them in his Word Bank.

Guide the journal time using the *Journal Entry Idea* on page 33 and the information given in the front of this manual. Elicit remembrances from your student of times he has lost in contests of various kinds (even a footrace or a race to get his room cleaned). The more discussion you have with him, the easier it will be for him to write. (BATs: 3b Mind, 3c Emotional control, 4d Victory)

Fifth Day

Guide the study time.

Dictate the word list for the final test.

Give the following dictation sentences.

1. The president received a **telegram** when he was visiting **Colombia**.
2. The scientist studied the strange **microbe** under his **microscope**.
3. The network decided to **telecast** a program about life in the **Congo**.

In order for your student to see the significance of the Jewish celebration described in this section, explain that the words *Yōm Kippōōr* mean "Day of Atonement." *Atonement* means "to make amends for an injury."

Use *The King's English* on page 33. After your student reads this section silently, read it with him orally. The subject matter for this lesson is extremely difficult, so explain and ask questions as you go along. Tie the offering of the sacrifice to the fact that Christ offered Himself as the sacrifice for our sins and died, shedding His blood. Tie the scapegoat into the fact that God says if a person accepts the sacrifice of Christ as payment for his sin, God removes his sin from him—as far as the East is from the West. God looks on that person as if he had never sinned. The following questions can be used:

1. Explain what the word *scapegoat* means to you.
2. What did a goat symbolically do in the Jewish celebration Yom Kippur?
3. Who bore the sins of mankind on Calvary's cross? (BATs: 1a Understanding Jesus Christ, 1b Repentance and faith)

Journal Entry Idea

"Our choir was the best! I know we must have won! I prayed that we would!"

Have you ever said something like that? What if the person who prayed to win lost instead? Has that ever happened to you? You could think of so many good things that would happen if your team or choir won. Could you also see good things as the results of your losing? Can you think of a time when you prayed to win, wanted to win, even thought you *had* to win, but lost? Write about it. Look back and try to find some results of losing that brought glory to God.

The King's English
scapegoat

In Leviticus 16, the Lord told Moses to have lots cast over two goats, choosing one for a sin offering. At the same time, a bullock was chosen for a burnt offering. Both the bullock and the goat on which the lot fell were killed. Aaron laid his hands on the remaining goat, placing the sins of Israel upon him. Then he sent the goat into the wilderness.

The Hebrew word *azazel*, which probably means "a complete removal," is translated as **scapegoat**. In the Jewish ceremony, Yom Kippur, the goat symbolically bore the sins of Israel. After the ceremony it was released into the wilderness. This showed that God had removed the people's sins and that they were forgiven forever. One year the scapegoat wandered back into Jerusalem. Since the people feared this as bad luck, the successive goats were taken to a high mountain. A man cast the goat down the slope, which was steep enough and rough enough to cause its certain death. The goat's death showed that the "sins of Israel" would not return!

Leviticus 16:8-26
Isaiah 53:1-12

33

Unit 9

Worktext pages 34-37
Dictionary page 155

───────── Generalization emphasis ─────────

1. **/jē • ŏ/ spelled *geo* at the beginning of a word**–/jē • ŏ/ at the beginning of a word is spelled *geo*, if the meaning of the word is related to "earth." *geology*

2. **/mə • nŏ'/ or /mŏn' ə/ spelled *mono* at the beginning of a word**–/mə • nŏ'/ or /mŏn'ə/ at the beginning of a word is spelled *mono*, if the meaning of the word is related to "single." *monopoly*

3. **/grăf/ spelled *graph*–**/grăf/ at the beginning or end of a word is spelled *graph*, if the meaning of the word is related to "written." *autograph*

4. **/ô' tə/ or /ô' tō/ spelled *auto* at the beginning of a word–**/ô' tə/ or /ô' tō/ at the beginning of a word, is spelled *auto*, if the meaning of the word is related to "self." *autobiography, automobile*

───────── Materials ─────────

• A world map or an atlas
• The *C* and *D* volumes of an encyclopedia

First Day

Give the pretest. After you have given the pretest and your student has checked and corrected it, give him time to choose two of the words from his Word Bank and write them as this week's *Word Bank Entries*.

After reading words 1-2 on page 34 to your student, apply generalization number one in the following way, using the suggested questions and statements:

• How are the spellings of the words *geology* and *geological* alike? (*Their first six letters are the same.*)
• Do you know what either of these words means?
• Can you think of another word that begins with the letters *geo*? (*geography*) What does that word mean? (*a study of parts of the earth and the people on earth*)
• Relate each of the words to the meaning of the Latin prefix *geo*. The following definition will be helpful:
   geology, geological: "of or pertaining to the scientific study of the origin and structure of the earth"
• Ask your student how /jē • ō/ (or /jē • ô/) is spelled if it comes at the beginning of a word that has a meaning related to "the earth." (*geo*)

After reading words 3-6 to your student, follow exactly the same steps to apply generalization number two to those words that you did when you applied number

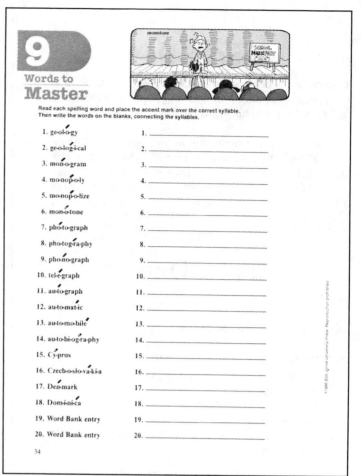

9
Words to
Master

Read each spelling word and place the accent mark over the correct syllable.
Then write the words on the blanks, connecting the syllables.

1. ge-ol-o-gy
2. ge-o-log-i-cal
3. mon-o-gram
4. mo-nop-o-ly
5. mo-nop-o-lize
6. mon-o-tone
7. pho-to-graph
8. pho-tog-ra-phy
9. pho-no-graph
10. tel-e-graph
11. au-to-graph
12. au-to-mat-ic
13. au-to-mo-bile
14. au-to-bi-og-ra-phy
15. Cy-prus
16. Czech-o-slo-va-ki-a
17. Den-mark
18. Dom-i-ni-ca
19. Word Bank entry
20. Word Bank entry

1. ___
2. ___
3. ___
4. ___
5. ___
6. ___
7. ___
8. ___
9. ___
10. ___
11. ___
12. ___
13. ___
14. ___
15. ___
16. ___
17. ___
18. ___
19. ___
20. ___

34

one. The following definitions will be helpful:
   monogram: "a design that gives the initials of one name"
   monopoly, monopolize: "of or pertaining to the exclusive control by one person or group"
   monotone: "a succession of sounds uttered in one tone"
• Ask your student how /mŏn'ə/ (or /mə • nŏ'/) is spelled if it comes at the beginning of a word that has a meaning related to "one." (*mon*)

Apply generalization number three to words 7-11, following exactly the same steps that you used for applying the first two generalizations. The following definitions will be helpful:

   photograph, photography: "of or pertaining to the reproduced image recorded (written) on a photosensitive surface"
   phonograph: "a machine that reproduces (writes) on a disc"
   autograph: "writing one's own name"
• Ask your student how /grăf/ is spelled if it comes at the end of a word that has a meaning related to "to write." (*graph*)

After reading words 12-14 to your student, follow exactly the same steps to apply generalization number

four to those words as you did when you applied the other three generalizations. The following definitions will be helpful:

> automatic: "self moving"
> automobile: "a self-propelled passenger vehicle"
> autobiography: "the life story a person writes about himself"

- Ask your student how /ô′ tō/ or /ô′ tə/ is spelled if it comes at the beginning of a word that has a meaning related to "self." *(auto)*

Introduce words 15-18 on page 34.

- Point out that the country *Cyprus* is spelled differently from the *cypress* that is a type of tree.
- Write the respelling for *Czechoslovakia* on a piece of paper (/chĕk′ ə • slə • vä′ kē • ə/), and compare it to the word. Ask your student to notice the letters that spell /chĕk/, as well as the three schwas in this word.

Guide a research activity: *Where in the World?* Help your student locate the countries with names in the spelling list on a world atlas or map. Ask him to use the *C* volume of an encyclopedia to expand his geographic and general country knowledge according to the ideas and optional activities presented in Unit 1.

Use the handwritten list. After your student has written each of the words in the list on the appropriate line, check his list for spelling and legibility. Instruct him to place an accent mark correctly in each multi-syllable word in the printed list.

Second day

Use the Bible verse activity on page 35.

Have fun with the *Word for Word* **section on page 35.**

Use worktext pages 35 and 36 to reinforce word meaning and the skills of the unit. Read the directions and give help, if needed, as your student completes the pages.

Guide a spelling activity: *All About Me.* Inform your student that a biography is a written account or story of a person's life, and that an autobiography is a biography of a person written by himself. Direct your student to write an autobiography including where and when he was born and the places he has lived. Ask him to describe your family and pets and the activities he enjoys doing. Tell him to make his autobiography interesting by including a description of an event that was meaningful or exciting. He should include either photographs or drawings of himself, those he loves, and places he has visited. Assist him in mounting his final written copy and picture on a large colored background. He may want to place it on his bedroom door for relatives and visitors to enjoy.

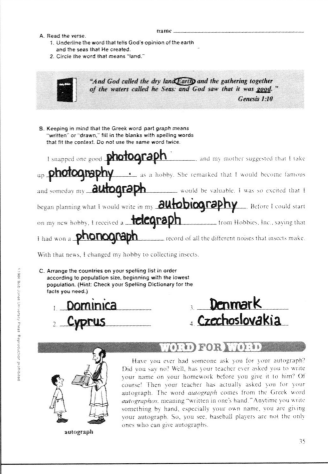

Third Day

Give your student time to study the words, using the study method printed on the back cover of the spelling worktext.

Dictate the word list for the trial test.

Give the following dictation sentences:

1. The **geology** teacher spoke in a **monotone**.
2. Both the **telegraph** and the **phonograph** were invented in the nineteenth century.
3. I didn't mean to **monopolize** the conversation with all my own ideas about **photography.**

> Dictionary skill: The *pronunciation key,* which is located on every page or every other page of a dictionary, gives a sample word for each sound. You can use it to read the respelling of the entry word.

Use page 155 to teach this week's dictionary skill. After you are certain that your student understands the skill, guide him as he completes the exercise.

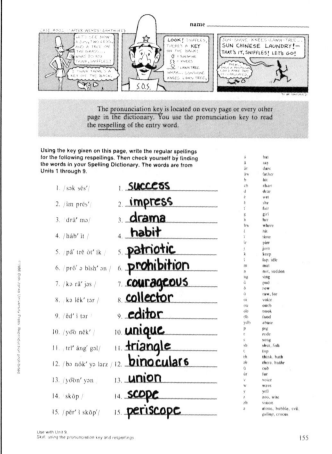

Fourth Day

Return last week's journal. Give your student time to correct the misspelled words in his previous journal entry and record them in his Word Bank.

Guide the journal time using the _Journal Entry Idea_ on page 37 and the information given in the front of this manual. Get out the photo albums and have a good time discussing the various events recorded there in pictures. Elicit from your student comments about his favorite photos. Ask him to bring out and show you any collection that he has and tell you what he remembers about where he got each piece in the collection. The more he talks about the journal idea, the easier it will be for him to write about it.

Fifth Day

Guide the study time.

Dictate the word list for the final test.

Give the following dictation sentences.
1. The new **automobile** had **automatic** door locks.
2. The men had to **photograph** the land for the **geological** survey.
3. I asked the piano teacher from **Czechoslovakia** to **autograph** my music book.

Use _The King's English_ on page 37. After your student reads this section silently, read it with him orally. Use the Bible verses, discussion, and good comprehension questions to make certain he understands the material. The following questions and statements can be used:
1. What does the Greek word for _paradise_ mean?
2. Describe the features that make a park special and unique.
3. What is the higher meaning for the word _paradise?_
4. Describe what you think heaven will be like.

Journal Entry Idea

Look at this one! I took it when our family went to a major league baseball game in Chicago. And this one is me under the St. Louis Arch. If you hold it in the light, you can almost see me. That's my whole family looking for sandpipers at the beach; see the Atlantic Ocean? Yes, that's a real castle. Look at these postcards: I try to get one from every place we visit.

Tell about your best collection or the one you would like to start.

The King's English
paradise

If you drew a picture of the Garden of Eden, what would you include? Crystal streams? Flowers? Animals roaming freely across the grass? If so, your picture could also have illustrated a _paradeisos,_ which is a Greek word that means "park."

Long ago, traveling Greeks were fascinated by the beautiful _paradeisos_ of ancient Persia. When transcribing the Greek version of the Old Testament, the writers had difficulty translating the Hebrew word _pardes._ Unable to find a word that better described the earthly park where Adam and Eve had been privileged to live, they chose to call it _paradeisos,_ or **paradise.**

In time, the word _paradise_ gained a higher meaning. In Luke 23, Jesus told the thief on the cross that he would be with Him in paradise. And in Revelation 2:7, John spoke of heaven as "the paradise of God."

Jesus told us in John 14, "And if I go and prepare a place for you, I will come again, and receive you unto myself; that where I am, there ye may be also."
Luke 23:43
II Corinthians 12:4
Revelation 2:7

37

Unit 10

Worktext pages 38-41
Dictionary page 156

Generalization emphasis
---

1. **/dīn/ spelled *dyn* at the beginning of a word–**/dīn/ at the beginning of a word is spelled *dyn* if the meaning of the word is related to "power." *dynamo*

2. **/hĭd/ or /hĭd • rō/ spelled *hyd* or *hydro*–**/hĭd/ or /hĭd • rō/ at the beginning of a word is spelled *hyd* or *hydro* if the meaning of the word is related to "water." *hydrant, hydroplane*

3. **/bī • ŏ/ or /bī • ə/ spelled *bio* at the beginning of a word–**/bī • ŏ/ or /bī • ə/ at the beginning of a word is spelled *bio* if the meaning of the word is related to "life." *biology, biological*

4. **/âr/ spelled *aer*–**/âr/ can be spelled *aer* when it comes at the beginning of a word that has a meaning related to "air." *aeronautics, aerodynamics*

Materials

- A world map or an atlas
- The *D* and *E* volumes of an encyclopedia

First Day

Give the pretest. After you have given the pretest and your student has checked and corrected it, give him time to choose two of the words from his Word Bank and write them as this week's *Word Bank Entries.*

After you read words 1 and 2 to your student, apply generalization number one to the words following the same steps you did for the other generalizations, using the following information:

- The words *dynamic* and *dynamo* come to us through the French word *dynamique* from the Greek word *dunamis,* which means "power." The word part *dyn,* while not properly a prefix, often indicates a meaning in our English words that is related to "power."
- Ask your student how /dīn/ is spelled if it comes at the beginning of a word that has a meaning that is related to "power." *(dyn)*

10 Words to Master

Read each spelling word and place the accent mark over the correct syllable. Then write the words on the blanks, connecting the syllables.

1. dy·na·mo	1. _____
2. dy·nam·ic	2. _____
3. hy·drant	3. _____
4. hy·drau·lic	4. _____
5. hy·dro·gen	5. _____
6. hy·dro·pho·bi·a	6. _____
7. hy·dro·plane	7. _____
8. bi·og·ra·phy	8. _____
9. bi·o·graph·i·cal	9. _____
10. bi·ol·o·gy	10. _____
11. bi·o·log·i·cal	11. _____
12. aer·i·al	12. _____
13. aer·o·nau·tics	13. _____
14. aer·o·dy·nam·ics	14. _____
15. Do·min·i·can Re·pub·lic	15. _____
16. Ec·ua·dor	16. _____
17. El Sal·va·dor	17. _____
18. E·gypt	18. _____
19. Word Bank entry	19. _____
20. Word Bank entry	20. _____

38

After reading words 3-7 to your student, apply generalization number two to these words, following the same steps that you did applying the first generalization. The following definitions will help:

> hydrant: "an upright pipe used to draw water from a water main"
> hydraulic: "the act of moving water (or fluid) under pressure"
> hydrogen: "a colorless, highly flammable gaseous element found in water"
> hydrophobia: "fear of water"
> hydroplane: "a sea plane," "to skim along on the top of water"

- Ask your student what four letters are found at the beginning of all the words with meanings related to water. *(hydr)*

After reading words 8-11 to your student, apply generalization three to those words, following the same steps you did for the first and the second generalizations. The following definitions will help:

> biography, biographical: "of or pertaining to a written account of a person's life"
> biology, biological: "of or pertaining to the study of the science of living organisms and the life process"

- Ask your student how /bī • ō/ is spelled if it comes at the beginning of a word that has a meaning related to "life." *(bio)*

After reading words 12-14 on page 38 to your student, apply generalization number four in the following way, using the suggested following statements and questions:

- Ask your student if he knows what an *aerial* is. *(He may say "an antenna.")*
- Guide your student as he finds *aerial* in a college dictionary. The first definition is "of, in, or caused by air." Read over the other definitions with him until he comes to the one he gave. Point out that a word we might think has only one meaning can actually have many.
- Teach the meanings of the *aer* words. The following definitions will help:

  aeronautics: "the theory and practice of aircraft navigation"

  aerodynamics: "the study of how the atmosphere interacts with moving objects"
- Ask your student how /âr/ is spelled if it comes at the beginning of a word that has a meaning related to "air." *(aer)*

Introduce words 15-18 on page 38.

- *Ecuador* has an unusual spelling.
- /ĭ/ in *Egypt* is spelled with a *y*.

Guide a research activity: *Where in the World?* Help your student locate the countries with names in the spelling list on a world atlas or map. Ask him to use the *D* and *E* volumes of an encyclopedia to expand his geographic and general country knowledge according to the ideas and optional activities presented in Unit 1.

Egypt plays an important part in the Bible. Read with your student the story of Joseph and his role in Egypt beginning in Genesis 39. The story of Moses and the Israelites leaving Egypt is a fascinating one to read in Exodus 12-14.

Use the handwritten list. After your student has written each word on the line provided, check his list for spelling and legibility. Instruct him to place an accent mark on the correct syllable of each word in the printed list.

Second Day

Use the Bible verse activity on page 39. Discuss the verse with your student, using the following questions:

1. What does *warreth* mean?
2. What does it mean to *entangle* yourself in the affairs of this life?
3. Who are we supposed to try to please? (Bible Promise: I God as Master)
4. What can we learn from this verse? (BAT: 1c Separation from the world)

Have fun with the *Word for Word* section on page 39.

Use worktext pages 39 and 40 to reinforce word meaning and the skills of the unit. Read the directions and give individual help, if needed, as your student completes the pages.

Guide an activity to develop word meaning: *Who-What?* Ask your student to use spelling words to answer the riddles as you read them.

Who-What?

1. I am a special kind of upright pipe that firemen like. What am I? *(hydrant)*
2. I am a colorless, flammable, very light gas. What am I? *(hydrogen)*
3. I often refer to something that is operated by means of water. What word am I? *(hydraulic)*
4. I am a kind of study that deals with living things. What am I? *(biology)*
5. I am usually made of metal and can receive electromagnetic waves. What am I? *(aerial)*
6. I am a kind of motorboat that skims the water at high speeds. What am I? *(hydroplane)*
7. I am a written account of a person's life history. What am I? *(biography)*

A. Read the verse.
1. Underline the thirteen words that tell why a Christian should not entangle himself in the affairs of this life.
2. Circle the word that means "the manner or period of existing."

"No man that warreth entangleth himself with the affairs of this life, that he may please him who hath chosen him to be a soldier."
II Timothy 2:4

Look at the following list of word parts from your spelling words. Do you know other words that begin the same way? What about *dynasty, dynamite, biotic, biopsy, aerogram,* and *aerosol?* In some words, like *aerodynamics,* two Greek word parts are combined. When you know the meaning of the Greek word part, you can soon figure out the meaning of the word as it appears in English. Study the meanings given below.

dyn means "power"   *bio* means "life"
hydr means "water"   *aero* means "air"

B. Under the following headings, write the spelling words that you think belong together.

aero	dyn	bio
aerodynamics	dynamo	biography
aerial	dynamic	biographical
aeronautics	aerodynamics	biology or biological

	hydr	
hydrophobia	hydrant	hydrogen
hydroplane	hydraulic	

WORD FOR WORD

Are you the kind of person who hates to take a bath? Did your mother ever teasingly say that you have hydrophobia? Maybe you wondered why she made that remark..The word *hydrophobia* comes from the Greek and literally means "water fear." A phobia is a kind of fear that doesn't make sense but is real to the person who is afraid. Most children get over their dislike of water, but some grown-ups miss the good fun found in water sports because of their hydrophobia. So be tough on yourself and step into that bathtub!

hydrophobia

39

C. Choose countries from your spelling list to answer the following questions.

1. What country is mentioned in the Bible?
2. What three countries are located south of the United States?

1. Egypt
2. Dominican Republic
   Ecuador
   El Salvador

D. Using the vertical message below as a guide, arrange spelling words on the blanks.

```
A E R O N A U T I C S
        B I O G R A P H Y
        B I O L O G Y
        H Y D R A N T
        A E R I A L
    H Y D R O G E N
        H Y D R O P H O B I A
A E R O D Y N A M I C S

        D Y N A M O

    D Y N A M I C
    B I O G R A P H I C A L
        H Y D R A U L I C
  A E R O N A U T I C S
A E R O D Y N A M I C S
    H Y D R A N T

        E C U A D O R
    H Y D R O P L A N E
        B I O L O G I C A L
    E L S A L V A D O R
        E G Y P T
```

Words to Master

dynamo	hydrophobia	biological	Ecuador
dynamic	hydroplane	aerial	El Salvador
hydrant	biography	aeronautics	Egypt
hydraulic	biographical	aerodynamics	
hydrogen	biology	Dominican Republic	

40

Third Day

Give your student time to study the words, using the study method printed on the back cover of the spelling worktext.

Dictate the word list for the trial test.

Give the following dictation sentences:

1. The car began to **hydroplane** on the wet road, and then it ran into a fire **hydrant**.
2. This **biography** contains an **aerial** picture of the missionary's home in **Ecuador**.
3. The Wright brothers had a **dynamic** effect on the science of **aeronautics.**

Dictionary skill: Some words have both *primary* and *secondary accent marks.* The primary accent gets the greatest stress.

Use page 156 to teach this week's dictionary skill. After teaching your student the skill of the lesson, guide him as he completes the exercises on the page.

In words of more than three syllables, there often are two points of stress. In this example, *Af ghan' i stan',* the strongest stress, or primary accent, comes on the second syllable, and the weaker stress, or secondary accent, comes on the last syllable. The accents can be found in the respelling of the entry word.

Find the following words in your Spelling Dictionary and notice their two points of stress. In the first blank after each word, put the number of the syllable on which the primary accent falls. In the next blank, do the same for the secondary accent. The first example is done for you.

Word	Primary	Secondary
1. technicality	3	1
2. individual	3	1
3. Argentina	3	1
4. patriotic	3	1
5. prohibition	3	1
6. exhibition	3	1
7. telescopic	3	1
8. Bangladesh	3	1
9. telecast	1	3
10. unicycle	1	3
11. televise	1	3
12. television	1	3
13. periscope	1	3

156

Use with Unit 10
Skill: Identifying primary and secondary accents

Fourth Day

Return last week's journal. Give your student time to correct the misspelled words in his previous journal entry and record them in his Word Bank.

Guide the journal time using the *Journal Entry Idea* on page 41 and the information given in the front of this manual. Guide a discussion about the many wonderful aspects of this country. Elicit many ideas from your student about the fascinating places he would like to visit or has visited.

Fifth Day

Guide the study time.

Dictate the word list for the final test.

Give the following dictation sentences.

1. The pilot read books about **aerodynamics** and **hydraulic** landing gear.
2. My **biology** textbook has a section on **hydrophobia** in wild animals.
3. I am looking for **biographical** information on the last king of **Egypt**.

Use *The King's English* on page 41. After your student has read this section silently, read it orally with him. Make certain that he understands the material completely through the use of the Bible verses, discussion, and good questions. Bring out the concept that a person's conscience is a helper to him because it warns him of danger, but that person must listen to his conscience. If your student is a Christian, he should be learning to let God control his conscience. The following questions can be used:

1. What does your *conscience* do?
2. What happens to an unsaved person's conscience?
3. When does a conscience operate as God intended it to? (BATs: 6c Spirit-filled, 6d Clear conscience)

Journal Entry Idea

You're walking down an ancient street in Philadelphia, and suddenly you see a man dressed in old-fashioned clothes yelling from a window. Your family stares in awe as a drama from 1776 unfolds around you.

On this trip across the United States, you have walked the fields of Gettysburg, strolled down the lanes of Mount Vernon, and stared up at the Statue of Liberty. What a great country you live in!

Tell about an experience *you* had that made you realize how much you love your country.

The King's English
conscience

Have you ever felt that what you or your friends were planning to do was wrong even though the activity was not specifically forbidden by God's Word? That was your **conscience** prompting you to distinguish between right and wrong. The word *conscience* comes from the Latin word *conscientia*, from *conscire*, "to know."

I John 3:20 calls the conscience the "heart." "For if our heart condemn us, God is greater than our heart, and knoweth all things." Everyone has a conscience, but the conscience of an unsaved person is not the same as a Christian's. If this conscience is constantly thwarted, or suppressed, then it becomes "hardened." A person who constantly listens to wrong advice has a "conscience seared with a hot iron."

The Christian can be thankful that he has the Holy Spirit to govern his conscience. Only when the conscience operates under the influence of the Holy Spirit does it work as God intended for it to work.

John 8:9
I Peter 3:16, 21
I Corinthians 8:7, 10, 12

41

Unit 11

Worktext pages 42-45
Dictionary page 157

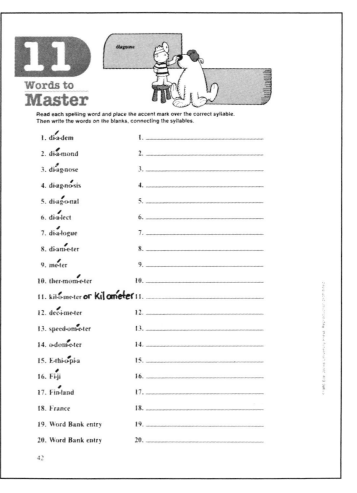

Generalization emphasis

1. **/dī • ə/ or /dī • ă'/ spelled *dia* at the beginning of a word—**/dī • ə/ or /dī • ă'/ at the beginning of a word is spelled *dia*, if the meaning of the word is related to "across" or "through." *dialogue, diagonal*

2. **/mē • tər/ or /mə • tər/ spelled *meter* at the beginning or end of a word—**/mē • tər/ or /mə • tər/ at the beginning or end of a word is spelled *meter*, if the meaning of the word is related to "measure." *meter, diameter*

Materials

- A world map or an atlas
- The *E* and *F* volumes of an encyclopedia

First Day

Give the pretest. After you have given the pretest and your student has checked and corrected it, give him time to choose two of the words from his Word Bank and write them as this week's *Word Bank Entries.*

After reading words 1-8 on page 42 to your student, apply generalization number one to words 1-8 in the following way, using the suggested questions and statements:

- What do words 1-8 have in common? *(All begin with the spelling* dia.*)*
- Draw a circle where your student can see it and draw a line through it. Ask your student what we call a line that cuts across a circle. *(diameter)*
- Read the word *diadem* and then discuss with your student its meaning. For example, after you read *diadem,* ask your student what he thinks it means. He will probably say that a *diadem* is a crown that goes across the top of the head. Explain (through the use of the dictionary or without it) that when you take the parts of the word back to their origins, you find that *dia* means "across" and *dem* means "bind"; so *diadem* technically means "to bind across."
- Follow the same steps with each of the *dia* words, except *diamond.* The following definitions will be helpful:

  diagnose: "to identify a disease" in other words, "to cut through the disease until it can be separated from other diseases"

  diagnosis: "the findings once the disease has been cut through to the extent that it can be separated from other diseases"
  diagonal: "of or pertaining to a slanted straight line that seems to cut a rectangle in two"
  dialect: "a language cut from a larger family of languages (a language branch)"
  dialogue: "a conversation between two or more people"
  diameter: "a line segment passing through the center of a figure"

- Ask your student how /dī • ə/ or /dī • ă'/ is spelled if it comes at the beginning of a word that has a meaning related to "through, across, or between." *(dia)*

> The meaning of "diamond" is discussed in the *Word for Word* section of the student text.

After reading words 8-14 to your student, apply generalization number two. Follow exactly the same steps as you did when you applied generalization number one. Inform your student that the Latin word *metrun,* means "to measure." The following definitions will help:

> meter: "a fundamental unit of length or a device that measures time, distance, speed, or intensity"
>
> thermometer: "an instrument that measures temperature"
>
> kilometer: "one thousand meters"
>
> decimeter: "one-tenth of a meter"
>
> speedometer: "an instrument for measuring speed"
>
> odometer: "an instrument that measures distance traveled in a vehicle"

- Ask your student how /mə • tər/ or /mē • tər/ is spelled if it comes at the end of a word that has a meaning related to "measure." *(meter)*

Introduce words 15-18 on page 42.

- Since *Fiji* is not included in the Spelling Dictionary, mention that it is a country composed of about 320 islands, located in the southwestern Pacific Ocean.
- Point out the schwa sound in the second syllable of *Finland.*

Guide a research activity: *Where in the World?* Help your student locate the countries with names in the spelling list on a world atlas or map. Ask him to use the *E* and *F* volumes of an encyclopedia to expand his geographic and general country knowledge according to the ideas and optional activities presented in Unit 1.

Have your student do some research to find out the relationship between the Statue of Liberty and France. Ask him to write a short paper on the facts he gathers and share it with your family.

Use the handwritten list. After your student has written each word on the appropriate line, check his list for spelling and legibility. Instruct him to place an accent mark in each multi-syllable word of the printed list.

Second Day

Use the Bible verse activity on page 43. Talk about the meaning of this verse; explain that a person becomes a "crown of glory" and a *royal diadem,* not by being born or being good. That position is obtained only by placing one's faith in Christ's shedding of His blood and calling upon God to save him from punishment.

Have fun with the *Word for Word* section on page 43.

Use worktext pages 43 and 44 to reinforce word meaning and the skills of the unit. Read the directions and give individual help, if needed, as your student completes the pages.

A. Read the verse.
1. In whose hand will the people be a crown or a diadem? Underline two words that refer to Him.
2. Circle the three-syllable word that means "a crown or headband worn as a sign of royalty."

name _____

"Thou shalt also be a crown of glory in the hand of the <u>Lord</u>, and a royal diadem in the hand of thy <u>God</u>."   Isaiah 62:3

The two Greek word parts that make up *diameter* ("across-measure") will give you clues for understanding the words in this unit. The prefix *dia-* has many meanings, but *dia-* can be a useful decoding tool.

B. Use the italicized words in the sentences below to give you clues for spelling words beginning with *dia-*.

1. The geometry teacher told us to *measure across* the circle   1. **diameter**
2. The young princess liked to *bind across* her hair a circlet of rubies.   2. **diadem**
3. Take a short-cut by going *across* the square from *angle to angle*.   3. **diagonal**

You are already familiar with the word *meter* as a measuring term in math. One of the most interesting *meter* words on your list is *odometer.* Its first three letters come from a French word derived from the Greek, which means "road" or "journey." Look at your *meter* words. Do you know any other words that have *meter* in them?

C. Write spelling words to answer the questions below.

1. What measures speed?   1. **speedometer**
2. What means one-tenth of a meter?   2. **decimeter**
3. What measures heat?   3. **thermometer**

WORD FOR WORD

diamond

What does the word *diamond* mean to you? A boy might think of a baseball diamond, which is named for its diamond shape. A girl may dream of an expensive ring displaying the gem that is famous for its glittering beauty. Besides being beautiful and having an interesting shape, diamonds are the hardest natural substance known to man. That is why the ancient Greeks used a word for them that means "invincible" and called diamonds "the untamed stone." A diamond may be a valuable gem, but don't let anyone ever accuse you of having a heart like one.

43

D. Use your dictionary and this week's spelling words to complete the following crossword puzzle.

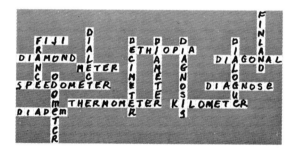

Down
1. A country in Northern Europe
2. A language that belongs especially to one certain group of people
3. A country in Western Europe
4. Equal to one-tenth of a *meter*
5. A straight line that measures the distance *across* the center of a circle
6. The act of identifying a disease *apart* from other diseases
7. A conversation *between* two or more people
12. An instrument that *measures* distance

Across
3. An island in the southwest Pacific
8. A country of northeastern Africa
9. A hard, clear gem
10. A line *across* a figure from one angle to another
11. An instrument for measuring
13. An instrument that records speed
14. To recognize a disease *apart* from other diseases
15. An instrument for measuring temperature
16. Equal to 1,000 meters
17. A headpiece that goes *across* the forehead; often a sign of royalty

---

Words to Master

diadem	dialect	kilometer	Fiji
diamond	dialogue	decimeter	Finland
diagnose	diameter	speedometer	France
diagnosis	meter	odometer	
diagonal	thermometer	Ethiopia	

44

Third Day

Give your student time to study the words, using the study method printed on the back cover of the spelling worktext.

Dictate the word list for the trial test.

Give the following dictation sentences:

1. The **odometer** on my bike shows that I have gone less than a **kilometer** on this trip.
2. The doctor from **Ethiopia** gave us his **diagnosis** of Bill's illness.
3. A **thermometer** is a useful tool in helping to **diagnose** an illness.

> Dictionary skill: When you have to choose between several *definitions* of an entry word, try to decide which one best fits the context of what you are writing or saying.

Use page 157 to teach this week's dictionary skill(s). After you are certain that your student understands the skill, guide him as he completes the exercise.

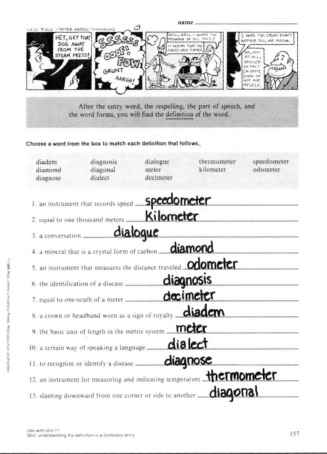

Fourth Day

Return last week's journal. Give your student time to correct the misspelled words in his previous journal entry and record them in his Word Bank.

Guide the journal time using the *Journal Entry Idea* on page 44 and the information given in the front of this manual. Get your student excited about writing by telling him some things you are thankful for. Call on him then to talk about his blessings. The more he talks about his ideas, the easier it will be for him to express them in writing. Read Ephesians 5:20 to remind your student that thanks is given to God for all things. Read other verses that teach the Christian character trait of gratitude. (BATs: 7c Praise, 7d Contentment)

Fifth Day

Guide the study time.

Dictate the word list for the final test.

Give the following dictation sentences.
1. The queen of **France** wore a golden **diadem** that had a large **diamond** in it.
2. This table is exactly one **meter** in **diameter**.
3. My dad checked his speed on the **speedometer** and the number of miles on the **odometer**.

Use *The King's English* on page 45. After your student reads this section silently, read it with him orally. Use the Bible verses, discussion, and good comprehension questions to make certain he understands the material. Make certain that your student understands what *surety* means in financial terms. Explain the principle behind a *down payment* or *earnest* money. Now is a good time to teach (or remind) him that when one places his trust in Jesus Christ and calls upon God to save him, God places in him His Holy Spirit, an earnest, to assure him of a place in heaven. He then places that person in the hands of the Lord Jesus, as taught in Hebrews 7:22. The following questions can be used:

1. What is the most common form of pledging?
2. What does the verse mean, "Christ is our surety"? (Bible Promises: D. Identified in Christ, F. Christ as Intercessor)
3. How did Christ become a Christian's surety? (BATs: 1a Understanding Jesus Christ, 1b Repentance and faith)

Journal Entry Idea

"Please don't make me do it," you plead with your teacher. She wants you to give your composition as a speech in the Thanksgiving program. The title is "Count Your Blessings." You don't mind *feeling* "thankful"; you don't mind *writing* "thankful"; you just don't want *everyone* to hear you *talk* "thankful." So then the teacher asks a Korean girl to do hers, and she joyfully says yes. You feel ashamed when you hear her say that she wants everyone to know that she is counting her blessings.

In your journal this week, tell about the things you are thankful for. Count your blessings!

The King's English

surety

Our word **surety** comes from the Latin word *securus*. It means to pledge or deposit a pledge for something or someone. The most common form of pledging is financial. In Moses' time, a person who pledged in favor of the debtor had to meet all the responsibilities of the debtor. In this way, the creditor was protected.

The first time surety is recorded in the Bible concerns a situation in which one person pledged himself for another. In Genesis 43:9, Judah tells his father that he will be "surety" for Benjamin and will bring him back from Egypt safely. When Joseph accused Benjamin of stealing his silver cup, Judah offered himself in his brother's place.

In a larger sense, Christ is our surety. Hebrews 7:22 tells us that Jesus was "made a surety of a better testament." As our mediator, He made Himself responsible for us.

Genesis 43:9
Hebrews 7:22
Psalm 119:122

45

Unit 12

Worktext pages 46-49

───────── Generalization emphasis ─────────

Generalization statements can be found in Units 7-11.

───────── Materials ─────────

- Prepare the following activity for Day 2.

Sense or Nonsense

1. The speedoscope in Tom's car showed that he was disobeying the law. *(speedometer)*
2. A mining company wants to make a(n) unlogical survey of Uncle Perry's ranch. *(geological)*
3. I used my micronoculars to watch the parachutists jump. *(binoculars)*
4. Malaria is a disease that is caused by a telescopic organism. *(microscopic)*
5. At the circus we saw an amazing dynial trapeze act. *(aerial)*
6. Mrs. Lawrence was elected to the county council by a(n) bianimous vote. *(unanimous)*
7. Jonathan Jones spent a whole year writing his micro-biography. *(autobiography)*
8. Sam's favorite science course is triology. *(biology)*
9. The submarine captain was angry when I broke his perimeter. *(periscope)*
10. Who can ever understand our biune God? *(triune)*
11. "Please use a(n) aerphone when you speak," said the old man. *(microphone)*
12. The famous astronomer told us about a geoscopic star that he was studying. *(telescopic)*
13. The gold miners used a powerful stream of water for a tool; they called it autoaulic mining. *(hydraulic)*
14. Aunt Martha is a hydramic little woman who never seems to get tired. *(dynamic)*

For review, apply the generalizations found in Lessons 7-11 to the word list on page 46.

Use worktext page 46 to reinforce word meaning and the skills of the unit. Read the directions and give individual help, if needed, as your student completes the page.

Review 12
Words to Master

1. unanimous	9. geological	17. diagnosis	25. Colombia
2. unique	10. monopolize	18. dialogue	26. Costa Rica
3. binoculars	11. photography	19. diameter	27. Czechoslovakia
4. triune	12. autobiography	20. thermometer	28. Denmark
5. periscope	13. dynamic	21. diamond	29. Ecuador
6. telescopic	14. hydraulic	22. speedometer	30. Egypt
7. microscopic	15. biology	23. Chad	31. Ethiopia
8. microphone	16. aerial	24. Chile	32. Fiji

A. BACKWARD SHIFT CIPHER. Decode this cipher by counting back three letters in the alphabet to find the correct letter for spelling each word. *D* represents *A*, *C* represents *Z*, and so on.

Secret message:

WKHGLDPRQGIURPHFXDGRU

LVKLGGHQLQWKHSHULVFRSH.

Decoded message:

The diamond from Equador is hidden in the periscope.

B. Use review words to complete these analogies:

1. earth : geography :: life : _biology_
2. city : Detroit :: islands : _Fiji_
3. rectangle : width :: circle : _diameter_
4. Europe : France :: Central America : _Costa Rica_
5. sight : binoculars :: sound : _microphone_
6. distance : odometer :: heat : _thermometer_
7. different : same :: common : _unique_

46

Second Day

Use the Bible verse activity on page 47. Discuss the verse with your student, using the following questions:

1. What does *a pen of iron* mean?
2. How can you write something with *a point of a diamond*?
3. What kind of table is a *table of the heart*?
4. What are the *horns of the altar*?
5. What can we learn from this verse?
   (BATs: 1a Separation from the world, 4a Sowing and reaping, 4b Purity, 4c Honesty)

If your student cannot explain the meanings of these expressions, teach him that a metaphor is a figure of speech, a comparison, a saying that does not mean what it says but gives the idea the author wanted to give, or a saying not to be taken literally. Point out the four metaphors in the verse: *pen of iron, point of a diamond, upon the tables of their heart, upon the horns of your altar.* Tell your student that God had His prophet Jeremiah use these metaphors so that there would be no doubt that His people would get the message. Now ask your student if he can say the verse using his own words. *(God is saying that the sin of His chosen people will never be forgotten because God is going to record it where it can never be erased.)* Bring out the fact that, indeed, it has never been forgotten because it is recorded in His Word, the Bible.

Use worktext pages 47 and 48 to reinforce word meaning and the skills of the unit. Read the directions and give individual help, if needed, as your student completes the pages.

Use an activity to develop word meaning: *Sense or Nonsense.* Provide a copy of the activity found in the *Materials* section. Notice that the Latin and Greek word parts are mixed up in these sentences. Write the correct word after each sentence.

---

name _____

C. Read the verse.
1. Underline two phrases that tell where the sin of Judah was written.
2. Circle the word that means "an extremely hard, clear gem."

"The sin of Judah is written with a pen of iron, and with the point of a diamond it is graven upon the table of their heart, and upon the horns of your altars."
Jeremiah 17:1

D. Write the four-syllable spelling words (not names of countries) that have the stress on the second syllable.
1. binoculars   4. biology
2. monopolize   5. thermometer
3. photography   6. speedometer

E. Write the three-syllable spelling words (not names of countries) that have the stress on the first syllable.
1. periscope   3. dialogue
2. microphone   4. diamond

F. Look for words that have the -ic and -ical endings. Write them in syllables.
1. mi cro scop ic   3. ge o log ical
2. hy drau lic   4. tel e scop ic

G. Classify eight of the countries on your spelling list according to the continents listed below.
1. AFRICA: _____
Chad, Egypt, Ethiopia
2. SOUTH AMERICA: _____
Chile, Colombia, Ecuador
3. EUROPE: _____
Czechoslovakia, Denmark

47

Remember These?		
geo-: earth	tri-: three	bi-: two
uni-: one	auto-: self	dia-: between, among, across

H. Answer the questions below with review words, using the information in the box and the clues given by the italicized words.

1. What word is a conversation *between* two or more people?
2. What word means the process of choosing *between* several diseases to decide on the correct one?
3. What word describes our God, who is *three* persons in one?
4. What word has to do with the study of the *earth*?
5. What word means *one* of a kind?
6. What word refers to a device designed to be used by *both (two)* eyes at once?
7. What word refers to many people being of *one* opinion?
8. What word means an account written by someone about *himself*?

1. dialogue
2. diagnosis
3. triune
4. geological
5. unique
6. binoculars
7. unanimous
8. autobiography

I. Find a spelling word that each of the following sets brings to mind.

1. submarine, mirror, reflector
2. dominate, control, exclude
3. powerful, compelling, commanding
4. air, radio, television

periscope
monopolize
dynamic
aerial

Words to Master

unanimous	geological	diagnosis	Colombia
unique	monopolize	dialogue	Costa Rica
binoculars	photography	diameter	Czechoslovakia
triune	autobiography	thermometer	Denmark
periscope	dynamic	diamond	Ecuador
telescopic	hydraulic	speedometer	Egypt
microscopic	biology	Chad	Ethiopia
microphone	aerial	Chile	Fiji

48

Third Day

Give your student time to study the words, using the study method printed on the back cover of the spelling worktext.

Guide a spelling activity: *SETtle It!*

Read each **set** of words to your student, and have him choose the word from Unit 12 that each *set* of clues brings to mind.

1. conversation, exchange, talk: *dialogue*
2. different, special, only: *unique*
3. measure, rate, guide: *speedometer*
4. hard, stone, sparkling: *diamond*
5. powerful, influential, impressive: *dynamic*
6. self, story, write: *autobiography*
7. three, deity, one: *triune*
8. measure, heat, temperature: *thermometer*
9. body, science, study: *biology*
10. one, hoard, self: *monopolize*
11. far, look, study: *telescopic*
12. pyramids, Cairo, Africa: *Egypt*
13. high, lofty, antenna: *aerial*
14. two, eyes, glasses: *binoculars*
15. picture, record, cameras: *photography*
16. South America, Pacific Ocean, Santiago: *Chile*

Dictate the word list for the trial test.

Give the following dictation sentences:

1. I took a picture of the **unique** mushroom for my **photography** class.
2. The child from **Chad** and the child from **Chile** carried on an interesting **dialogue**.
3. Mrs. Smith asked the boys not to **monopolize** the **periscope** of the museum.

Fourth Day

Return last week's journal. Give your student time to correct the misspelled words in his previous journal entry and record them in his Word Bank.

Guide the journal time using the *Journal Entry Idea* on page 49 and the information given in the front of this manual. Discuss with your student what things might be important enough to be put in a time capsule. Then discuss with him what things he would want to include. Move on to discuss what things Christians of future generations would want to have included. (BAT: 5c Evangelism and missions; Bible Promise: I. God as Master)

Fifth Day

Guide the study time.

Dictate the word list for the final test.

Give the following dictation sentences:

1. I could not see as far with my **binoculars** as my brother could with his **telescope.**
2. The **geological** study shows that there might be a **diamond** mine in those hills.
3. We had an **aerial** view of the mountains of **Colombia** from our small plane.

Use *The King's English* on page 49. After your student reads this section silently, read it with him orally. Use the Bible verses, discussion, and good comprehension questions to make certain he understands the material. The following questions and statements can be used:

1. What are we doing when we say *hallelujah?*
2. What should we always remember to do in our prayers? (BATs: 7b Exaltation of Christ, 7c Praise)
3. Read Psalm 150 and explain what it says.

Journal Entry Idea

The year is 2076, the 300th birthday of the United States of America. The ceremony will be televised for the whole world to see. Millions of people wait breathlessly as the president of the United States, accompanied by everybody-who-is-anybody, opens the time capsule to reveal what the powers-that-be thought were important representations of the century just past. The first thing removed is . . . well, what do *you* think it would be? Write about what you would include in a time capsule to be buried this year and opened in 2076.

The King's English
hallelujah

The Hebrew word *hallelōōyah* came from *hĕllēl,* meaning "to praise," and *Yah,* which means "Jehovah."

"Praise ye Jehovah" or "Praise ye the Lord" begins ten of the psalms. Because the words were used so frequently, they became a popular expression of praise. The ten psalms that begin with the praise are known as the **Hallelujah** Psalms.

In Psalm 106 the psalmist praises the Lord for His goodness and for His mercy. He reminds us that the Lord is so great that no one can praise Him enough. Sometimes our prayers drift into a series of requests of God. We should take time in our prayers to thank the Lord for what He has done for us and to praise Him.

The last psalm, Psalm 150, tells us why, where, and how to praise the Lord. We are to praise Him both in His sanctuary and in the firmament of His power. We are to praise Him for the things He does and for His greatness. We are to praise Him with music, using both song and instruments.

Find and read the "Hallelujah Psalms." Then, when you pray, try to remember to praise the Lord as the psalmist has done.
Psalm 106
Psalm 150

49

Unit 13

Worktext pages 50-53
Dictionary page 158

——— Generalization emphasis ———

1. **Adding a suffix beginning with a vowel letter to a word ending with a consonant letter**–When a suffix beginning with a vowel letter is added to a word ending with a consonant letter, the spelling of the base word does not change. *legal, legalism*

2. **Dividing a word with two consonant letters**–A word with the pattern VCCV is usually divided between the two consonant letters. *an • noy*

3. **Dividing a word with a single consonant letter between two vowel letters**–A word with the pattern VCV is sometimes divided after the first vowel letter. *ma • jor*

4. **Dividing a word with a single consonant between two vowel letters**–A word with the pattern VCV is sometimes divided after the consonant letter. *legal • ity*

5. **Dividing a word with two vowel letters that work together to make one sound**–A word with the VV pattern is divided after the two letters if they work together to make one sound. *oy: an • noy • ance*

——— Materials ———

- A world map or an atlas
- The *B* and *C* volumes of an encyclopedia

First Day

Give the pretest. After you have given the pretest and your student has checked and corrected it, give him time to choose two of the words from his Word Bank and write them as this week's *Word Bank Entries*.

After reading words 1-14 on page 50 to your student, apply generalization number one in the following way, using the suggested questions:

- Look at the words *assist, minor, major, legal,* and *character.* What do these words have in common? *(They all end with consonant letters.)*
- How is the word *annoy* different? *(It ends with y, which can be a vowel or consonant. In this case it is a blend with the o; but when a suffix is added, it works the same as a consonant.)*
- Look at the words formed from these words: *assistant, assistance, annoyance, minority, majority, legalism,* and *characteristic.* How were the spellings of the base

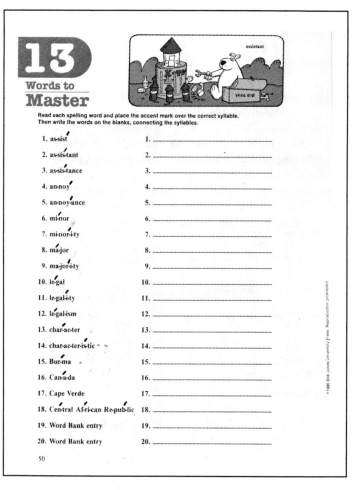

words changed when the suffixes were added? *(The spellings were not changed.)*

- To emphasize the generalization, ask what happens when a suffix that begins with a vowel letter is added to a word that ends with a consonant letter. *(The spelling of the base word is not changed.)*
- For practice, write the following on a piece of paper and ask your student to add either *-ance, -ant, -ity,* or *-ism.*

deliver	*equal*	*rigid*
temper	*vigil*	*ideal*
partial	*valid*	*inhabit*
buoy	*author*	
further	*timid*	

Apply generalizations number two through five to words 1, 4, 6, 8, 10, 13, 15, and 16, using the following activity:

- Write the following patterns on a piece of paper in three columns and ask your student to put words 1, 4, 6, 8, 10, 13, 15, or 16 under one of the headings. Direct him to use dots to show syllable division.

VC/CV	V/CV	VC/V
as • sist	mi • nor	Can • ada
an • noy	le • gal	char • acter
Bur • ma	ma • jor	

Introduce words 15-18 on page 50.

- Broadly speaking, all four of the countries' names in this week's lesson follow spelling generalizations.
- You may want to point out the silent *e* at the end of both parts of *Cape Verde*.

Guide a research activity: *Where in the World?* Help your student locate the countries with names in the spelling list on a world atlas or map. Ask him to use the *B* and *C* volumes of an encyclopedia to expand his geographic and general country knowledge according to the ideas and optional activities presented in Unit 1.

Since *Canada* is our nearest northern neighbor, have your student spend extra time reading about this country. Ask him to organize some facts about it and give an oral report to your family at the dinner table.

Use the handwritten list. After your student has written each word on the appropriate line, check his list for spelling and legibility. Instruct him to place an accent mark in each multi-syllable word of the printed list.

Second Day

Use the Bible verse activity on page 51. Use this verse to teach how important the Bible is in a Christian's life. Ask the following questions to get him to think:

1. What is the *law of the Lord?*
2. Why is the law perfect?
3. What does *convert* mean?
4. What does *the testimony of the Lord is sure* mean?
5. How does God's testimony make wise the simple?
6. What should this verse encourage you to do daily?
   (BATs: 6a Bible study, 6b Prayer, 8b Faith in the power of the Word of God)

Have fun with the *Word for Word* section on page 51.

Use worktext pages 51 and 52 to reinforce word meaning and the skills of the unit. Read the directions and give help, if needed, as your student completes the pages.

---

name _____

A. Read the verse.
   1. Underline the three words that describe the work of God's perfect law.
   2. Circle the word that has the Biblical meaning "direction given by God" and today usually means "a set of rules pertinent to a certain people."

> *"The law of the Lord is perfect, converting the soul: the testimony of the Lord is sure, making wise the simple."*
> *Psalm 19:7*

A limerick is a short, nonsensical verse that has five lines and often contains an element of humor or surprise. Usually, its first, second, and fifth lines rhyme and have the same number of syllables; its third and fourth lines rhyme and have the same number of syllables.

B. Use the base words *annoy* and *assist* and the word forms of these two words to complete the following limerick.

There was an __1__ named Roy,
Who did less to __2__ than __3__;
But he gave his __4__,
And it met no resistance,
Because his __5__ brought joy.

1. assistant
2. assist
3. annoy
4. assistance
5. annoyance

C. In the following limerick, use *character*, *legal*, and *minor* as you think they would fit into the verse.

A __1__ Tom was — just a child;
With __2__ gentle and mild.
He thought that he should
Stay __3__ and good,
And he never did anything wild.

1. minor
2. character
3. legal

WORD FOR WORD

annoy

Just as you doze off on a warm summer night, a mosquito whines past your cheek. You slap at it in the darkness, duck under the sheet and then back out again. Suddenly there's a screeching aerial attack and — stab! You've been bitten. You switch on the light, searching angrily for your tormentor.

At this moment you can understand the original meaning of the Latin word for *annoy:* "to be hateful, odious, offensive." It certainly describes the "monster" who is keeping you awake. During the past few hundred years, *annoy* has become a much milder term, and today it means only "to bother or irritate."

51

D. From your spelling list, choose the correct form of each italicized word and write it on the answer blank.

I have to admit that the reason I agreed to *assistance*[1] Ol' McGuffey with his yardwork is that he lives right next to the ball field. Yesterday he remarked with his *character*[2] grin, "Hope it doesn't *annoyance*[3] you, boy, havin' a ball game goin' on while you're tryin' to weed."

I grinned back, glad that he understood my longing to play baseball in the *majority*[4] leagues some day. My dad used to be a pitcher for a *minority*[5] league team, but something happened, and now he's only an *assist*[6] coach. Once Ol' McGuffey told me that some kind of *legal*[7] had kept Dad from becoming a star player. From the *annoy*[8] on the old man's face, I could tell that he doesn't think much of our *legalism*[9] system. The kids say that McGuffey's a mean old *characteristic*[10] but I know better.

1. assist
2. characteristic
3. annoy
4. major
5. minor
6. assistant
7. legality
8. annoyance
9. legal
10. character

E. Use your Spelling Dictionary to help you match each country on your spelling list with its capital city.

1. Praia
2. Rangoon
3. Bangui
4. Ottawa

1. Cape Verde
2. Burma
3. Central African Republic
4. Canada

F. Given the following base words from Unit 13, first write the words that are forms of that word and then put *yes* if the base word spelling stayed the same and *no* if it did not.

1. minor   1. minority-yes
2. major   2. majority-yes
3. legal   3. legality-yes   legalism-yes

Words to Master

assist	minor	legality	Canada
assistant	minority	legalism	Cape Verde
assistance	major	character	Central African Republic
annoy	majority	characteristic	_____
annoyance	legal	Burma	_____

52

Third Day

Give your student time to study the words, using the study method printed on the back cover of the spelling worktext.

Dictate the word list for the trial test.

Give the following dictation sentences:

1. My **assistant** will check on the **legality** of your claim.
2. He played the **character** of a little old man from **Burma**.
3. These flies have become a **major annoyance**.

> Dictionary skill: When looking for the definition of a word in the dictionary, read each definition and then *choose the best definition* for the word you want to use.

Use page 158 to teach this week's dictionary skill(s). After you are certain that your student understands the skill, guide him as he completes the exercise. This is a very important skill. After your student has completed the exercise, go over his answers with him, not for a "grade" but as a teaching tool.

In a standard-size dictionary, most entry words are followed by more than one definition. To know which definition you need for any particular word, you must look at its context. The rest of the sentence will help you decide on the correct definition.

In the following sentences, spelling words from Unit 13 are underlined. Find each underlined word in your Spelling Dictionary and give the number (such as 1) or the number and letter (such as 1b) of the definition that fits best. Look for the definitions that go with the part of speech given at the end of the sentence. If there is only one definition, put 0.

1. The Bible character Obadiah wrote a very short book and is considered a minor prophet. (adjective)   1. **2**
2. The whole neighborhood banded together to assist the new family that needed help so badly. (verb)   2. **1**
3. By firmly defending the truth, that man has shown that he has character. (noun)   3. **3**
4. The wicked king allowed his men to do things that were not legal. (adjective)   4. **2**
5. The little dog's constant barking began to annoy the elderly lady. (verb)   5. **1**
6. Everybody in town voted for Mr. Collins; therefore he received an overwhelming majority. (noun)   6. **2a**
7. The church will give you financial assistance if your family doesn't have enough money for food. (noun)   7. **2**
8. The faucet dripped all night and was a continual annoyance. (noun)   8. **1**
9. One characteristic of that hardworking family was getting up at sunrise. (noun)   9. **0**
10. Men are in the minority in this group, which mostly consists of women. (noun)   10. **1**
11. That has become a major problem. (adjective)   11. **1**
12. He is an assistant to the principal and helps with much of the work at our school. (noun)   12. **0**

158

Use with Unit 13.
Skill: choosing the best definition

Fourth Day

Return last week's journal. Give your student time to correct the misspelled words in his previous journal entry and record them in his Word Bank.

> You may, as a home teacher, prefer not to use the journal entry idea on page 53. Following the paragraph about the journal idea in the worktext is an alternate journal entry idea.

Guide the journal time using the *Journal Entry Idea* on page 53 (optional) and the information given in the front of this manual. Discuss the dreams, plans, and opportunities for the future after graduation in six years. Is there an area of study or a job possibility that has captured your student's imagination? In what areas of study do your student's abilities lie, and what kinds of jobs would include those abilities?

Guide the journal time, using an alternate journal entry idea. Ask your student to write about his plans for college and a career. Lead a discussion in which you and he mention friends and relatives that have interesting jobs–medical missionary, camp director, linguistics expert, artist, social worker, etc. Ask him to tell you why any career he mentions is of interest to him. The more he can verbalize his ideas, the easier it will be for him to write them.

Fifth Day

Guide the study time.

Dictate the word list for the final test.

Give the following dictation sentences.
1. The **majority** of Americans believe in our **legal** system.
2. Cold weather is **characteristic** of this part of **Canada.**
3. We sent money to **assist** our missionary in the **Central African Republic.**

Use *The King's English* on page 53. After your student reads this section silently, read it with him orally. Use the Bible verses, discussion, and good comprehension questions to make certain he understands the material. The following questions can be used:

1. What does *adorn* mean?
2. Where does true beauty come from?
3. What are some ways you can adorn your heart? (BATs: 2b Servanthood, 6a Bible study, 6b Prayer, 6c Spirit-filled, 7d Contentment, 7e Humility, 8d Courage)

Journal Entry Idea

A letter jacket? A class ring? A commencement award? A diploma? Are you looking forward to earning these by completing thirteen years in the school you are attending? Will you be proud to say, "I graduated from ____"? You'll probably invite all your family and friends to see you take the walk that is the commencement of your life-after-eighteen. But what about right now? Tell, as honestly as you know how, your feelings about the school you attend. Give examples that illustrate why you feel the way you do.

The King's English

adorn

The Romans used the word *ornatus* as a military term for honor bestowed on a soldier. The definition also indicates the medal or wreath that constituted the token of honor.

Later, the prefix *ad-* was added for emphasis. The word *adornatus*, then, gave us the word **adorn.** Today, the word *adorn* means to make something or someone more beautiful by adding to, or wearing something special.

Have you ever heard the sayings "beauty is only skin deep" or "handsome is as handsome does"? The wisdom of ages past has taught us that true beauty comes not from outward show or adornment of self but by having a spirit in tune with God.

Peter wrote that the adornment of women should be an adorning of the heart and not of the person. A believer is to show by his life what it means to be a genuine Christian.

Do you prepare your *heart* first in the morning by having a quiet time alone with God, before you tend to your physical appearance?
Titus 2:9-10
I Peter 3:3-4
Isaiah 61:10

53

Unit 14

Worktext pages 54-57
Dictionary page 159

Generalization emphasis

1. **Adding a suffix beginning with a vowel letter to a word ending in *e*–**When a suffix beginning with a vowel letter is added to a word ending in *e*, the *e* is usually dropped before adding the suffix. *appreciate, appreciation*

2. **Changing *-le* to *-ility*–**When the ending *-ity* is added to some words that end in *-le*, the *le* is changed to *il* before the ending is added. *possible, possibility*

Materials

- A world map or an atlas
- The *G* and *H* volumes of an encyclopedia
- Prepare the following activity for Day 2.

Context Conclusions

1. My dad wanted his sons to be __ambitious__ enough to go looking for a job.
2. I gave her the gift to show my __appreciation__.
3. There was not one __possibility__ that I could win that trophy.
4. Mom always insisted that we eat __nutritious__ lunches.
5. The __probability__ of our winning that prize is one in a million.
6. We all celebrated Dad's getting the __promotion__.
7. To find my watch, I looked in every __possible__ place that I might have left it.
8. In health class we studied __nutrition__.
9. My brother's __ambition__ is to be a great trumpet player.
10. Thank you; I __appreciate__ your help.
11. The teacher asked us to do all we could to __promote__ good will between classes.
12. Dad let us go on the trip but told us to use extreme __caution__.
13. It was the only answer that was close to being __probable__.
14. We were __cautious__ as we opened the cellar door.

First Day

Give the pretest. After you have given the pretest and your student has checked and corrected it, give him time to choose two of the words from his Word Bank and write them as this week's *Word Bank Entries.*

After reading words 1-4 on page 54 to your student, apply generalization number one. Use the following questions:

- Look at the words *appreciate* and *promote*. What do these words have in common? *(They both end in* e.*)*

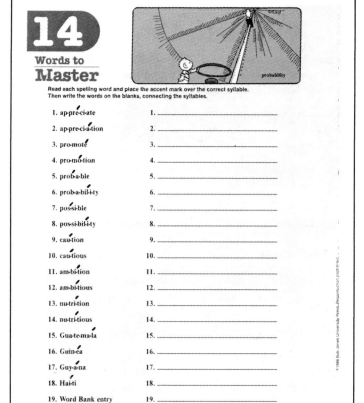

Words to Master 14

Read each spelling word and place the accent mark over the correct syllable. Then write the words on the blanks, connecting the syllables.

1. ap-pre-ci-ate   1. _____
2. ap-pre-ci-a-tion   2. _____
3. pro-mote   3. _____
4. pro-mo-tion   4. _____
5. prob-a-ble   5. _____
6. prob-a-bil-i-ty   6. _____
7. pos-si-ble   7. _____
8. pos-si-bil-i-ty   8. _____
9. cau-tion   9. _____
10. cau-tious   10. _____
11. am-bi-tion   11. _____
12. am-bi-tious   12. _____
13. nu-tri-tion   13. _____
14. nu-tri-tious   14. _____
15. Gua-te-ma-la   15. _____
16. Guin-ea   16. _____
17. Guy-a-na   17. _____
18. Hai-ti   18. _____
19. Word Bank entry   19. _____
20. Word Bank entry   20. _____

54

- Look at *appreciation* and *promotion.* What happened to the base words when the suffixes were added? *(In each word, the* e *was dropped before the suffix was added.)*
- What generalization can you form from these words? *(To add a suffix beginning with a vowel letter to a word ending in silent* e, *drop the* e *before adding the suffix.)*
- For practice, write the following words on a piece of paper and ask your student to add *-ion.*

complete	ignite
supervise	saturate
delete	confuse
precise	accommodate
contrite	televise
lubricate	locate

 Point out the similarities in the spellings of the following pairs of words: *caution, cautious; ambition, ambitious; nutrition, nutritious.*

After reading words 5-8 to your student, apply generalization number two, using the following questions:

- Ask your student to look carefully at the two base words *probable* and *possible* and tell you what they have in common. *(Each ends in* ble.*)*
- Now ask him to look at the words made from those two words: *probability* and *possibility* and tell you what happened to the base word for each when *-ity* was added to it. *(The* le *in each word was changed to* il *before* -ity *was added.)*

Introduce words 15-18 on page 54.

- *Guatemala* has three *a*'s and one *e*.
- In *Guatemala* the *u* can be heard after the *g*, but in *Guyana* and *Guinea*, the *u* cannot be heard, although it makes the *g* hard.
- The word *guinea* can also refer to a gold coin, a bird, a pig, or a worm.
- /ā/ in *Haiti* is spelled *ai*.

Guide a research activity: *Where in the World?* Help your student locate the countries with names in the spelling list on a world atlas or map. Ask him to use the *G* and *H* volumes of an encyclopedia to expand his geographic and general country knowledge according to the ideas and optional activities presented in Unit 1.

Use the handwritten list. After your student has written each word on the appropriate line, check his list for spelling and legibility. Instruct him to place an accent mark in each multi-syllable word of the printed list.

Second Day

Use the Bible verse activity on page 55. Ask your student to say the verse in his own words. Make certain he understands what the verse is teaching: not to compromise, but to display the fruit of the Spirit.

Have fun with the *Word for Word* **section on page 55.**

Use worktext pages 55 and 56 to reinforce word meaning and the skills of the unit. Read the directions and give help, if needed, as your student completes the pages.

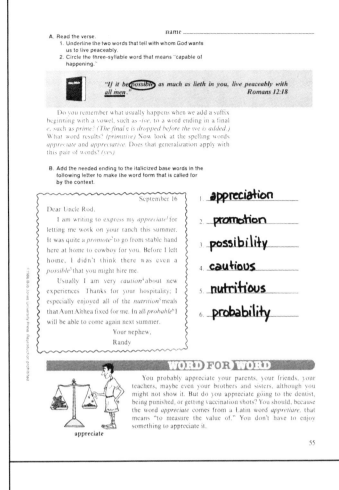

name ....

A. Read the verse.
1. Underline the two words that tell with whom God wants us to live peaceably.
2. Circle the three-syllable word that means "capable of happening."

"If it be possible as much as lieth in you, live peaceably with all men."   Romans 12:18

Do you remember what usually happens when we add a suffix beginning with a vowel, such as *-ive*, to a word ending in a final *e*, such as *prime*? *(The final e is dropped before the ive is added.)* What word results? *(primitive)* Now look at the spelling words *appreciate* and *appreciative*. Does that generalization apply with this pair of words? *(yes)*

B. Add the needed ending to the italicized base words in the following letter to make the word form that is called for by the context.

September 16

Dear Uncle Rod,

I am writing to express my *appreciate*[1] for letting me work on your ranch this summer. It was quite a *promote*[2] to go from stable hand here at home to cowboy for you. Before I left home, I didn't think there was even a *possible*[3] that you might hire me.

Usually I am very *caution*[4] about new experiences. Thanks for your hospitality; I especially enjoyed all of the *nutrition*[5] meals that Aunt Althea fixed for me. In all *probable*[6] I will be able to come again next summer.

Your nephew,
Randy

1. appreciation
2. promotion
3. possibility
4. cautious
5. nutritious
6. probability

WORD FOR WORD

You probably appreciate your parents, your friends, your teachers, maybe even your brothers and sisters, although you might not show it. But do you appreciate going to the dentist, being punished, or getting vaccination shots? You should, because the word *appreciate* comes from a Latin word *appretiare*, that means "to measure the value of." You don't have to enjoy something to appreciate it.

appreciate

55

C. Cross out the incorrect word in each sentence and substitute a suitable spelling word.

1. Sonja worked hard and got a ~~raise~~ at the end of the year. — promotion
2. A spinach-and-liver sandwich was Aunt Peggy's idea of a ~~terrible~~ lunch. — nutritious
3. Sometimes we don't ~~know~~ all the good things our parents do for us. — appreciate
4. It's always ~~possible~~ that we could have a rainy summer. — possible
5. The clever old coon was extremely ~~careful~~ when he stole our corn. — cautious
6. Dr. Bartun pointed out the ~~chance~~ of the volcano's erupting. — probability
7. Tom's ~~dream~~ was to be class president. — ambition

D. Decide what spelling base word you would look up in the dictionary if you wanted to find the meaning of each of the words listed below. Write the base words on the blanks.

1. cautionary
2. possibly
3. probably
4. appreciative
5. promoting
6. nutritional
7. ambitiousness
8. cautiousness

1. caution
2. possible
3. probable
4. appreciate
5. promote
6. nutrition
7. ambitious
8. cautious

E. Rearrange the syllables in the following list to make spelling words. Remember to capitalize the names of countries.

1. eaguin — Guinea
2. laguamate — Guatemala
3. naaguy — Guyana
4. tihai — Haiti
5. tiousbiam — ambitious
6. bilsiiposty — possibility

Words to Master

appreciate	probability	ambition	Guinea
appreciation	possible	ambitious	Guyana
promote	possibility	nutrition	Haiti
promotion	caution	nutritious	
probable	cautious	Guatemala	

56

Third Day

Give your student time to study the words, using the study method printed on the back cover of the spelling worktext.

Dictate the word list for the trial test.

Give the following dictation sentences:

1. Warn the reporter in **Guatemala** to use **caution** when talking with soldiers.
2. It is **possible** even for a **cautious** person to make a mistake.
3. You must not let your **ambition** cause you to forget to show **appreciation** to others.

> Dictionary skill: Some entry words are listed *more than one time.* You need to read the definitions to find the one that fits the context of the material you are reading or writing.

Use page 159 to teach this week's dictionary skill. After you are certain that your student understands the skill, guide him as he completes the exercise. Spend some time with your student with this skill. After he completes the exercise, check his work. Do not "grade" it but use it as a teaching tool.

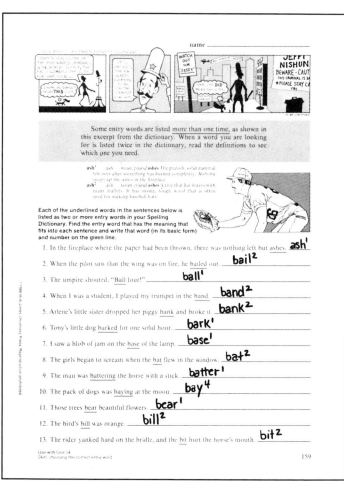

Fourth Day

Return last week's journal. Give your student time to correct the misspelled words in his previous journal entry and record them in his Word Bank.

Guide the journal time using the *Journal Entry Idea* on page 57 and the information given in the front of this manual. Get excited about your favorite place to be alone to read, listen to music, or just think. Elicit your student's ideas on this subject, keeping the discussion lively. Talk with him about the different kinds of reading material: books, magazines, newspapers. As you explain the benefits of reading, listening to good music, and meditating, make them applicable to his experience.

Fifth Day

Guide the study time.

Dictate the word list for the final test.

Give the following dictation sentences.

1. That **ambitious** man might get a **promotion**.
2. We **appreciate** the **nutritious** meals that Mom makes.
3. It is **probable** that many children in **Haiti** suffer from poor **nutrition**.

Use *The King's English* on page 57. After your student reads this section silently, read it with him orally. Use the Bible verses, discussion, and good comprehension questions to make certain he understands the material. The following questions can be used:

1. What does *promote* mean? Give some examples of your answer.
2. When can a promotion be a negative event?
3. How can you be confident that a promotion is for your benefit?
4. Should you be careful about your promotions?
5. Should you be careful about the people and ideas you promote?
6. How does the Lord promote you?
7. Where does wisdom begin, and where do you get wisdom? (BATs: 6a Bible study, 6b Prayer)

Journal Entry Idea

"If you need me, just call me! I'll be in my special spot!" Have you ever said something like that on a scrumptious Saturday at home? You have found a place that only you know about. It's a wear-your-old-clothes place, a curl-up-warm-and-cozy place, a custom-built-for-you place, a "take-it-easy" place, a nobody-knows-where-I-am place, a *reading* place. A place where you can take your latest adventure, science fiction, or mystery novel and really get into it. There you can live in a world of amazing inventions, a world of impossible experiences, a world of exciting space encounters. You are alone with your book and your dreams. Tell about your private place to read.

The King's English

promote

The Latin word *promovere* means "to advance," or to move forward. When we think of the word **promote**, we think of moving forward into the next grade.

Another meaning of *promote* is "to advance in rank or honor." When Esther became queen, she did not make known her relationship to Mordecai. He rose in rank because of his honesty and diligence, not because he was Esther's uncle. Esther 10:2 tells us "the king advanced him."

God had control of the situation in which Mordecai was advanced. However, it is wise to be careful of people who desire to promote us. Remember, Balak promised to promote Balaam to gain his own desires. We should weigh every situation against the Word of God.

In Proverbs 4 we learn that if we seek wisdom and get understanding, she, Wisdom, will promote us. Since we know that the beginning of wisdom is the fear of the Lord, we know where to begin. James 1:5 tells us that if we lack wisdom, we should ask it of God.

Esther 10:2
Proverbs 4:7-8
Daniel 3:30

57

Unit 15

Worktext pages 58-61
Dictionary page 160

Generalization emphasis

1. **Adding an ending to a base word that causes an internal change in spelling**—Sometimes when a base word is changed to a word form, an internal change in spelling takes place. *require, requisition*

2. **Adding a suffix beginning with *i* to a word ending with /k/ spelled *c*—**When a suffix beginning with *i* is added to a word ending with /k/ spelled *c*, the *c* sound changes from /k/ to /sh/. *optic, optician*

3. **Dropping the *y* before adding a suffix beginning with a vowel letter**—When a word ends in a *y*, in most cases the *y* is dropped before adding the suffix. *melody, melodic*

Materials

- A world map or an atlas
- The *H* and *I* volumes of an encyclopedia
- Write the names of the countries studied so far on index-type cards in preparation for the game *Concentration* to be played on Day 2.

First Day

Give the pretest. After you have given the pretest and your student has checked and corrected it, give him time to choose two of the words from his Word Bank and write them as this week's *Word Bank Entries*.

After reading words 1-4 and words 7 and 8 to your student, apply generalization number one, using the following questions:

- What do words 1 and 3 have in common? *(They both end in* quire.*)*
- How did the spellings of *require* and *acquire* change when the ending *-tion* was added to each? *(In each the* re *became* si.*)*
- What unusual spelling does the word *technique* have? *(/k/ is spelled* que.*)*
- How does the spelling of the base word change when the suffix *-ian* is added? *(The* que *becomes* c *before the* -ian *is added; this changes /k/ to /sh/.)*

After reading words 5-6 to your student, apply generalization number two. The following questions can be included:

- Look at words 5 and 6 closely. What spelling do they have in common? *(The first five letters are the same.)*

15 Words to Master

politician

Read each spelling word and place the accent mark over the correct syllable. Then write the words on the blanks, connecting the syllables.

1. re·quire	1. _____
2. req·ui·si·tion	2. _____
3. ac·quire	3. _____
4. ac·qui·si·tion	4. _____
5. mel·o·dy	5. _____
6. me·lod·ic	6. _____
7. tech·nique	7. _____
8. tech·ni·cian	8. _____
9. mag·ic	9. _____
10. ma·gi·cian	10. _____
11. op·tic	11. _____
12. op·ti·cian	12. _____
13. pol·i·tics	13. _____
14. pol·i·ti·cian	14. _____
15. Hon·du·ras	15. _____
16. Hun·ga·ry	16. _____
17. Ice·land	17. _____
18. In·di·a	18. _____
19. Word Bank entry	19. _____
20. Word Bank entry	20. _____

58

- Why do you suppose that is true? *(The word* melody *is the base word of the word* melodic.*)*
- How did the spelling of *melody* change when the suffix *-ic* was added? *(The* y *was dropped.)*
- Add the suffix *-ic* to the following words to practice this generalization:

specify *(specific)*	economy
symphony	history
irony	harmony

After you have read words 9-14 on page 58 to your student, apply generalization number one. You may use questions such as the following:

- What do the three words *magic, optic,* and *politics* have in common? *(They all end with /k/ spelled* c.*)*
- Did the spelling of the base words change when the suffix *-ian* was added to make *magician, optician,* and *politician?* *(no)*
- How does the sound of *c* change? *(It is /k/ and becomes /sh/.)*

Introduce words 15-18 on page 58.

- Guide your student in discovering that the four countries in this week's list are spelled the way they sound.

Guide a research activity: *Where in the World?* Help your student locate the countries with names in the spelling list on a world atlas or map. Ask him to use the *H* and *I* volumes of an encyclopedia to expand his geographic and general country knowledge according to the ideas and optional activities presented in Unit 1.

Direct your student to choose an optional activity he has not done for a while or one he has never done to find out more about one of these countries.

Use the handwritten list. After your student has written each word on the appropriate line, check his list for spelling and legibility. Instruct him to place an accent mark in each multi-syllable word of the printed list.

Second Day

Use the Bible verse activity on page 59. Ask your student what he thinks the phrase *speaking to yourselves in songs and hymns and spiritual songs* means? Ask him who can help him to be *singing and making melody* in his heart to the Lord. (BAT: 6c Spirit-filled)

Have fun with the *Word for Word* section on page 59.

Use worktext pages 59 and 60 to reinforce word meaning and the skills of the unit. Read the directions and give help, if needed, as your student completes the pages.

Guide a spelling activity: *Concentration*. Review with your student all of the countries included so far in the spelling units. Have your student play a game of Concentration where prepared cards (the name of a country is written on two index-type cards) are turned face down in a random order. He turns over two cards at a time trying to get a match.

Extend the game for your student by adding the following optional activity:

> When your student makes a match, he spells the word and then receives points if he is correct. He receives an additional ten points if he accurately tells something about the country (location, capital, etc.). You may give a special award, treat, or activity to your student for a majority of correct responses totaling a certain number of points. Keep the cards and add to them each unit, playing the game as a special activity.

---

name _____

A. Read the verse.
  1. Underline the name of the person to whom we should sing.
  2. Circle the word that has the Biblical meaning "something played on a stringed instrument," but today means "a series of musical tones."

"Speaking to yourselves in psalms and hymns and spiritual songs, singing and making melody in your heart to the Lord."
Ephesians 5:19

The word pairs on your spelling list are examples of how an ending can change a word so much that it becomes a different part of speech. Compare the verb *require* with its noun form *requisition*. The ending *-sition* makes a considerable difference, but the two words are still related in meaning and similar in spelling.

B. In each sentence group below, look at the heading first. The italicized word will be the first part of speech mentioned in the heading. Write a related word in the blank, making sure that it is the second part of speech mentioned in the heading.

A word that changes from *verb* to *noun*

1. Tim's boss told him that if his job should *require* supplies, he would have to fill out a _____.   1. **requisition**

Words that are *nouns*, but that change into other *nouns* that represent people

2. My dad is in *politics*, but I never think of him as a _____.   2. **politician**

3. Because my sister uses a special *technique* in her job at the hospital, she is referred to as a laboratory _____.   3. **technician**

A word that changes from *noun* to *adjective*

4. If a song has a pretty *melody*, it is said to be _____.   4. **melodic**

WORD FOR WORD

Which lines are parallel?

Which line is longer?

a   b

optical

These figures are optical illusions. An optical illusion is deceptive because it makes you think you see something that may not truly be there. The word *optic* comes from the Greek word *optos*, which means "visible." An illusion is something you think you see. For instance, all the diagonal lines in figure *a* are parallel. In figure *b* the lines are equal in length. Did either optical illusion fool you?

59

C. Use spelling words to complete these newspaper headlines.

| George Camden enters __1__; will run for governor |
| Museum's new __2__ worth thousands |
| Contestant names mystery __3__ for $10,000 |
| Local __4__ wins national optical award |
| Doctor defends new surgical __5__ |

1. **politics**
2. **acquisition**
3. **melody**
4. **optician**
5. **technique**

D. Replace the scrambled words in the sentence below with spelling words. Be sure to capitalize the names of countries.

I searched from hdsrnoau¹ to gyunrah², from ldecani³ to iaidn⁴, questioning every gimanica⁵ how he did his gimca⁶ tricks, but all I managed to riueacq⁷ was a painful disease of the otcpi⁸ nerve.

1. **Honduras**   5. **magician**
2. **Hungary**   6. **magic**
3. **Iceland**   7. **acquire**
4. **India**   8. **optic**

E. Write the two words from which *-re* was dropped when *-sition* was added.

1. **requisition**
2. **acquisition**

Words to Master

require	melodic	optic	Hungary
requisition	technique	optician	Iceland
acquire	technician	politics	India
acquisition	magic	politician	
melody	magician	Honduras	

60

Third Day

Give your student time to study the words, using the study method printed on the back cover of the spelling worktext.

Dictate the word list for the trial test.

Give the following dictation sentences:

1. You **acquire** good piano **technique** only with constant practice.
2. The **acquisition** of **Hungary** took place just before the war ended.
3. His **magic** tricks **require** him to be quick with his hands.

> Dictionary skill: A *synonym* of a word is another word that has a meaning so close to the word that it could be used in place of that word.

Use page 160 to teach this week's dictionary skill(s). After you are certain that your student understands the skill, guide him as he completes the exercise.

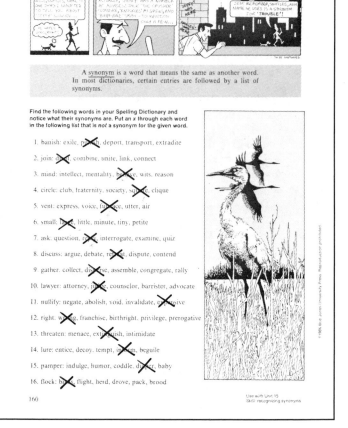

A synonym is a word that means the same as another word. In most dictionaries, certain entries are followed by a list of synonyms.

Find the following words in your Spelling Dictionary and notice what their synonyms are. Put an *x* through each word in the following list that is *not* a synonym for the given word.

1. banish: exile, punish, deport, transport, extradite
2. join: divert, combine, unite, link, connect
3. mind: intellect, mentality, believe, wits, reason
4. circle: club, fraternity, society, square, clique
5. vent: express, voice, furnace, utter, air
6. small: large, little, minute, tiny, petite
7. ask: question, relate, interrogate, examine, quiz
8. discuss: argue, debate, repeat, dispute, contend
9. gather: collect, disperse, assemble, congregate, rally
10. lawyer: attorney, judge, counselor, barrister, advocate
11. nullify: negate, abolish, void, invalidate, explosive
12. right: wrong, franchise, birthright, privilege, prerogative
13. threaten: menace, extinguish, intimidate
14. lure: entice, decoy, tempt, inform, beguile
15. pamper: indulge, humor, coddle, dismiss, baby
16. flock: butt, flight, herd, drove, pack, brood

160

Use with Unit 15
Skill: recognizing synonyms

Fourth Day

Return last week's journal. Give your student time to correct the misspelled words in his previous journal entry and record them in his Word Bank.

Guide the journal time using the *Journal Entry Idea* on page 61 and the information given in the front of this manual. Reminisce with your student about Christmas in the home of your parents when you were a child. Persuade him to do the same about his Christmases in your home. Allow him to describe to you as many remembrances of Christmas as he can. Ask him to give you some words that describe Christmas and list them on a piece of paper. Tell him he can use these words in his writing if he chooses.

Fifth Day

Guide the study time.

Dictate the word list for the final test.

Give the following dictation sentences.

1. The lab **technician** lost his job because of an injury to his **optic** nerve.
2. I know a young **optician** who has decided to go into **politics**.
3. The snake charmer from **India** played a **melody** in front of a basket on the floor.

Use *The King's English* on page 61. After your student reads this section silently, read it with him orally. Use the Bible verses, discussion, and good comprehension questions to make certain he understands the material. The following questions can be used:

1. What did the original word for melody refer to?
2. Why do you think God gave us such a thing as melody? (BATs: 6c Spirit-filled, 7b Exaltation of Christ, 7c Praise)
3. Why would following Ephesians 6 help someone to be happy even in the midst of sadness? (Bible Promises: G. Christ as Friend, H. God as Father, I. God as Master)
4. How can music be used to glorify God? (BATs: 4d Victory, 5c Evangelism and missions)
5. What are some of the melodies that you like to sing just because you're happy?

Journal Entry Idea

The spirit of Christmas! What is it? Is it getting to visit your grandma, who is the givingest giver in the whole world? Is it enjoying her wonderful cooking at a table that is bright with candles and brimming with the best food you ever tasted—and a batch of fun-loving cousins you haven't seen for ages? Maybe the spirit of Christmas to you is giggling over secrets and watching a loved one open something special. Or the singing of lovely songs that you know so well you don't have to use the book. Tell why Christmas is one of your favorite times.

The King's English
melody

Have you ever heard a choir sing *a cappella?* The words *a cappella* mean to use only the voices, no instruments, to make music. The word **melody** came from the Greek word *melōidia,* meaning "choral song."

Hebrew music was usually sung, and it was usually accompanied by the lyre. The first mention of music in the Bible occurred in Genesis; it was used as merrymaking for guests. Miriam led one of the first songs of worship when she celebrated with music the crossing of the Red Sea. And who can forget the maidens' song, "David has slain his ten thousands"?

Sometimes an occasion is so sad that music is not appropriate. When the Babylonian conquerers required a song from the Israelites, they refused, saying they could not sing in a strange land.

A person who sings to himself presents a picture of a happy and contented person. Ephesians 6 tells us to be filled with the Spirit, "speaking to yourselves in psalms and hymns and spiritual songs, singing and making melody in your heart to the Lord."
Isaiah 51:3
Ephesians 5:19
Psalm 137:3-4

61

Unit 16

Worktext pages 62-65
Dictionary page 161

Generalization emphasis
---

1. **Adding an ending composed of two syllables**–Sometimes an ending composed of two syllables is added to a word to make a form of the word. *alter, alternative*

2. **Adding a suffix beginning with a vowel letter to a word ending in *e***–When a suffix beginning with a vowel is added to a word ending in *e*, the *e* is dropped before the suffix is added. *sense, sensation*

Materials

- A world map or an atlas
- The *I* volume of an encyclopedia

First Day

Give the pretest. After you have given the pretest and your student has checked and corrected it, give him time to choose two of the words from his Word Bank and write them as this week's *Word Bank Entries*.

After you have read words 1 and 2 to your student, use the following questions to apply generalization number one:

- How are words 1 and 2 related? (*Alter is the base word for* alternative.)
- What was added to *alter* to make the word *alternative*? (*native*)
- Did the spelling of the base word change when the suffix was added? (*no*)

After you have read words 3, 4, and 8-13, apply generalization number two in the following way, using the suggested questions:

- How did the spelling of the base word *execute* change when the suffix *-ion* was added to make *execution*? (*The* e *was dropped.*)
- How did the spelling of the base word *guide* change when the suffix *-ance* was added? (*The* e *was dropped.*)
- How did the spelling of the base word *grieve* change when the suffixes *-ance* and *-ous* were added? (*The* e *was dropped.*)
- How did the spelling of the base word *insure* change when the suffix *-ance* was added? (*The* e *was dropped.*)

16 Words to Master

Read each spelling word and place the accent mark over the correct syllable. Then write the words on the blanks, connecting the syllables.

1. al·ter
2. al·ter·na·tive
3. ex·e·cute
4. ex·e·cu·tion
5. sense
6. sen·si·tive
7. sen·sa·tion
8. guide
9. guid·ance
10. grieve
11. griev·ance
12. griev·ous
13. in·sure
14. in·sur·ance
15. In·do·ne·sia
16. I·ran
17. I·raq
18. Ire·land
19. Word Bank entry
20. Word Bank entry

62

After reading words 5-7 to your student, discuss their spellings, using the following questions:

- What happened to the spelling of the base word *sense* when the ending *-itive* was added to make the word *sensitive*? (*The* e *was dropped.*)
- What happened to the spelling of the base word *sense* when the ending *-ation* was added to make the word *sensation*? (*The* e *was dropped.*)

Introduce words 15-18 on page 62.

- Point out that *Indonesia* will not be difficult to remember if the student thinks of it in syllables; the only unusual syllable is the last: /shə/ spelled *sia*.
- *Iran* is easy to spell by listening to the sounds, or the student can think of it as a sentence: *I ran*.
- Your student will need to remember that *Iraq* ends with a *q* without the usual *u* following it.
- Your student must remember that the first syllable of *Ireland* is spelled *Ire*. The ending of the word will be easy.

Guide a research activity: *Where in the World?* Help your student locate the countries with names in the spelling list on a world atlas or map. Ask him to use the *I* volume of an encyclopedia to expand his geographic and general country knowledge according to the ideas and optional activities presented in Unit 1.

Many citizens of the United States have ancestors from Ireland. Direct your student to spend some time reading about why so many of the Irish immigrated here. Ask him to find out about the problems that divide this beautiful country today. Have him share the information with your family.

Use the handwritten list. After your student has written each word on the appropriate line, check his list for spelling and legibility. Instruct him to place an accent mark in each multi-syllable word of the printed list.

Second Day

Use the Bible verse activity on page 63. Discuss the verse with your student, using the following questions:
1. What does the word *grieve* mean?
2. Where does the *Holy Spirit of God* live? (BAT: 6c Spirit-filled)
3. What does it mean to be *sealed unto the day of redemption?* (BAT: 8b Faith in God's promises)
4. What is God telling us in this verse? (BAT: 1c Separation from the world; Bible Promise: A. Liberty from Sin)
5. What can we learn from this verse? (BATs: 6a Bible study, 6b Prayer)

This is a good opportunity to tell your student that God gives the Holy Spirit to a person when he accepts Christ. Because He has given us His Spirit, we can rest easily in the assurance that He will also give us the eternal life He promises. Explain *sealed* with illustrations of canned goods and packages that are sealed safely.

Have fun with the *Word for Word* section on page 63. Make certain your student understands that the word *execute* means "to follow out" so that he can apply it in a variety of sentence settings.

Use worktext pages 63 and 64 to reinforce word meaning and the skills of the unit. Read the directions and give help, if needed, as your student completes the pages.

A. Read the verse.
  1. Underline the six words that tell what the Holy Spirit does for the believer.
  2. Circle the word that has the long e sound spelled ie and means "to afflict."

"And grieve not the holy Spirit of God, whereby ye are sealed unto the day of redemption."
Ephesians 4:30

When we talk about an *etymology*, or the origin of a word, we are referring to information that you will find at the end of the dictionary entry in most dictionaries. This section gives the language in which the word was originally found and the changes it went through until it became the word we use today. Knowing the etymology of a word will often help you to spell that word correctly.

B. After looking at each of the following Latin and French words, take an intelligent guess at the two or three spelling words that each foreign word represents. Write them on the blanks provided.

1. Medieval Latin, *alterare* — **alter, alternative**
2. Latin, *sensus* — **sense, sensitive, sensation**
3. Latin, *gravare* — **grieve, grievance, grievous**
4. Medieval Latin, *executare* — **execute, execution**
5. Old French, *enseurer* — **insure, insurance**

C. Find the following verses in the Bible, and write the spelling word or the form of a spelling word that appears in each.

  1. Proverbs 15:1   3. Ephesians 4:30
  2. John 16:13   4. Romans 13:4

1. **grievous**
2. **guide**
3. **grieve**
4. **execute**

WORD FOR WORD

execute

Have you ever heard anyone say that a certain court official was going to "execute the law"? What do you think that odd expression means?

The word *execute* comes from a Latin word *executare*, meaning "to follow out." When someone executes a law, he is carrying it out or obeying it. The more common meaning of *execute*, "to put to death," refers to the death sentence being carried out on a condemned prisoner.

63

Homonyms are words that have the same sound and often the same spelling as each other, but have different meanings. For example, the words *strait* and *straight* are homonyms. They both sound like strāt , but their meanings are entirely different. You need to know the separate spellings of commonly used homonyms.

D. Write the spelling words that are homonyms of the words given.

1. cents   1. **sense**   3. **guide**
2. altar   2. **alter**   4. **grieve**
3. guyed
4. greave

Look at the words *insure* and *insurance*, and decide what letter had to be dropped before the ending *-ance* was added. (e) Can you think of other word pairs that do this? *(promote, promotion; celebrate, celebration; persecute, persecution)* Many words follow this pattern. Usually when a suffix beginning with a vowel is added to a word that ends in e, the e is dropped before the suffix is added.

Note: There are only seven answers to this section.

E. Keep this observation in mind and write the spelling words that dropped the final e before their ending was added.

1. **insurance**   5. **sensation**
2. **grievous**   6. **guidance**
3. **execution**   7. **grievance**
4. **sensitive**   8.

F. Arrange the countries on your spelling list in order according to population size, beginning with the highest population. Use your Spelling Dictionary.

1. **Indonesia**   3. **Iraq**
2. **Iran**   4. **Ireland**

Words to Master

alter	sensitive	grievance	Iran
alternative	sensation	grievous	Iraq
execute	guide	insure	Ireland
execution	guidance	insurance	
sense	grieve	Indonesia	

64

Third Day

Give your student time to study the words, using the study method printed on the back cover of the spelling worktext.

Dictate the word list for the trial test.

Give the following dictation sentences:

1. My little sister is so **sensitive** that any sharp words will **grieve** her.
2. Please **insure** this letter that is going to **Iran**.
3. The **guide** on our trip to **Ireland** was a woman.

> Dictionary skill: *Homographs* are words that are spelled the same as each other; they even sound the same. They have different meanings, though, because they have different origins, or come from different root words.

Use page 161 to teach this week's dictionary skill. After you are certain that your student understands the skill, guide him as he completes the exercise. Your student may need some guidance to understand and work with homographs. Point out that the first part of the word means "same" and the last part means "to write." Bring out the fact that homographs are words that are "written the same," or spelled the same.

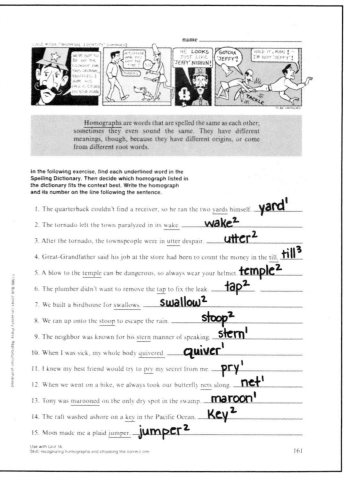

> Homographs are words that are spelled the same as each other; sometimes they even sound the same. They have different meanings, though, because they have different origins, or come from different root words.

In the following exercise, find each underlined word in the Spelling Dictionary. Then decide which homograph listed in the dictionary fits the context best. Write the homograph and its number on the line following the sentence.

1. The quarterback couldn't find a receiver, so he ran the two yards himself. __yard¹__
2. The tornado left the town paralyzed in its wake. __wake²__
3. After the tornado, the townspeople were in utter despair. __utter²__
4. Great-Grandfather said his job at the store had been to count the money in the till. __till³__
5. A blow to the temple can be dangerous, so always wear your helmet. __temple²__
6. The plumber didn't want to remove the tap to fix the leak. __tap²__
7. We built a birdhouse for swallows. __swallow²__
8. We ran up onto the stoop to escape the rain. __stoop²__
9. The neighbor was known for his stern manner of speaking. __stern¹__
10. When I was sick, my whole body quivered. __quiver¹__
11. I knew my best friend would try to pry my secret from me. __pry¹__
12. When we went on a hike, we always took our butterfly nets along. __net¹__
13. Tony was marooned on the only dry spot in the swamp. __maroon¹__
14. The raft washed ashore on a key in the Pacific Ocean. __key²__
15. Mom made me a plaid jumper. __jumper²__

Use with Unit 16.
Skill: recognizing homographs and choosing the correct one

161

Fourth Day

Return last week's journal. Give your student time to correct the misspelled words in his previous journal entry and record them in his spelling dictionary.

Guide the journal time using the *Journal Entry Idea* on page 65 and the information given in the front of this manual. Open a lively discussion during which you tell your student about one of your physical or personality features that you wish you didn't have. Talk about how you have used that feature for good or overcome it, etc. Discuss with him how a feature that seems bad to you can actually be the very feature that helps you succeed. Elicit his ideas about features of his that he dislikes and how he can use them to his good. Point out to him that if a person does not have a problem, he will never learn how to deal with one. That could be a big problem! After he has talked about his ideas, ask him to write about them. (BAT: 3a Self-concept)

Fifth Day

Guide the study time.

Dictate the word list for the final test.

Give the following dictation sentences.
1. Life in prison is sometimes an **alternative** to **execution** for a crime.
2. I could **sense** the Lord's **guidance** in my life.
3. The old man decided to **alter** his **insurance** plan.

Use *The King's English* on page 65. After your student reads this section silently, read it with him orally. Use the Bible verses, discussion, and good comprehension questions to make certain he understands the material. The following questions can be used:
1. Who was the greatest teacher and guide that ever lived?
2. What did Jesus say about the Pharisees?
3. What has God given us by which we can always be guided? (BAT: 6a Bible study; Bible Promise G. Christ as Friend)
4. Can you be a guide to someone else? (BATs: 5d Communication, 5e Friendliness)

Journal Entry Idea

"Oh! If I would only grow taller!" Or bigger? Or smaller? Or shorter? Or, "Oh! If I had hair like hers, I could wear braids!" Or, "If I had bigger hands, I could handle the ball better." "Why is it that I didn't get the body I wanted?" This might be your attitude, or you might think, "I never get *anything* I want." Do you get angry with yourself because you are slow and *that* keeps you from doing what you want to do? Could you turn from being a "slowpoke" to being "slow and steady"? That's a good quality. Write about a *problem* you have and how you could try to turn it into a *promotion.*

The King's English
guide

When Lewis and Clark began their exploration of the American West, they needed a **guide** to show them the way. The word *guide* comes from the Middle English word *guida,* which was taken from the Old English word *witan,* meaning "to know."

Sometimes we need a guide to lead us, not through strange lands but into new knowledge. Someone who knows the subject, knows the language, or knows how to perform what another person wishes to learn can be a **guide** to another person.

Your teacher is an example of such a guide. Psalm 32:8 gives the commitment of a willing teacher—"I will instruct thee and teach thee in the way which thou shalt go: I will guide thee with mine eye."

The greatest teacher is our Lord. When He was on earth, He used many parables to illustrate His messages. His words, recorded in the New Testament, still guide those who are willing to learn. He criticized the Pharisees of that day because they had failed to be good guides of their people. Jesus said they were "blind leaders of the blind." What kind of a guide are you?

Psalm 32:8
Isaiah 58:11
John 16:13

65

Unit 17

Worktext pages 66-69
Dictionary page 162

Generalization emphasis

1. **Using morphophonemics as an aid in spelling**—The spelling of a word is made more obvious by the pronunciation (stress) of a related word. *similar, similarity*

2. **Adding the suffix -ity to words ending in -ile**—When the suffix *-ity* is added to a word ending in *-ile* the *e* is dropped before the suffix is added. *mobile, mobility*

3. **Adding the suffix -ity to words ending in -ble**—When the suffix *-ity* is added to a word ending in *-ble*, the *le* is changed to *il* before the suffix is added. *changeable, changeability*

Materials

- An atlas or a world map
- The *I* and *J* volumes of an encyclopedia
- Prepare the following activity for Day 2.

Thinkalogies
1. kind : friendly :: cruel : _hostile_
2. unlike : different :: like : _similar_
3. building : stable :: vehicle : _mobile_
4. wedding : rejoice :: funeral : _grieve_
5. Athens : Greece :: Rome : _Italy_
6. feet : tough :: eyes : _sensitive_
7. God : constant :: man : _changeable_
8. Nassau : Bahamas :: Teheran : _Iran_
9. teach : instruct :: lead : _guide_
10. praise : compliment :: complaint : _grievance_
11. requirement : fulfill :: law : _execute_
12. unaccepted : shameful :: accepted : _respectable_

First Day

Give the pretest. After you have given the pretest and your student has checked and corrected it, give him time to choose two of the words from his Word Bank and write them as this week's *Word Bank Entries.*

After you have read words 1 and 2 to your student, apply generalization number one to the words in the following way, using the following questions:

- Ask your student to say *similar* and *similarity* and tell you on which syllable the stress comes in each word. *(In* similar *the stress is on the first syllable; in* similarity *it is on the third.)*
- Can one of those words help you spell the other? *(Yes, in* similarity *you can hear that the syllable* lar *is spelled with an* a.)

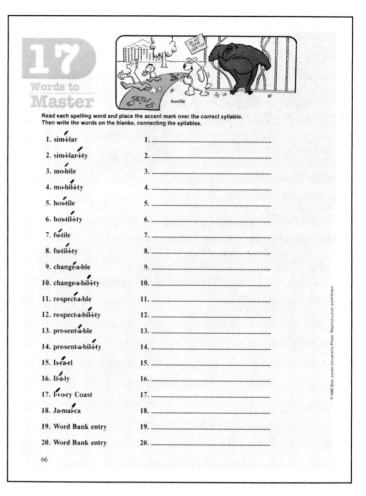

After you have read words 3-8 on page 66 to your student, apply generalization number two to the words in the following way, using the suggested questions and statements:

- What do words 3, 5, and 7 have in common? *(all end with* ile)
- What happened to the spelling of each when the suffix *-ity* was added? *(The final* e *was dropped before the suffix was added.)*
- Bring out the fact that the spelling of /əl/ is *ile.*

After you have read words 9-14 to your student, apply generalization number three to the words in the following way, using the suggested questions:

- What spelling do words 9, 11, and 13 end with? *(able)*
- What happens to the *able* spelling when the suffix *-ity* is added? *(The* le *is changed to* il *before the suffix* -ity *is added.)*

Introduce words 15-18 on page 66.

Help your student with the following suggestions:

- Point out that *Israel* has three syllables; and if your student thinks of it as /Is′ rā el/, its spelling will be easier to remember. The actual pronunciation is /Iz′ rē • əl/.

- *Italy* is easy, except for the second syllable, which is a schwa. If your student thinks of the related word *Italian*, he can hear that the second syllable is an *a*.
- *Ivory Coast* is spelled as it sounds.
- Your student can try to remember that *Jamaica* has three *a*'s. The middle syllable that has *ā* is spelled *ai*.

Guide a research activity: *Where in the World?* Help your student locate the countries with names in the spelling list on a world atlas or map. Ask him to use the *I* and *J* volumes of an encyclopedia to expand his geographic and general country knowledge, according to the ideas and optional activities presented in Unit 1.

Assist your student in using a map of Israel to find where Jesus was born, where He lived, and where He practiced His ministry. Ask him to find the Sea of Galilee. Direct him to draw a map of Israel and locate these cities and other important features.

Use the handwritten list. After your student has written each word on the appropriate line, check his list for spelling and legibility. Instruct him to place an accent mark in each multi-syllable word of the printed list.

Second Day

Use the Bible verse activity on page 67. Talk with your student about how the word *respect* is used in the verse and what it means. Ask him what he thinks the word *blessed* means? Some Bible teachers say it means "happy." The way the words *bless, blessed,* and *blessing* are used in the Bible, we know that only God can bless, only by God can a person be blessed, and a blessing is something only God can give a person. If you think of it in that light, being blessed is very special; and one will be happy if he is blessed by God.

Have fun with the *Word for Word* section on page 67.

Use worktext pages 67 and 68 to reinforce word meaning and the spelling skills of the unit. Read the directions and give help, if needed, as your student completes the pages.

Developing word meaning: *Thinkalogies.* This activity will build on your student's understanding of analogies. It is similar to the activity found in Unit 6, *Analogies Anonymous*. Complete each analogy by determining the relationship between the first pair of words and applying it to the second pair of words. Follow up the activity by choosing a set of four words to illustrate. Fold a piece of plain paper in quarters; then draw a picture for each of the four words. Add labels. (Note: Some pictures will be more easily illustrated than others.)

A. Read the verse.
1. Underline the word that describes the man who makes the Lord his trust.
2. Circle the word that has the Biblical meaning "looks on or acknowledges," but today means "admires or honors."

"Blessed is that man that maketh the Lord his trust, and respecteth not the proud, nor such as turn aside to lies." Psalm 40:4

Look at the words *similar* and *similarity*. How does the stress change when *-ity* is added to the base word? (*It moves to the third syllable.*) Notice that in *similar*, the third syllable (unstressed) has the schwa sound that is difficult to hear and to spell. In *similarity*, however, that syllable is stressed, allowing you to hear the *ar* sound. Remembering this pattern will help you spell several of the words on your list.

B. Given the following word pairs and the above reminder, read the statements below and write the correct word in each blank. The first one is done for you.

similar, similarity
The word _1_ helps you spell the word _2_

1. _similarity_
2. _similar_

mobile, mobility
The word _3_ helps you spell the word _4_

3. _mobility_
4. _mobile_

hostile, hostility
The word _5_ helps you spell the word _6_

5. _hostility_
6. _hostile_

futile, futility
The word _7_ helps you spell the word _8_

7. _futility_
8. _futile_

Filling a bucket with water isn't much of a project, but have you ever tried to fill a bucket that has a hole in it? "That's hopeless," you'll say. The ancient Romans would have described it with the Latin word *futilis*, meaning "leaky, untrustworthy, useless." Our English word *futile* means almost the same thing. It still describes something that is hopeless or unproductive or has no useful result.

futile

67

C. Watch out for the schwa sound in the respellings below. Write a correct spelling word for each one.

1. / pri-zĕn-tə-bəl / _presentable_
2. / iz-rē-əl / _Israel_
3. / sim-ə-lər / _similar_
4. / chān-jə-bəl / _changeable_
5. / mō-bəl / _mobile_
6. / ī-və-rē kōst/ _Ivory Coast_
7. / hŏs-təl / _hostile_
8. / ĭt-ə-lē / _Italy_
9. / ri-spĕk-tə-bĭl-i-tē / _respectability_
10. / jə-mā-kə / _Jamaica_

D. Add vowels to make spelling words. Remember to capitalize each name of a country.

1. srl _Israel_
2. rspctbl _respectable_
3. chngbl _changeability_
4. jmc _Jamaica_
5. ftlt _futility_
6. tl _Italy_
7. prsntbl _presentability_
8. hstlt _hostility_
9. ftl _futile_
10. vr cst _Ivory Coast_

E. Underline the word in each set that does not belong. On the blank that follows each set, write a sentence telling what the other three words have in common.

1. futile, similar, hostile, mobile _They all have the ending -ile._

2. changeable, hostile, respectable, presentable _they all have the ending -able._

3. futility, similarity, hostile, mobility _they all have the ending -ity._

Words to Master

similar	hostility	respectable	Italy
similarity	futile	respectability	Ivory Coast
mobile	futility	presentable	Jamaica
mobility	changeable	presentability	
hostile	changeability	Israel	

68

Third Day

Give your student time to study the words, using the study method printed on the back cover of the spelling worktext.

Dictate the word list for the trial test.

Give the following dictation sentences:

1. It is **futile** to reason with someone who is so **changeable**.
2. Because of the **hostility** of the crowd, the king saw the **futility** of making his speech.
3. I want my outfit to be **respectable** and **presentable**.

 Dictionary skill: Certain words or phrases in a dictionary are labeled *idiom, slang,* or *informal*. Sometimes these words or phrases are expressions that do not mean *exactly* what they say, or they are not generally acceptable for use in formal writing.

Use page 162 to teach this week's dictionary skill. After you are certain that your student understands the skill, guide him as he completes the exercise. Enjoy this exercise with your student. When he is finished, instruct him to be looking for *idioms* in other material that he reads. Ask him to keep a list of the idioms that he finds. Challenge him to try some of them when talking with the family at supper or at any other time.

Certain words or phrases in a dictionary are labeled idiom, slang, or informal. Sometimes these words or phrases are expressions that do not mean *exactly* what they say, or they are not generally acceptable for use in formal writing.

Locate the following words or phrases in your Spelling Dictionary. Then find the matching informal meaning in the second column and put its letter in front of each word. If it is a phrase (more than one word), look for the underlined word in your Spelling Dictionary.

J	1. smack-dab	A. acting in a reckless and impulsive way
S	2. skip	B. a person who cleverly works his way into another's favor
B	3. smoothie	C. difficult or unpleasant
R	4. show	D. overly sentimental
I	5. shrink	E. to serve yourself
F	6. pan	F. face
E	7. help yourself	G. scribble
P	8. hard up	H. an informer
L	9. ham	I. a psychiatrist
W	10. galore	J. directly, squarely
Y	11. beyond doubt	K. immediately
A	12. off the deep end	L. an amateur radio operator
U	13. hot rod	M. friendly
M	14. matey	N. a wonderful person
V	15. mob	O. undoubtedly dead
		P. poor, needy
		Q. a taxicab
		R. to arrive
		S. to leave in a hurry
		T. clothes
		U. an automobile rebuilt to go faster
		V. a crime organization
		W. in great number
		X. without question
		Y. a person with great skill

162

Use with Unit 17.
Skill: recognizing slang, idioms, and informal language

Fourth Day

Return last week's journal. Give your student time to correct the misspelled words in his previous journal entry and record them in his Word Bank.

Guide the journal time, using the *Journal Entry Idea* on page 69 and the information given in the front of this manual. Guide a lively discussion about things that your family does on Sunday. Elicit from your student why he likes Sunday. Accept any reason, encouraging him to talk more and more. The more he verbalizes his ideas, the easier it will be for him to write them in his journal.

Fifth Day

Guide the study time.

Dictate the word list for the final test.

Give the following dictation sentences.

1. The shape of **Italy** is **similar** to that of a boot.
2. We met with **hostile** ships near the **Ivory Coast**.
3. The children of **Israel** had a **mobile** way of life in the wilderness.

Use *The King's English* on page 69. After your student reads this section silently, read it with him orally. Use the Bible verses, discussion, and good comprehension questions to make certain he understands the material. The following questions can be used:

1. Who received many gifts in Bible times?
2. Why then was Jesus brought gifts at his birth?
3. What does God want us to give Him?
4. What is the greatest gift that God gave us? (BAT: 1a Understanding Jesus Christ; Bible Promise: E. Christ as Sacrifice)

Journal Entry Idea

Waking up! What an awful thing! But no, it's Sunday. It isn't a school day, after all. Oh, I like Sunday! Dad will be with us all day today, we'll go to Sunday school and church, and then we'll have a big dinner. After church at night, we always have piping-hot popcorn.

Is that how you feel about Sunday? What do you do on Sunday that you like? Is there something special that Sunday brings to mind? Is it the funny papers that you like? Or having time to sit quietly and stare out of your window? Or going to see your friends at Sunday school? Tell what you like about Sunday.

The King's English

present

What do you enjoy most about a birthday party? The games, the food, or the gifts? The games are soon over, the food quickly disappears, but the gifts remain after the guests are gone. A Hebrew word for gift, or **present**, is *minchah*. It was customary in Biblical times to bring gifts to the king. When Jesus was a young boy, wise men brought Him gold, frankincense, and myrrh—gifts fit for a king.

When the second syllable of the word *present* is accented, the word can mean "to present yourself." Romans 12 tells us to present our bodies "a living sacrifice, holy, acceptable unto God." In this sense, *present* is not a gift but a "reasonable service," for we have been bought with a price.

That price, the greatest gift of all, was given by God. He "gave his only begotten Son, that whosoever believeth in him should not perish, but have everlasting life."

Romans 12:1-2
Job 2:1
John 3:16

69

Unit 18

Worktext pages 70-73

Generalization emphasis

Generalization statements can be found in Units 13-17.

Materials

- Newspapers and magazines

First Day

For review, apply the generalizations found in Lessons 13-17 to the word list on page 70.

Use worktext page 70 to reinforce word meaning and the skills of the unit. Read the directions and give help, if needed, as your student completes the page.

Review 18
Words to Master

1. assistance	9. nutritious	17. guidance	25. Guyana
2. annoyance	10. acquisition	18. grievance	26. Haiti
3. legalism	11. technician	19. similarity	27. Honduras
4. characteristic	12. magician	20. changeability	28. Hungary
5. appreciate	13. optician	21. hostility	29. Iraq
6. possibility	14. politician	22. presentability	30. Ireland
7. probability	15. execution	23. Canada	31. Israel
8. ambitious	16. sensation	24. Central African Republic	32. Jamaica

GRID NUMBER CIPHER

Use the number grid to break this cipher. Each letter of the alphabet is represented by two numbers: the first number refers to its row in the grid, and the second refers to its column. For example, B is 1 (the row number) and 2 (the column number), written as 12. Continuing through the alphabet, C is 13, D is 14, and so on. Notice that Y and Z are both in the same square; it will not be hard for *zou* to decide which one to use.

A. In the space below each number, write the letter it represents. After deciphering the message, write it on the blank lines at the bottom of the page.

	1	2	3	4	5
1	A	B	C	D	E
2	F	G	H	I	J
3	K	L	M	N	O
4	P	Q	R	S	T
5	U	V	W	X	Y/Z

11 13 42 51 24 44 24 45 24 35 34/ 35 21/
A C Q U I S I T I O N   O F

11 33 12 24 45 24 35 51 44/ 45 15 13 23 34 24 13 24 11 34/
A M B I T I O U S   T E C H N I C I A N

21 35 43/ 13 15 34 45 43 11 32/ 11 21 43 24 13 11 34
F O R   C E N T R A L   A F R I C A N

43 15 41 51 12 32 24 13/ 11/ 41 35 44 44 24 12 24 32 24 45 55/
R E P U B L I C   A   P O S S I B I L I T Y

53 35 51 32 14/ 11 41 41 43 15 13 24 11 45 15/
W O U L D   A P P R E C I A T E

11 44 44 24 44 45 11 34 13 15/
A S S I S T A N C E

Acquisition of ambitious technician for Central African Republic a possibility; would appreciate assistance.

70

Second Day

Use the Bible verse activity on page 71. Discuss the verse with your student, using the following questions:

1. What is a *drought?*
2. What does it mean when it says that the Lord shall *satisfy thy soul in drought?*
3. What does *make fat thy bones* mean?
4. What is God telling us in this verse? (BATs: 7a Grace, 8a Faith in God's promises)
5. What can we learn from this verse? (Bible Promise: H. God as Father)

Use worktext pages 71 and 72 to reinforce word meaning and the skills of the unit. Read the directions and give help, if needed, as your student completes the pages.

Third Day

Give your student time to study the words, using the study method printed on the back cover of the spelling worktext.

Dictate the word list for the trial test.

Give the following dictation sentences:

1. **Iraq** was involved in **hostility** with Iran.
2. The **characteristic** of a **nutritious** meal is a variety of low-fat foods from the four food groups.
3. There is a **possibility** that we will visit **Ireland** next summer.

Guide a spelling activity: *Words in the News.* Using newspapers or magazines, instruct your student to try to find as many of the review words as he can. Cut out the articles or sections where the words are found and underline them. Mount the articles making a collage or print. (A collage is a random overlapping of pictures or articles in an artistic way.)

---

name _____

B. Read the verse.
  1. Underline the word that tells how often the Lord will guide His people.
  2. Circle the word that means "to lead."

> *"And the Lord shall guide thee continually, and satisfy thy soul in drought, and make fat thy bones: and thou shall be like a watered garden, and like a spring of water, whose waters fail not."*   Isaiah 58:11

C. In each of the following sentences, a synonym for a spelling word is underlined. Find the spelling word that could replace the underlined word in each sentence and write it on the appropriate blank.

  1. The man had no feeling in his legs.
  2. The busy teacher was glad for the mother's help.
  3. I told my mother that I had been eating nourishing meals.
  4. The youth worker noticed that the gang members were full of antagonism.
  5. The new baby had red hair, which was a common trait in that family.
  6. We wrote to the company about our complaint.
  7. My latest purchase for my coin collection was a 1935 silver dollar.

1. sensation
2. assistance
3. nutritious
4. hostility
5. characteristic
6. grievance
7. acquisition

D. In the following list you will find an early form of each spelling word and the language from which it came. Decide which review word each one represents and write the word.

  1. Old French, *anoier*
  2. Greek, *tekhnikos*
  3. Greek, *politikos*
  4. Latin, *legalis*
  5. Old French, *assister*
  6. Latin, *optica*
  7. French, *similaire*

1. annoyance
2. technician
3. politician
4. legalism
5. assistance
6. optician
7. similarity

71

E. Use your dictionary and the review spelling words to help you complete this crossword puzzle.

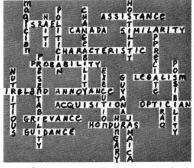

Down

1. one who uses tricks
2. enmity
3. person in public office
4. flexibility
5. country of the West Indies; capital — Port-au-Prince
10. value highly
12. readiness to be presented
14. chance
15. nourishing
16. a carrying out
17. republic of NE South America; capital — Georgetown
23. country of SW Asia; capital — Baghdad
25. country of central Europe; capital — Budapest
26. island in the Caribbean; capital — Kingston

Across

6. help
7. country of SW Asia; capital — Jerusalem
8. country of N North America; capital — Ottawa
9. likeness
11. trait
13. likelihood
18. according to the law
19. island of the British Isles; capital — Dublin
20. irritation
21. a taking over
22. sells eyeglasses
24. hardship
27. country of N Central America; capital — Tegucigalpa
28. leadership

Words to Master

assistance	nutritious	guidance	Guyana
annoyance	acquisition	grievance	Haiti
legalism	technician	similarity	Honduras
characteristic	magician	changeability	Hungary
appreciate	optician	hostility	Iraq
possibility	politician	presentability	Ireland
probability	execution	Canada	Israel
ambitious	sensation	Central African Republic	Jamaica

72

Fourth Day

Return last week's journal. Give your student time to correct the misspelled words in his previous journal entry and record them in his Word Bank.

Guide the journal time using the *Journal Entry Idea* on page 73 and the information given in the front of this manual. Discuss with your student some of the different older people he knows and the special characteristics they have. Relive some of the experiences that he has shared with them.

Fifth Day

Guide the study time.

Dictate the word list for the final test.

Give the following dictation sentences:

1. I **appreciate** the **assistance** that the kind **technician** gave us.
2. Tell your **grievance** to that **ambitious** young **politician**.
3. The **acquisition** of more land enlarged our mission in the **Central African Republic.**

Use *The King's English* on page 73. After your student reads this section silently, read it with him orally. Use the Bible verses, discussion, and good comprehension questions to make certain he understands the material. Tell your student that one of the meanings of the word part *con* is "with." Show him how the two word parts *con* and *gregare* join to make the word *congregation*. The following questions and statement can be used:

1. What does the Latin word *gregare* mean?
2. What does "to flock together" make you think of?
3. How does a person become "separated unto the Lord"?
4. Explain how you think our Lord is like a shepherd. (Bible Promises: H. God as Father, I. God as Master)

Journal Entry Idea

"When can we sing at the retirement home again?" Is that the way *you* feel about it? What about that older man who lives on your block—the one with the flashy Ferrari? Why, he must be over eighty! He is the one you take your bike to when the tire is going flat, and he *always* wants to talk. He talks in an excited, whispery voice, and you lean over to hear him. He has the best stories about back when there wasn't even any electricity and he was a telegraph operator. Do you have a favorite older person? Describe that person and tell why you like him or her.

The King's English
congregation

Have you ever thought of sheep as a **congregation?** The Lord did, for the Latin word *gregare* means "to flock together." A congregation is a group of people who are gathered together, just like sheep.

And, just like sheep, they need a leader. In the Old Testament, the Hebrew word *kähal* often referred to the people of Israel. Moses led his congregation out of Egypt physically and gave them guidance and laws to keep them on the right path spiritually. He was the shepherd of his flock of people.

Now, when we talk about a congregation, we usually mean a group of people gathered together in a church.

When we are separated unto the Lord, He calls us the congregation of the righteous. Psalm 1:5 tells us that sinners shall not stand in that congregation, for the Lord knows the way of the righteous. He sees our hearts and knows our names, just as a shepherd knows the name of each sheep in his flock.

Psalm 1:5
   Leviticus 4:21
    Exodus 16:2

73

Unit 19

Worktext pages 74-77
Dictionary page 163

Generalization emphasis

1. **/ăst/ or /əst/ spelled *ast* at the beginning of a word**—/ăst/ or /əst/ at the beginning of a word is spelled *ast*, if the meaning of the word is related to "star." *astronomy*

2. **/sĕn/ or /sĕnt/ spelled *cen* or *cent* at the beginning of a word**—/sĕn/ or /sĕnt/ at the beginning of a word is spelled *cen* or *cent*, if the meaning of the word is related to "hundred." *centigrade, century*

3. **/mĭl/ or /məl/ spelled *mill* at the beginning of a word**—/mĭl/ or /məl/ at the beginning of a word is spelled *mill*, if the meaning of the word is related to "thousand." *millimeter, millenium*

Materials

- A world map or atlas
- The *J* and *K* volumes of an encyclopedia
- Prepare the following activity for Day 2.

Say It in a Word
1. Jon has always wanted to be a(n) <u>person who studies the stars</u>. *(astronomer)*
2. The caterpillar that I found was (a) <u>one-thousandth of a meter</u> longer than Gail's. *(millimeter)*
3. On Thursday a(n) <u>person trained to pilot a spaceship</u> visited our school. *(astronaut)*
4. It seemed like a <u>hundred years</u> before the ambulance arrived. *(century)*
5. Grandma has a pink <u>daisylike flower</u> growing in her garden. *(aster)*
6. Andrew found another <u>worm with numerous legs</u> for his collection. *(centipede)*
7. Our science teacher insisted that we use a thermometer that was <u>divided into a hundred degrees</u>. *(centigrade)*
8. It is an <u>immense</u> distance from Venus to Mars. *(astronomical)*
9. Many brave men and women have died for Christ in the past <u>thousand years</u>. *(millennium)*
10. My favorite book is about Marcus, a <u>leader of one hundred men</u> who lived in Rome. *(centurion)*

First Day

Give the pretest. After you have given the pretest and your student has checked and corrected it, give him time to choose two of the words from his Word Bank and write them as this week's *Word Bank Entries*.

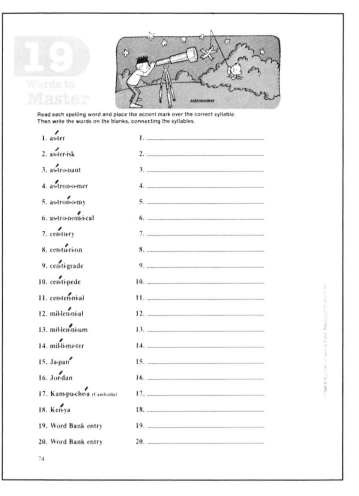

Read each spelling word and place the accent mark over the correct syllable. Then write the words on the blanks, connecting the syllables.

1. ás·ter	1. _____
2. ás·ter·isk	2. _____
3. ás·tro·naut	3. _____
4. as·trón·o·mer	4. _____
5. as·trón·o·my	5. _____
6. as·tro·nóm·i·cal	6. _____
7. cén·tu·ry	7. _____
8. cen·tú·ri·on	8. _____
9. cén·ti·grade	9. _____
10. cén·ti·pede	10. _____
11. cen·tén·ni·al	11. _____
12. mil·lén·ni·al	12. _____
13. mil·lén·ni·um	13. _____
14. míl·li·me·ter	14. _____
15. Ja·pán	15. _____
16. Jór·dan	16. _____
17. Kam·pu·che·a (Cambodia)	17. _____
18. Kén·ya	18. _____
19. Word Bank entry	19. _____
20. Word Bank entry	20. _____

74

After reading words 1-6 on page 74 to your student, apply generalization number one to these words in the following way, using the suggested questions:

- What do the first six words have in common? *(All of them begin with* ast.*)*
- Can you tell what all of these words are related to by thinking of their meanings? *(Your student might come up with the idea that they all have something to do with stars or the sky. Bring out the meaning of the root* aster*–star.)*
- If he does not see any connection, ask him what one of the words means, such as *astronomer*. *(a scientist who studies astronomy, or a scientist who studies celestial bodies–stars)*
- After you discuss with him one of the words he knows the meaning of, move to the others and show how they are all related to the word *aster* which means "star." Use the following definitions:

  > aster: "a many-colored flower that resembles a star"
  > asterisk: "a star-shaped figure"
  > astronaut: "a person trained to navigate a ship in space–two word parts go together in the following way: aster=star, naut=sail"

astronomy: "the study of the universe–heavenly bodies"

astronomical: "of or pertaining to astronomy; inconceivably large"

- Ask your student how /ăst/ or /əst/ is spelled if it comes at the beginning of a word that has a meaning that is related to "star." (ast)

After reading words 7 through 11 to your student, apply generalization number two to these words in exactly the way you applied generalization number one. The following definitions will be helpful:

century: "one hundred years"

centurion: "leader of one hundred Roman soldiers in New Testament times"

centigrade: "of or pertaining to a temperature scale that registers the freezing point of water as 0 degrees and the boiling point as 100 degrees"

centipede: "any of several wormlike creatures with numerous legs"

centennial: "of or pertaining to a period of 100 years"

- Ask your student how either /sĕn/ or /sĕnt/ is spelled if it comes at the beginning of a word with a meaning that is related to "one hundred." (cent)

After reading words 12-14 to your student, apply generalization number three to these words using exactly

the same method you did to apply generalization number one. The following definitions will be helpful:

millennial, millenium: "of or pertaining to a period of 1000 years"

millimeter: "a unit of length equal to one thousandth of a meter"

- Ask your student how /mĭl/ or /məl/ is spelled if it comes at the beginning of a word with a meaning that is related to "one thousand." (mill)

Introduce words 15-18 on page 74.

- In this unit, the four countries are spelled according to the way they sound.
- You might point out that the /ch/ in the third syllable of *Kampuchea* is spelled with a *ch*.

Guide a research activity: *Where in the World?* Help your student locate the countries with names in the spelling list on a world atlas or map. Ask him to use the *J* and *K* volumes of an encyclopedia to expand his geographic and general country knowledge according to the ideas and optional activities presented in Unit 1.

Japan has been both friend and foe to the United States. Ask your student to read about this fascinating country and the relationship it has had with America.

Use the handwritten list. After your student has written each word on the appropriate line, check his list for spelling and legibility. Instruct him to place an accent mark in each multi-syllable word on the printed list.

Second Day

Use the Bible verse activity on page 75. Discuss the verse with your student, making certain he understands the context of the verse and the emotion that might have been felt by the centurion.

Have fun with the *Word for Word* section on page 75.

Use worktext pages 75 and 76 to reinforce word meaning and the skills of the unit. Read the directions and give help, if needed, as your student completes the pages.

Developing word meaning: *Say It in a Word.* Use the activity found in the *Materials* section. Write a spelling word that means the same as the underlined phrase.

A. Read the verse.
 1. Underline the words that the centurion and those with him said about Jesus.
 2. Circle the word that means "a leader of 100 men."

name _____

 "Now when the Centurion and they that were with him, watching Jesus, saw the earthquake, and those things that were done, they feared greatly, saying, Truly this was the Son of God."
Matthew 27:54

****

In our language we have many interesting words that begin with *aster-*. They are derived from the Latin *aster*, which comes from the Greek word meaning "star." Four hundred years ago, the English spoke of stars as "asters," but now that particular use of the word has become obsolete. Today, our English word *aster* refers to a white, blue, or pink daisylike flower that looks like a star, if you have a good imagination.

****

B. Use the Latin words *aster* (star), *centum* (hundred), and *mille* (thousand) to help you match spelling words with the definitions below.

 1. comes from the Greek word for "a little star"
 2. the study of the stars
 3. an adjective that refers to a span of 1,000 years
 4. occurring every 100 years

1. asterisk
2. astronomy
3. millennial
4. centennial

C. Match the countries on your spelling list with the locations below. Use your Spelling Dictionary.

 1. NE Asia
 2. E Central Africa
 3. SW Asia

1. Japan
2. Kenya
3. Jordan

WORD FOR WORD

Have you ever wanted to be an astronaut? Would you be surprised if someone told you that even in our space program, we don't have any true astronauts?

The word *astronaut* comes from two Greek words that mean "sailor of the stars." Since the nearest star (our sun) is 93,000,000 miles away, no one has actually "sailed to the stars" — not yet. Just think, if you ever traveled to the sun, you would be the world's first true astronaut!

astronaut

75

D. Use spelling words to fill in the blanks. Use each word only once.

On my last trip to __1__ (Cambodia), I met an __2__ who claimed that while studying __3__, he had discovered how to travel to any __4__ he chose. He said that his best friend was a Roman __5__ who kept a pet __6__ inside his helmet. Once, as they rode into battle, an arrow missed him by only a __7__.

I've always liked traveling and want to be an __8__, so at first I listened attentively. Then, as he showed me around his study, he paused at a vase that held a __9__ thermometer and a blue flower that I think was an __10__. "This is my secretary, Grace," he explained. "She speaks softly, but in another __11__ or so, you can listen to her on my new equipment." Sadly I went on my way, concluding that his __12__ claims were a trifle far-out.

1. Kampuchea
2. astronomer
3. astronomy
4. century
5. centurion
6. centipede
7. millimeter
8. astronaut
9. centigrade
10. aster
11. millennium
12. astronomical

E. Use the first letter of each word in the following sentences to form a spelling word. Write it on the corresponding blank. On the lines at the bottom, try writing your own sentence that forms a spelling word.

 1. A storage tank, remaining open, normally announces urgent trouble.
 2. Could everyone now turn, unless receiving instructions on navigating?
 3. Maybe in leaving last, I might enjoy the end round.
 4. Call every number that's in green, reading all decimals exactly.

1. astronaut
2. centurion
3. millimeter
4. centigrade

Answers will vary.

_____

_____

Words to Master

aster	astronomical	centennial	Jordan
asterisk	century	millennial	Kampuchea (Cambodia)
astronaut	centurion	millennium	Kenya
astronomer	centigrade	millimeter	
astronomy	centipede	Japan	

76

Third Day

Give your student time to study the words, using the study method printed on the back cover of the spelling worktext.

Dictate the word list for the trial test.

Give the following dictation sentences:
1. A **millennium** is ten times as long as a **century**.
2. A famous **astronaut** led our town's **centennial** parade.
3. The **centurion** sent his army across the **Jordan** River.

Dictionary skill: In the dictionary, entry words are divided into syllables. You can use the dictionary to discover how a word can be divided.

Use page 163 to teach this week's dictionary skill. After you are certain that your student understands the skill, guide him as he completes the exercise.

name _____

In the dictionary, entry words are divided into syllables. Generalization patterns and rules are used to divide words into syllables correctly.

Use the generalizations and patterns below to find out why the spelling words from Units 1-18 are divided as they are. Put the letter of the rule or pattern that fits each syllable division above the period that divides the syllables. The first example is completed for you.

A. In dividing a word with the VCCV (vowel, consonant, consonant, vowel) pattern, we divide between the two consonants: VC/CV. (for·mal)

B. In dividing a word with the VCV pattern, the consonant will often go with the *second* syllable: V/CV. This sometimes puts the stress on the syllable *before* the CV, which contains a long vowel sound and is therefore an open syllable. (bi·ceps)

C. In dividing a word with three or four consonants, usually the syllable division is after the first consonant: VC/CC. (im·press)

D. In dividing words with two vowels together, when each vowel makes its own sound, we divide between the two vowels: V/V. (ge·ol·o·gy)

E. Do *not* divide between letters that work together to make one sound. (punc·tu·al)

1. suc · ces · sion — A

2. im · pres · sion — C A

3. tri · une — D

4. tech · nique — E

5. bi · sect — B

6. pa · tri · ot — E D

7. mi · crobe — B E

8. me · ter — B

9. ho · ri · zon — B B

10. cou · ra · geous — E B

11. ad · van · tage — A A

12. col · lec · tor — A A

13. u · ni · cy · cle — B B B

14. bi · ceps — B

15. an · noy — A

Use with Unit 19.
Skill: using patterns and rules to divide words into syllables

163

Fourth Day

Return last week's journal. Give your student time to correct the misspelled words in his previous journal entry and record them in his Word Bank.

Guide the journal time using the *Journal Entry Idea* on page 77 and the information given in the front of this manual. After you and your student read the paragraph, try to really ''get into'' telling your student about an experience you have had in your life like the one in the book. Try to get him to tell about an experience that he has had like that. After he has related it to you, allow him to write about it. (BATs: 2a Authority, 3c Emotional control, 4d Victory, 8a Faith in God's promises)

Fifth Day

Guide the study time.

Dictate the word list for the final test.

Give the following dictation sentences.
1. This type of **aster** is grown in **Japan.**
2. This **centipede** is found in the jungles of **Kenya** and has a harmful sting.
3. There is an **asterisk** by that man's name in my **astronomy** book.

Use *The King's English* on page 77. After your student reads this section silently, read it with him orally. Use the Bible verses, discussion, and good comprehension questions to make certain he understands the material. The following questions can be used:
1. What do you think the cherubim looked like when they guarded the garden of Eden?
2. What are cherubim associated with in the Bible?

Journal Entry Idea

Your back is rigid, and you aren't breathing! They are just about to tell who made it into the finals of the tournament. Did he read your name or didn't he? No — it will be next. But he has stopped. The ones who made it are waiting to be congratulated. The ones who didn't are standing in stunned silence. How could this happen?

Have you ever had an experience like this? Tell about it, how you felt about it then and how you feel about it now.

The King's English
cherubim

Cherubim first appear in the book of Genesis. God placed them at the entrance of the Garden of Eden so that man could not return to the Garden and eat of the tree of life. In Exodus 25:18, the Israelites were instructed to make golden cherubim that would cover the mercy seat with their wings. From Ezekiel 10, we understand that the cherubim are beings that have a mixture of human and animal parts. Cherubim (from the Hebrew *kerubim* and Greek *cheroubim*) are not to be confused with any earthly creature.

The Israelites engraved cherubim on the ark of the covenant and embroidered them on the tabernacle curtains. In Solomon's temple, two large cherubim of olive wood represented God's greatness and holiness. Cherubim became part of the tabernacle furnishings, but they were never worshiped by the Israelites.

The cherubim stood guard at the Garden of Eden and prevented man from partaking of the tree of life. They were part of God's judgment. Therefore, from the beginning cherubim have been associated with judgment against those who violate God's holiness.

Genesis 3:24
Exodus 25:18
I Samuel 4:4

77

Unit 20

Worktext pages 78-81
Dictionary page 164

Generalization emphasis

1. **/tĕr • ə/ or /tər/ spelled *terri* or *ter*–**/tĕr • ə/ or /tər/ is spelled *terri* or *ter*, if the word's meaning is related to "earth." *terrain, territory*

2. **/mŭl • tə/ spelled *multi* at the beginning of a word–**/mŭl • tə/ at the beginning of the word is spelled *multi*, if the word's meaning is related to "many." *multiple*

3. **/krĕd/ or /krĭd/ spelled *cred* at the beginning of a word–**/krĕd/ or /krĭd/ at the beginning of a word is spelled *cred*, if the word's meaning is related to "to believe." *credible*

Materials

- A world atlas or map
- The *K* and *L* volumes of an encyclopedia

First Day

Give the pretest. After you have given the pretest and your student has checked and corrected it, give him time to choose two of the words from his Word Bank and write them as this week's *Word Bank Entries*.

After reading words 1-5 on page 78 to your student, apply generalization number one in the following way, using the suggested questions and statements:

- What do the first five words have in common? *(They all begin with the spelling* terr.*)*
- Ask your student if he knows what *terrain* means? *(ground)*
- If he does not know the meaning of that word, allow him to tell what he thinks are the meanings of any of the *ter* words.
- Follow this by relating each of the *ter* words to the meaning of *terri* or *ter*, "earth." The following definitions will be helpful:
  - terrarium: "a small closed container of soil in which small plants or animals are kept"
  - terrestrial: "of or pertaining to the earth or its inhabitants"
  - territory, territorial: "of or pertaining to an area of land"
- Ask your student how to spell either /tĕr • ə/ or /tər/ if it comes at the beginning of a word that has a meaning related to "earth." *(terr)*

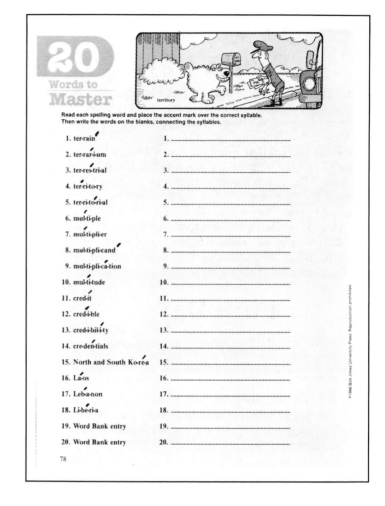

After reading words 6-10 to your student, apply generalization number two to these words in exactly the same way you applied generalization number one.

- Show how each of the words relates to the meaning of *multi*, "many." The following definitions will be helpful:
  - multiple: "of or pertaining to more than one individual"
  - multiplier: "the number by which the multiplicand is multiplied"
  - multiplicand: "the number that is multiplied by another"
  - multiplication: "the act of multiplying"
  - multitude: "a great indefinite number"
- Ask your student how /mŭl • tə/ is spelled if it comes at the beginning of a word that has a meaning related to "many." *(multi)*

After reading words 11-14 to your student, apply generalization number three to these words, in exactly the same way that you applied generalization number one.

- Show him how each of these words relates to the meaning of *cred*, "to believe." The following definitions will be helpful:

credit: "belief or confidence in the truth of something"

credible, credibility: "of or pertaining to the capability of being believed"

credentials: "those things that prove one is worthy of being believed"

- Ask your student how to spell /krĕd / or /krĭd/ if it comes at the beginning of a word that has a meaning related to "to believe." *(cred)*

Introduce words 15-18 on page 78.

- Since most of the countries' names can be found in the Spelling Dictionary, use it as a tool and have your student try to pronounce the name of each country in this unit.
- Point out the three possible pronunciations for *Laos.*

Guide a research activity: *Where in the World?* Help your student locate the countries with names in the spelling list on a world atlas or map. Ask him to use the *K* and *L* volumes of an encyclopedia to expand his geographic and general country knowledge according to the ideas and optional activities presented in Unit 1.

Use the handwritten list. After your student has written each word on the appropriate line, check his list for spelling and legibility. Instruct him to place an accent mark in each multi-syllable word of the printed list.

Second Day

Use the Bible verse activity on page 79. Spend some time after your student reads the verse and follows the directions given to discuss the meaning of the verse. Ask him to explain what the *bodies terrestrial,* the *bodies celestial,* the *terrestrial glory,* and the *celestial glory* might be.

Have fun with the *Word for Word* section on page 79.

Use worktext pages 79 and 80 to reinforce word meaning and the skills of the unit. Read the directions and give help, if needed, as your student completes the pages.

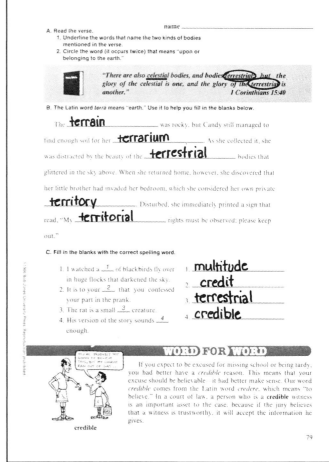

name _____

A. Read the verse.
1. Underline the words that name the two kinds of bodies mentioned in the verse.
2. Circle the word (it occurs twice) that means "upon or belonging to the earth."

"There are also celestial bodies, and bodies terrestrial: but the glory of the celestial is one, and the glory of the terrestrial is another."   *I Corinthians 15:40*

B. The Latin word *terra* means "earth." Use it to help you fill in the blanks below.

The **terrain** _____ was rocky, but Candy still managed to find enough soil for her **terrarium** _____. As she collected it, she was distracted by the beauty of the **terrestrial** _____ bodies that glittered in the sky above. When she returned home, however, she discovered that her little brother had invaded her bedroom, which she considered her own private **territory** _____. Disturbed, she immediately printed a sign that read, "My **territorial** _____ rights must be observed; please keep out."

C. Fill in the blanks with the correct spelling word.

1. I watched a __1__ of blackbirds fly over in huge flocks that darkened the sky.
2. It is to your __2__ that you confessed your part in the prank.
3. The rat is a small __3__ creature.
4. His version of the story sounds __4__ enough.

1. **multitude**
2. **credit**
3. **terrestrial**
4. **credible**

WORD FOR WORD

If you expect to be excused for missing school or being tardy, you had better have a *credible* reason. This means that your excuse should be believable—it had better make sense. Our word *credible* comes from the Latin word *credere,* which means "to believe." In a court of law, a person who is a **credible** witness is an important asset to the case, because if the jury believes that a witness is trustworthy, it will accept the information he gives.

credible

79

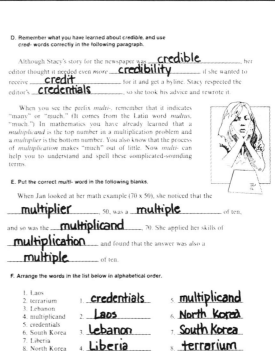

D. Remember what you have learned about *credible,* and use *cred-* words correctly in the following paragraph.

Although Stacy's story for the newspaper was **credible** _____, her editor thought it needed even *more* **credibility** _____ if she wanted to receive **credit** _____ for it and get a byline. Stacy respected the editor's **credentials** _____, so she took his advice and rewrote it.

When you see the prefix *multi-,* remember that it indicates "many" or "much." (It comes from the Latin word *multus,* "much.") In mathematics you have already learned that a *multiplicand* is the top number in a multiplication problem and a *multiplier* is the bottom number. You also know that the process of *multiplication* makes "much" out of little. Now *multi-* can help you to understand and spell these complicated-sounding terms.

E. Put the correct *multi-* word in the following blanks.

When Jan looked at her math example (70 × 50), she noticed that the **multiplier** _____, 50, was a **multiple** _____ of ten, and so was the **multiplicand** _____, 70. She applied her skills of **multiplication** _____ and found that the answer was also a **multiple** _____ of ten.

F. Arrange the words in the list below in alphabetical order.

1. Laos
2. terrarium
3. Lebanon
4. multiplicand
5. credentials
6. South Korea
7. Liberia
8. North Korea

1. **credentials**
2. **Laos**
3. **Lebanon**
4. **Liberia**
5. **multiplicand**
6. **North Korea**
7. **South Korea**
8. **terrarium**

Words to Master

terrain	multiple	credit	Laos
terrarium	multiplier	credible	Lebanon
terrestrial	multiplicand	credibility	Liberia
territory	multiplication	credentials	
territorial	multitude	North and South Korea	

80

Third Day

Give your student time to study the words, using the study method printed on the back cover of the spelling worktext.

Dictate the word list for the trial test.

Give the following dictation sentences:

1. A small band of soldiers covered some rough **terrain** in the jungles of **Laos.**
2. The lawyer had a **multitude** of **credible** witnesses from which to choose.
3. What is the **multiplicand** in this **multiplication** problem?

Dictionary skill: An accent mark in the respelling shows where the *stress* comes in an entry word.

Use page 164 to teach this week's dictionary skill. After you are certain that your student understands the skill, guide him as he completes the exercise. Ask your student to explain how the rule after Part *A* relates to each of the five words given before he decides what syllable the stress is on. Ask him to do this on his own for Parts *B* and *C*.

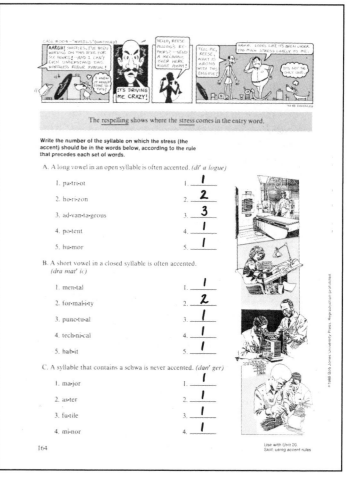

Fourth Day

Return last week's journal. Give your student time to correct the misspelled words in his previous journal entry and record them in his Word Bank.

Guide the journal time using the *Journal Entry Idea* on page 81 and the information given in the front of this manual. If your student cannot remember when he had such an experience, remind him of a time. Talk with him about owning something that someone else wanted and how it must feel. After he has discussed the idea with you for a while, ask him to write down exactly what he said to you in his journal.

Fifth Day

Guide the study time.

Dictate the word list for the final test.

Give the following dictation sentences.

1. There was a **territorial** dispute between **North** and **South Korea.**
2. The teacher gave John extra **credit** for the **terrarium** he had built and filled with plants.
3. My father escaped from enemy **territory** in **Lebanon.**

Use *The King's English* on page 81. After your student reads this section silently, read it with him orally. Use the Bible verses, discussion, and good comprehension questions to make certain he understands the material. The following questions can be used:

1. What do you think Jesus meant when He said to receive the kingdom of God as a little child? (BAT: 1b Repentance and faith)
2. Do you remember a time when you understood what God wanted you to do and completely changed the direction of your life, either when you became one of God's children or finally decided to live only for His glory? (BATs: 1a Understanding Jesus Christ, 1c Separation from the world)
3. What would you say if you tried to convert someone to believing in the Lord Jesus Christ? (BAT: 5c Evangelism and missions)

Journal Entry Idea

The choir teacher has just asked you to sing the next verse as a solo. You are elated! You wonder if you can sing with that enormous smile on your face. You get through the song, and afterwards your teacher says that you will sing a solo in the program. You can't wait to tell your friend, but when you do, *she* isn't excited at all!

You are chosen to be the only one in the *whole* school to use the new computer. Everyone, all of a sudden, is being mean to you. You wonder if it's worth it. Have you ever had something someone else wanted? How did you handle it? Tell about it.

The King's English
convert

The Latin word *convertere* means "to turn around, to transform." When we accept Christ as our Saviour, we repent of our sins, turn from them, and become transformed spiritually.

Shub is the Hebrew word that means "to turn about." When we witness to others, we are trying to turn them to the Lord, or **convert** them. The message we give to others is not hard to understand. When the disciples tried to spare Jesus by keeping the children away from Him, He rebuked His disciples, saying, "Whosoever shall not receive the kingdom of God as a little child shall in no wise enter therein."

Psalm 19:7 reminds us that "the law of the Lord is perfect, converting the soul: the testimony of the Lord is sure, making wise the simple." However, some harden their hearts and close their ears to the gospel, being unwilling to listen (Matthew 13:15; John 12:40).

It is important not to get discouraged in witnessing, for the rewards are great. When you win a soul to Christ, the angels in heaven rejoice, for you have "saved a soul from death."
Psalm 19:7
James 5:19-20
Acts 3:19

81

Unit 21

Worktext pages 82-85
Dictionary page 165

--- **Generalization emphasis** ---

1. **/ô • də/, /ô • dē/, or /ô • dĭ/ spelled *audi*, at the beginning of a word**–/ô • də/, /ô • dē/, or /ô • dĭ/ at the beginning of a word is spelled *audi*, if the word's meaning is related to "to hear." *audible, audience*

2. **/kôrp/ or /kôr/ spelled *corp* at the beginning of a word**–/kôrp/ or /kôr/ at the beginning or end of a word is spelled *corp*, if the meaning of the word is related to "body." *corpse*

3. **/vĭ/ spelled *vi* at the beginning of a word**–/vĭ/ at the beginning of a word is spelled *vi*, if the word's meaning is related to "to see." *visible*

--- **Materials** ---

- A world map
- The *L* and *M* volumes of an encyclopedia

First Day

Give the pretest. After you have given the pretest and your student has checked and corrected it, give him time to choose two of the words from his Word Bank and write them as this week's *Word Bank Entries.*

After reading words 1-4 on page 82 to your student, apply generalization number one to the words in the following way, using the questions and statements given below:

- What spelling do words 1-4 have in common? *(All begin with* audi.*)*
- Do you know what any of these words means? *(Your student may say an* audience *is a group of people; he may say an* auditorium *is a place where people come to see or hear something.)*
- Show him how the word part *audi* fits into these meanings: *A person in an* audience *is "hearing" something; in an* auditorium, *people are "hearing" something.*
- Go over the meanings of the other two words, showing how the word part fits into each: when a person is given an *audition,* he is being given a "hearing"; when something is *audible,* it is able to be "heard."
- Ask your student how /ô • dĭ/ is spelled if it comes at the beginning of a word that has a meaning related to "to hear." *(audi)*

21 Words to Master

Read each spelling word and place the accent mark over the correct syllable. Then write the words on the blanks, connecting the syllables.

1. au·di·ble   1. _____
2. au·di·ence   2. _____
3. au·di·tion   3. _____
4. au·di·to·ri·um   4. _____
5. corps   5. _____
6. corpse   6. _____
7. cor·po·rate   7. _____
8. cor·po·ra·tion   8. _____
9. cor·pus·cle   9. _____
10. vid·e·o   10. _____
11. vid·e·o·tape   11. _____
12. vi·sion   12. _____
13. vis·i·ble   13. _____
14. vis·i·bil·i·ty 14. _____
15. Lib·y·a   15. _____
16. Ma·la·wi   16. _____
17. Ma·lay·sia   17. _____
18. Mex·i·co   18. _____
19. Word Bank entry 19. _____
20. Word Bank entry 20. _____

82

> *corps* is pronounced as if the *p* and *s* were not there: (/kôr/).

After reading words 5-9 to your student, apply generalization number two, following the same steps as you used to apply generalization number one. Add the following questions and statements to those steps:

- Say the word *corps* again as your student looks at the word. Ask him if he notices anything different about the way the word is pronounced and the way it is spelled. *(The letters* p *and* s *are not heard.)*
- Pronounce the other words with *corp,* and ask your student if the *p* is silent in any of those. *(no)*
- Ask your student if he knows what any of these words mean. *(He may know that* corpse *means "a dead body.")*
- Using the word he knows the meaning for, move on to the other words discussing how their meanings include the meaning of *corp,* "body." The following meanings will help:

  corps: "a body of persons"
  corpse: "a dead body"

corporate, corporation: "of or pertaining to a body of persons acting together as one body"

corpuscle: "a small body within the human body, called a *cell,* that has the freedom of movement"

- Ask your student how /kôrp/ or /kôr/ is spelled when it comes at the beginning of a word that has a meaning related to "body." *(corp)*

After you have read words 10-14 to your student, apply generalization number three to those words, following the same steps that you did when you applied generalization number two. The following definitions will help:

video : "having to do with televised images that are seen"

videotape: "a relatively wide magnetic tape used to record television images that are seen"(In some dictionaries this is a two-word compound.)

vision, visible, visibility: "of or pertaining to the sense of sight"

- Ask your student how either /vĭd/ or /vĭz/ is spelled if it comes at the beginning of a word that has a meaning related to "to see." *(vid or vis)*

Introduce words 15-18 on page 82.

- Point out that the name *Libya* is a three-syllable word, and the y has a separate pronunciation, /ē/.
- *Malawi* ends in /ē/ and the last syllable of *Malaysia* is /zhə/.

Guide a research activity: *Where in the World?* Help your student locate the countries with names in the spelling list on a world atlas or map. Ask him to use the *L* and *M* volumes of an encyclopedia to expand his geographic and general country knowledge according to the ideas and optional activities presented in Unit 1.

Mexico is our nearest southern neighbor. Ask your student to spend extra time reading about this country and its influence on America's language and customs, particularly in the southwestern states of Texas, New Mexico, Arizona, and southern California. Have him share the information with your family in a written report.

Use the handwritten list. After your student has written each word on the appropriate line, check his list for spelling and legibility. Instruct him to place an accent mark in each multi-syllable word of the printed list.

Second Day

Use the Bible verse activity on page 83. Ask your student if he can tell you what the verse means. Make certain he understands the following words and phrases as used in the verse: *vision, perish, keepeth the law, happy.*

Have fun with the *Word for Word* section on page 83. Your student might want to prepare a song or a reading and pretend he is auditioning for a program or concert. He could do his auditioning for his family.

Use worktext pages 83 and 84 to teach word meaning and the skills of the unit. Read the directions and give help, if needed, as your student completes the pages.

Guide a spelling activity: *Remember, Remember.* Read three to five spelling words in random order from the spelling list. Ask your student to write the words. Award 100 points for each word remembered and 500 points for each word spelled correctly. The points are traded in for a special treat or activity.

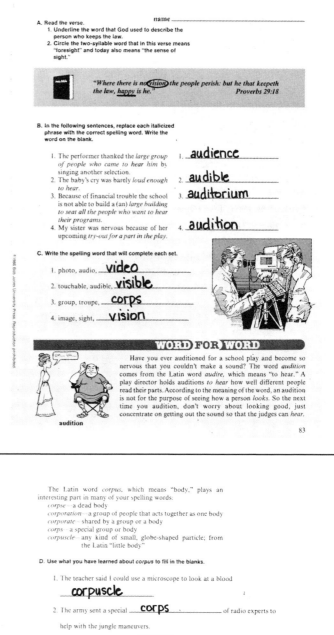

Third Day

Give your student time to study the words, using the study method printed on the back cover of the spelling worktext.

Dictate the word list for the trial test.

Give the following dictation sentences:

1. When **visibility** is good, we can see the Gulf of **Mexico.**
2. My uncle works for a small **corporation** in **Malaysia.**
3. The film was both **audible** and **visible** from where we sat.

> Dictionary skill: Some entry words are followed by *more than just one respelling.* This is because people pronounce the same word in different ways. The first respelling is usually the most correct one.

Use page 165 to teach this week's dictionary skill. After you are certain that your student understands the skill, guide him as he completes the exercise. When he has completed the page, check his work. It is not to be "graded" but to be used as a teaching tool.

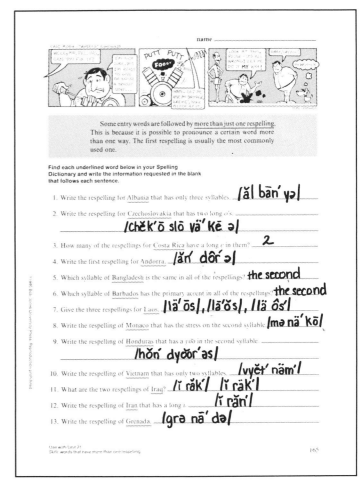

Fourth Day

Return last week's journal. Give your student time to correct the misspelled words in his previous journal entry and record them in his Word Bank.

Guide the journal time using the *Journal Entry Idea* on page 85 and the information given in the front of this manual. Reminisce with your student about the good times your family has had eating together, either at homes of friends and relatives or at restaurants. When he remembers a special meal your family has had, encourage him to talk about it before he begins writing.

Fifth Day

Guide the study time.

Dictate the word list for the final test.

Give the following dictation sentences.

1. They showed a **videotape** of our play in the school **auditorium.**
2. The blood **corpuscle** was **visible** under the microscope.
3. Will you be in the **audience** when I go for my **audition?**

Use *The King's English* on page 85. After your student reads this section silently, read it with him orally. Use the Bible verses, discussion, and good comprehension questions to make certain he understands the material. The following questions can be used:

1. To what does the paragraph liken "gaining an audience with God"? (BATs: 6a Bible study, 6b Prayer)
2. Why is it easier to gain an audience with God than with an important person here on earth? *(God can listen to as many individuals at one time as want to talk to Him.)*
3. Have you ever written something that someone else read? That person was your *audience*. Name some people with whom you gained an audience or who have read something you have written.
4. If you said, "Dad, I would like to talk to you," can you use the word *audience* to tell what you would be doing? (BAT: 4d Communication)

Journal Entry Idea

Tonight is a fantastically-fun-filled-family-feast night! The whole family's going out to eat. The occasion is Grandma's birthday and boy, are you thankful she was born, because you love to eat out. Mom's excited too because she won't have to cook. You just hope that your little brother won't drop a tomato in your lap like he did the last time.

Do you like to go out to eat with your family? Tell about an eating-out experience: where you went, what you ate, and anything funny that happened.

The King's English
audience

Being in a play can be fun, but sometimes it's even more fun to sit in the **audience.** Seated there, you can see and hear everything that is taking place on the stage. It is not surprising that the Latin word *audire* means "to hear."

Another meaning for *audience* is a meeting in which you wish to be "heard." When Moses and Aaron wanted to see the ruler of Egypt, they asked for an audience. They met with the Pharaoh and his court, and Moses asked for the Israelites' freedom. The Pharaoh heard the request, though it took many more audiences before he granted the request.

Sometimes gaining an audience with a king or an important leader takes patience and time. We, as children of God, gain audiences with our Lord every time we pray. And when we pray, He hears us and responds. Prayer is a privilege that we should treasure and use often.

The group of people who read what is printed is also called an audience. You are our audience, for you are reading what has been written here.

Exodus 5:1
I John 5:14-15
Esther 5:2-8

85

Unit 22

Worktext pages 86-89
Dictionary page 166

────── Generalization emphasis ──────

1. /pŏp • yə/ **spelled** *popu* **at the beginning of a word**–
   /pŏp • yə/ at the beginning of a word is spelled *popu*, if the meaning of the word is related to "people." *populate*

2. /sōl/ or /sŏl/ **spelled** *sol* **at the beginning of a word**– /sōl/ or /sŏl/ at the beginning of a word is spelled *sol* if the meaning of the word is related to "alone." *solo, solitude*

3. /vĕr/ or /vûr/ **spelled** *ver* **at the beginning of a word**–/vĕr/ or /vûr/ at the beginning of a word is spelled *ver*, if the meaning of the word is related to "true." *verify, verdict*

4. /măn/ **spelled** *man* **at the beginning of a word**– /măn/ is spelled *man* at the beginning of many words that originally had to do with "hand." *manual*

────────── Materials ──────────

- A world atlas or map
- The *M* volume of an encyclopedia

First Day

Give the pretest. After you have given the pretest and your student has checked and corrected it, give him time to choose two of the words from his Word Bank and write them as this week's *Word Bank Entries*.

After reading words 1-3 on page 86 to your student, apply generalization number one to the words in the following way, using the suggested statements or questions:

- What do the first three words have in common? *(They all begin with the six letters* popula.*)*
- Do you know what any of these words mean?
- If he wants to speculate on the meaning of one of the words, allow him to do so. Move from the one he knows to the others, showing how each of the words relates to the meaning "the people." The following definitions will help:
      populate: "to fill with people"
      populace: "the common people"
      population: "all the people in a certain place"
- Ask your student how /pŏp • yə/ is spelled if it comes at the beginning of a word that has a meaning related to "the people." *(popu)*

Words to Master

Read each spelling word and place the accent mark over the correct syllable.
Then write the words on the blanks, connecting the syllables.

1. pop·u·late	1. _____
2. pop·u·lace	2. _____
3. pop·u·la·tion	3. _____
4. sole	4. _____
5. so·lo	5. _____
6. sol·i·tude	6. _____
7. ver·i·fy	7. _____
8. ver·dict	8. _____
9. man·age	9. _____
10. man·ag·er	10. _____
11. man·a·ge·ri·al	11. _____
12. man·u·al	12. _____
13. man·i·fest	13. _____
14. man·u·script	14. _____
15. Mon·a·co	15. _____
16. Mon·go·li·a	16. _____
17. Mo·roc·co	17. _____
18. Mo·zam·bique	18. _____
19. Word Bank entry	19. _____
20. Word Bank entry	20. _____

86

After reading words 4-6 to your student, apply generalization number two to the words, using the same steps that you did when you applied generalization number one. The following definitions will help:
      sole: "being the only one"
      solo: "a musical passage for one voice or instrument"
      solitude: "the state of being alone"
- Ask your student how either /sōl/ or /sŏl/ is spelled if it comes at the beginning of a word with a meaning related to "alone." *(sol)*

After reading words 7-9 to your student, follow the same steps to apply generalization number three to these words as you did when you applied generalization number one. The following definitions will be helpful:
      verify: "to prove the truth by the presentation of evidence or testimony"
      verdict: "a decision reached by a jury at the conclusion of a trial; a judgment"
- Ask your student how either /vĕr/ or /vûr/ is spelled if it comes at the beginning of a word with a meaning related to "truth." *(ver)*

After reading 10-14 to your student, apply generalization number four to them in the following way, using the suggested questions and statements:

- What do these words all have in common? *(They all begin with the spelling* man.*)*
- Ask your student to comment on any of the meanings of the following words: *manage, manager, manual, manuscript.*
- Tell him that the Latin word part *manus* means "hand," but not many things today are made "by hand." The word *manage* is taken from that Latin word but means today "to control." The word *manager* means "one who controls or handles," and the word *managerial* describes a job at which someone "controls" people or things.

> See *The King's English* section on page 89 for more interesting information on the word *manager.*

- The word *manuscript* means "written by hand."
- The word "manual" used to mean "done by hand" but now the meaning is more broad.
- The word *manifest* is a little different; it now means "to show plainly." Remind them that the Bible tells us of a time when Jesus took three of the apostles to a special place, called the Mount of Transfiguration, where His glory was manifested. The Latin word for this is *manifestus.*

Introduce words 15-18 on page 86.

- The countries' names are spelled practically as they sound.
- In the word *Mozambique,* the last syllable sounds like /k/ but is spelled *que.*

Guide a research activity: *Where in the World?* Help your student locate the countries with names in the spelling list on a world atlas or map. Ask him to use the *M* volume of an encyclopedia to expand his geographic and general country knowledge according to the ideas and optional activities presented in Unit 1.

Use the handwritten list. After your student has written each word on the appropriate line, check his list for spelling and legibility. Instruct him to place an accent mark in each multi-syllable word of the printed list.

Second Day

Use the Bible verse activity on page 87. Make certain that your student understands what the verse is saying. For instance, talk with him about whom the Holy Spirit led to say these words (the writer of the book). Talk with your student about the Apostle Paul's writing this to the church at Colosse and what he desired to do. Ask your student what each of the following words and phrases means, and lead him from what he thinks it means to what it actually means: *utterance, bonds, manifest, open unto us a door of utterance, speak the mystery of Christ.*

Have fun with the *Word for Word* section on page 87.

Use worktext pages 87 and 88 to reinforce word meaning and the skills of the unit. Read the directions and give help, if needed, as your student completes the pages.

---

name _____

A. Read the verse.
1. Underline four words that tell what the writer wanted to speak after God opened a "door of utterance."
2. Circle the three-syllable word that means "apparent or evident."

"Withal praying also for us, that God would open unto us a door of utterance, to speak __the mystery of Christ__, for which I am also in bonds: That I may make it (manifest) as I ought to speak." Colossians 4:3-4

You have two spelling words that begin with *ver-*, from the Latin *verus* (true). The word *verify* literally means "make true." We use it when we present some kind of evidence to prove the truth: "George will *verify* that I stayed home last night." The literal translation of *verdict* is "true-speak." When a jury gives the verdict (its decision at the end of a trial), it tries to arrive at a decision or statement that is as close to the truth as possible.

Your spelling words beginning with *pop-* come from a Latin word that means "the people," and all of them have to do with people in one way or another.

B. Use *ver-* and *pop-* words correctly in the blanks below.

1. The jury's ___1___ declared that Uncle Pete was innocent.
2. We learned that India has a large ___2___ and a shortage of food.
3. Many years ago, Britain sent thousands of convicts to ___3___ Australia.
4. My neighbor will ___4___ Beth's statement that she owns five black cats.
5. The ___5___, or the common people, demanded tax reforms.

1. **verdict**
2. **population**
3. **populate**
4. **verify**
5. **populace**

C. Fill in the blanks, using spelling words that come from the Latin *solus*, which means "alone."

The **sole** _____ entry in the contest sang a **solo** _____.

WORD FOR WORD

Have you ever eaten sole? No, we are not talking about the sole of your foot or your shoe. This sole is a kind of fish. Both meanings of the word *sole* are derived from the Latin word *solea* (sandal), which comes from *solum* (bottom). Sole is a flat fish that tastes much like flounder, and its shape resembles the sole of a foot. So the next time someone offers you some *sole*, be certain which *sole* it is before you take a bite.

sole

87

The Latin word *manus* means "hand." You can see it in our words *manual* (something operated with the hands) and *manuscript* (something written or typed by hand). The dictionary gives us some other interesting words that are related to *manus*, such as *manicure* (hand care) and *manufacture* (handmade).

D. Use a spelling word beginning with *man-* to fill in the blank before each definition below. You may use a word more than once, since it may have more than one definition. Check definitions in your Spelling Dictionary.

1. **manual** — operated by using the hands
2. **manifest** — (noun) a list that shows cargo or passengers
3. **manage** — to control or direct
4. **manuscript** — something that is written or typed
5. **manifest** — (adjective) made apparent or clearly visible

E. Using the vertical message below as a guide, arrange spelling words on the blanks.

```
    P O P U L A T E
  M A N A G E R I A L
    M O Z A M B I Q U E
  V E R I F Y
    S O L E
  M A N U S C R I P T

      M O N A C O
      P O P U L A T I O N
  S O L I T U D E
      M A N A G E
          S O L O

    V E R D I C T
    M O R O C C O
    M O N G O L I A
  M A N A G E
  M A N I F E S T
```

Words to Master

populate	solitude	managerial	Mongolia
populace	verify	manual	Morocco
population	verdict	manifest	Mozambique
sole	manage	manuscript	_____
solo	manager	Monaco	_____

88

Third Day

Give your student time to study the words, using the study method printed on the back cover of the spelling worktext.

Dictate the word list for the trial test. Give the following dictation sentences:

1. Most of the **population** of **Monaco** speaks French.
2. Please ask your **manager** to **verify** this payment.
3. I hope I can **manage** to remember the music when I play my flute **solo.**

Use page 166 to teach this week's dictionary skill. Review the structural generalizations on the page and allow your student to work independently. Check his work after he has completed the page and use it for further teaching.

Review the following patterns for dividing words into syllables.

A. A word with the pattern *VCCV* is usually divided *VC/CV.* (ver·dict)
B. A word with the pattern *VCV* is usually divided *V/CV,* making the syllable with the lone vowel an open syllable. (na·tive)
C. A word with the pattern *VCV* is sometimes divided *VC/V,* making the syllable with the vowel followed by the consonant a closed syllable. (stom·ach)
D. A word with the pattern *VV* is divided *V/V* when each vowel makes its own sound. (tri·une)
E. Two letters that work together to make one sound should *not* be divided. (trans·late)

Divide the following words correctly as they are in your Spelling Dictionary. For each syllable division, write the letter of the rule or pattern that was used. Use the first example as a guide.

1. manuscript	1. _man u script_ C E
2. manual	2. _man u al_ CD
3. magic	3. _mag ic_ C
4. native	4. _native_ B
5. manage	5. _man age_ C
6. bifocals	6. _bi fo cals_ BB
7. microbe	7. _mi crobe_ B
8. hydrant	8. _hy drant_ B
9. solo	9. _so lo_ B
10. mobile	10. _mo bile_ B
11. video	11. _vid e o_ CD

166

Use with Unit 22.
Skill: reviewing rules and patterns for syllabication

Fourth Day

Return last week's journal. Give time for your student to correct his misspelled words in his previous journal entry and then record them in his spelling dictionary.

Guide the journal time using the *Journal Entry Idea* on page 89 and the information given in the front of this manual. Discuss with your student the "moves" that your family has made and how each has affected him. Encourage him to be open and free in his recollections of the different places your family has lived and how he has adjusted to each. If he has never had to move from a house, elicit his feelings about how he would react to a situation like that.

Fifth Day

Guide the study time.

Dictate the word list for the final test.

Give the following dictation sentences.

1. The old man worked on his **manuscript** in the **solitude** of his office.
2. Little bugs have begun to **populate** my **sole** remaining sack of flour.
3. We still have not reached a **verdict** on the new man for the **managerial** position.

Use *The King's English* on page 89. After your student reads this section silently, read it with him orally. Use the Bible verses, discussion, and good comprehension questions to make certain he understands the material. The following questions can be used:

1. What Bible character became a very good manager?
2. What character traits did Joseph have that enabled him to turn a bad situation into a good one? (BATs: 2a Authority, 2b Servanthood, 2c Faithfulness, 2d Goal setting, 4c Honesty, 4d Victory, 7d Contentment, 8d Courage)
3. Have you ever had to make the best of a bad situation?

Journal Entry Idea

"Oh, no, Mom, we can't move now!" That was what you said when your mother told you that your dad was getting transferred and your family would be moving to another part of the country. You truly felt like the ceiling was falling in. "Life is over!" you said to yourself. "Just when I finally found a good friend!" "Just when I made the team!" Have you ever had something happen that made you think life would *never* be the same again? Tell about an experience like that and then tell how it all came out and how you feel about it now.

The King's English
manager

Manager comes from the Latin word *manus,* which means "hand," and *manidiare,* which means "to handle." The Italians use the word *maneggiare* when talking about managing or handling a horse.

The owner of a large estate often needs to hire someone to care for his buildings, crops, and land. This person is called a manager. The skills that Joseph learned as manager of Potiphar's house aided him when Pharaoh set him over all the land of Egypt. Since God had already revealed the coming famine to Joseph, Joseph stored enough corn and food to last through the seven years. When food was needed, it was there. Joseph sold the food for money and for land, increasing the wealth of the Pharaoh. Joseph was an example of a good manager. He helped others, yet managed the Pharaoh's property wisely.

Compare yourself to Joseph. He had something happen to him that seemed bad, but because he managed his life well, it turned out for his good and the good of his people. Are you a good manager?
Genesis 39:4-5

89

Unit 23

Worktext pages 90-93
Dictionary page 167

Generalization emphasis

1. /ĕv • ə/ spelled *evi* at the beginning of a word–/ĕv • ə/ at the beginning of a word is spelled *evi*, if the meaning of the word is related to "to see." *evident*

2. /grăj/ spelled *grad* at the beginning or a word–/grăj/ at the beginning of a word is spelled *grad*, if the meaning of the word is related to "step" or "degree." *graduate*

3. /kûr/ or /kər/ spelled *curr* at the beginning of a word–/kûr/ or /kər/ at the beginning of a word is spelled *curr*, if the meaning of the word is related to "to run." *current*

4. /lĭb/ spelled *lib* at the beginning of a word–/lĭb/ at the beginning of a word is spelled *lib* if the meaning of the word is related to "free." *liberate*

Materials

- A world atlas or map
- The *N* volume of an encyclopedia
- Prepare the following activity for Day 2.

Tongue Twisters

1. Edward evidently explored Ecuador for evidence of extinct eggs.
2. The gifted graduate got a glimpse of a green gown at George's graduation .
3. The curriculum at Connie's college cultivates cursive writing.
4. The liberal lawyer loves liberty , so he will liberate the limping leopard.
5. Nan noticed Ned's news from the Netherlands while she navigated the North Sea.

First Day

Give the pretest. After you have given the pretest and your student has checked and corrected it, give him time to choose two of the words from his Word Bank and write them as this week's *Word Bank Entries*.

After reading words 1-4 on page 90 to your student, apply generalization number one to the words using the following steps and the suggested statements and questions:

- Ask your student whether he knows what any of the *evi* words mean?
- If he ventures an opinion on one or more of the words, use what he says to give him the exact meaning; if he

doesn't, go over the meanings given below with him. Show him how each of the words includes the meaning "to see."

> evident, evidently: "of or pertaining to something that is easily seen or understood"
> evidence, evidential: "of or pertaining to proof that can be seen"

- Ask your student how /ĕv • ə/ is spelled if it comes at the beginning of a word that has a meaning related to "to see." *(evi)*

After reading words 5-7 to your student, follow the same steps to apply generalization number two to these words as you did when you applied generalization number one. The following definitions will be helpful:

> graduate, graduation: "to complete a course that was done slowly, step by step"
> gradual: "to accomplish something slowly, step by step"

- Ask your student how /grăj/ is spelled if it comes at the beginning of a word that has a meaning related to "to step." *(grad)*

Read each spelling word and place the accent mark over the correct syllable. Then write the words on the blanks, connecting the syllables.

1. ev·i·dent	1. _____
2. ev·i·dence	2. _____
3. ev·i·dent·ly	3. _____
4. ev·i·den·tial	4. _____
5. grad·u·ate	5. _____
6. grad·u·al	6. _____
7. grad·u·a·tion	7. _____
8. cur·rent	8. _____
9. cur·ren·cy	9. _____
10. cur·ric·u·lum	10. _____
11. cur·sive	11. _____
12. lib·er·al	12. _____
13. lib·er·ty	13. _____
14. lib·er·ate	14. _____
15. Neth·er·lands	15. _____
16. New Zea·land	16. _____
17. Nic·a·ra·gua	17. _____
18. Ni·ger	18. _____
19. Word Bank entry	19. _____
20. Word Bank entry	20. _____

90

After reading words 8-11 to your student, follow the same steps to apply generalization number three to the words as you did when you applied generalization number one. The following definitions will be helpful:

> current: "something now in progress"; it could be thought of as "something now running"
>
> currency: "any form of money or exchange now in use"; it could be thought of as "money or exchange now running"
>
> curriculum: "all of the courses of study offered by a particular institution"; it could be thought of as a "running of the courses"

- Ask your student how /kûr/ or /kər/ is spelled if it comes at the beginning of a word that has a meaning related to "to run." *(curr)*

After reading words 12-14 to your student, apply generalization number four to the words following the same steps that you did to apply generalization number one, using the suggested question.

> liberal: "tending to give freely"
>
> liberty: "the condition of being free from restriction or control"
>
> liberate: "to set free"

- Ask your student how /lĭb/ is spelled if it comes at the beginning of a word that has a meaning related to "free." *(lib)*

Introduce words 15-18 on page 90.

- Point out the /ē/ spelled *ea* in *New Zealand.*
- In *Niger* the /j/ is spelled with a *g.*

Guide a research activity: *Where in the World?* Help your student locate the countries with names in the spelling list on a world atlas or map. Ask him to use the *N* volume of an encyclopedia to expand his geographic and general country knowledge according to the ideas and optional activities presented in Unit 1.

The Netherlands, which is sometimes called Holland, is a country known for its windmills, wooden shoes, dikes, and tulips. Ask your student to read about the Netherlands and then draw either a picture of this country or something that represents it, such as a windmill, etc. Direct him to write a short paragraph which explains his picture. Ask him to include factual information he has learned in his reading and then mount it with his picture on colored paper. Display it so others in your home can enjoy it.

Use the handwritten list. After your student has written each word on the appropriate line, check his list for spelling and legibility. Instruct him to place an accent mark in each multi-syllable word of the printed list.

Second Day

Use the Bible verse activity on page 91. Explain the meaning of the word *liberal* (as given above) and discuss with your student how any Christian can have a "liberal soul." Ask him what he thinks the phrase *he that watereth* means. Explain that if we help others when they need it, we will receive help when we need it.

Have fun with the *Word for Word* section on page 91.

Use worktext pages 91 and 92 to reinforce word meaning and the skills of the unit. Read the directions and give help, if needed, as your student completes the pages.

Note: In doing activity *B* on page 91, use the Latin sources and the information already given in the chart and the *Word for Word* section to complete this lesson.

Developing word meaning: *Tongue Twisters*. Provide a copy of the activity found in the *Materials* section. Write a spelling word that best fills in each blank of each tongue twister.

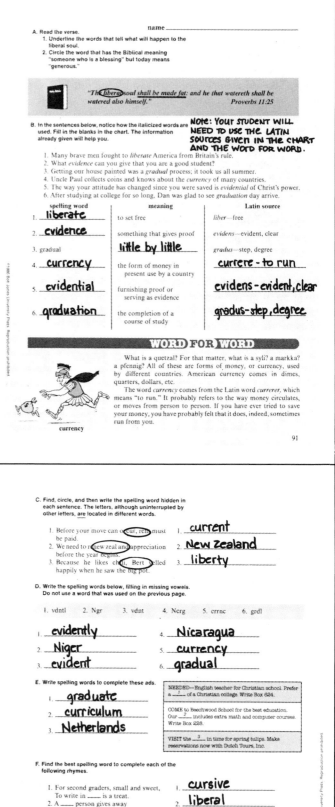

Third Day

Give your student time to study the words, using the study method printed on the back cover of the spelling worktext.

Dictate the word list for the trial test.

Give the following dictation sentences:

1. You will have to follow this **curriculum** if you are to **graduate.**
2. At my **graduation** my grandfather gave me a **liberal** amount of money.
3. Have the people of **Nicaragua** lost their **liberty?**

> Dictionary skill: The respelling gives you the sounds in a word. Use the *pronunciation key* to read the respelling of a word.

Use page **167 to teach this week's dictionary skill.** After you are certain that your student understands the skill, guide him as he completes the exercise.

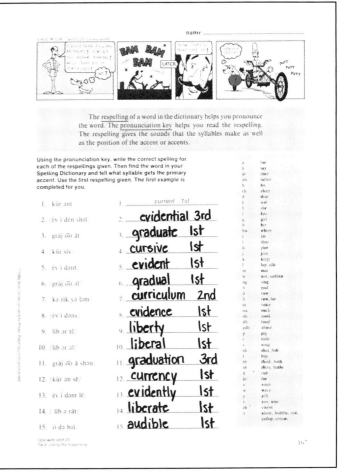

Fourth Day

Return last week's journal. Give your student time to correct the misspelled words in his previous journal entry and record them in his Word Bank.

Guide the journal time using the *Journal Entry Idea* on page 93 and the information given in the front of this manual. Elicit discussion from your student about how the anticipation of some event can be better than the event itself. Ask him to tell you about one time he remembers looking forward to something that did not turn out to be as much fun as he thought it would be.

Fifth Day

Guide the study time.

Dictate the word list for the final test.

Give the following dictation sentences.

1. Learning **cursive** writing is often **gradual** for children.
2. This **currency** is **evidently** worth less than it used to be.
3. Our **evidence** shows that the spy is from **New Zealand**.

Use *The King's English* on page 93. After your student reads this section silently, read it with him orally. Use the Bible verses, discussion, and good comprehension questions to make certain he understands the material. The following questions can be used:

1. What book tells you what you as a Christian are free to do and what you should not do?
2. Can you think of a time when you did something that hurt someone else?
3. Who came to earth to show us what God's truth about freedom was? (BAT: 1a Understanding Jesus Christ)

Journal Entry Idea

"Oh! Oh! Oh! This is truly the most superb, super-colossal situation I have ever been in!" Those were your words when your parents said you could go on vacation with your new friend's family, instead of going to camp. You would be living in luxury while your other friends were slaving away at camp. That feeling of wonder lasted less than two hours. After that, the trip went from "bad to worse." Why? Well, the car was hot and crowded, and you just couldn't keep from thinking about that camp with all your old friends up in those cool mountains.

Has anything you expected to be really good turned out to be not-so-great? Write about an experience like that.

The King's English
liberty

Most people want freedom. They want the right to think, believe, and act as they choose. The Latin word *liber,* from which we get the word **liberty,** means "free."

Our Constitution guarantees us certain freedoms; only by protecting the freedoms we have now can we make sure that they will be passed down to the next generation.

Is there a time, however, when freedom is not right? Some people think not. They believe that everyone should be free to "do his own thing." But what we do affects not just ourselves, but others. We should not cause a weaker brother to stumble.

Finally, it is Jesus Christ who has, in showing us truth about our Heavenly Father, shown us true liberty. John 8:32 says, "And ye shall know the truth, and the truth shall make you free." John 8:36 says, "If the Son therefore shall make you free, ye shall be free indeed."

I Corinthians 8:9-13
John 8:32, 36
I Peter 2:16

93

Unit 24

Worktext pages 94-97

Generalization emphasis

Generalization statements can be found in Units 19-23.

Materials

- Prepare the following activity for Day 2.
  ### Context Clues
  1. Because of the rough ___terrain___ we wore our hiking boots.
  2. Holland is a region of the country called the ___Netherlands___.
  3. The ship's ___manifest___ listed bananas, pineapples, and goats.
  4. Make sure that each visitor has the proper ___credentials___ before you let him into this office.
  5. Jim has five sisters and seldom gets a moment of ___solitude___.
  6. Our small plane could not take off because clouds hung low over the airport, making ___visibility___ poor.
  7. When Ken was younger, he thought that the country of ___Kenya___ was named after him.
  8. The frightened little girl's voice was barely ___audible___ when she told her story.
  9. Christ's ___millennial___ rule will last for a thousand years.
  10. The small country of ___Jordan or Lebanon___ is located in southwestern Asia.

First Day

For review, apply the generalizations found in Lessons 19-23 to the word list on page 94.

Use worktext page 94 to reinforce word meaning and the skills of the unit. Read the directions and give help, if needed, as your student completes the page.

Second Day

Use the Bible verse activity on page 94. This is a very well-known verse which discusses the heart of faith. Help your student to see that our faith is built on the hope of Jesus Christ and His love for us. Our faith is confidence in the unseen Holy Spirit at work in our lives, convicting us, guiding us, answering our prayers.

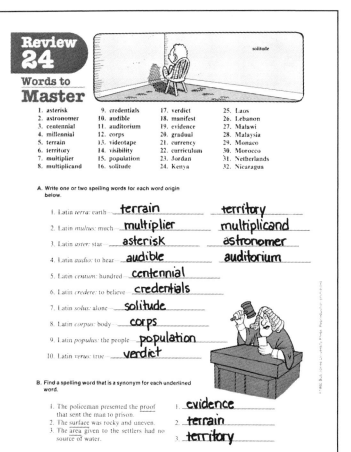

Review 24
Words to Master

solitude

1. asterisk
2. astronomer
3. centennial
4. millennial
5. terrain
6. territory
7. multiplier
8. multiplicand
9. credentials
10. audible
11. auditorium
12. corps
13. videotape
14. visibility
15. population
16. solitude
17. verdict
18. manifest
19. evidence
20. gradual
21. currency
22. curriculum
23. Jordan
24. Kenya
25. Laos
26. Lebanon
27. Malawi
28. Malaysia
29. Monaco
30. Morocco
31. Netherlands
32. Nicaragua

A. Write one or two spelling words for each word origin below.

1. Latin *terra:* earth — terrain / territory
2. Latin *multus:* much — multiplier / multiplicand
3. Latin *aster:* star — asterisk / astronomer
4. Latin *audio:* to hear — audible / auditorium
5. Latin *centum:* hundred — centennial
6. Latin *credere:* to believe — credentials
7. Latin *solus:* alone — solitude
8. Latin *corpus:* body — corps
9. Latin *populus:* the people — population
10. Latin *verus:* true — verdict

B. Find a spelling word that is a synonym for each underlined word.

1. The policeman presented the proof that sent the man to prison. — evidence
2. The surface was rocky and uneven. — terrain
3. The area given to the settlers had no source of water. — territory

94

Use worktext pages 95 and 96 to reinforce word meaning and the skills of the unit. Read the directions and give help, if needed, as your student completes the pages.

Guide a word meaning activity: *Context Clues.* Provide a copy of the activity found in the *Materials* section. Direct your student to write a spelling word in each blank, using the context to help him choose the correct one. Tell your student that *context* is the words around the blank. From the meaning of the other words and the word order, your student is able to pick an appropriate word. If he does not know the meaning of a word, he can usually use context to help determine its meaning.

Third Day

Give your student time to study the words, using the study method printed on the back cover of the spelling worktext.

Dictate the word list for the trial test.

Give the following dictation sentences:

1. We refer to the **population** of the **Netherlands** as the Dutch.
2. The **evidence** given at the trial led to a guilty **verdict**.
3. The **terrain** had a **gradual** slope to it.

Guide a spelling activity: *Letter by Letter.* Ask your student to study all thirty-two words; then choose a word at random and state the first letter. Your student guesses the second letter, you give the third, and he the fourth, etc., until the word is spelled. Your student begins with fifty points, and each time he makes a spelling error, he loses a point. He will count up the number of points at the end of the game and trade them in for a special treat or activity. You can take turns choosing the words and beginning the game. Sometimes you might begin one word, but because of identical beginnings, a different word will be spelled. If your student needs to write down the letters as they are spelled, that's fine.

C. Read the verse.
1. Underline the word that is defined by these words: "the substance of things hoped for, the evidence of things not seen."
2. Circle the word that has the Biblical meaning "conviction," but today means "the facts and signs that help one to form an opinion."

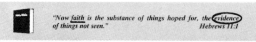

"Now faith is the substance of things hoped for, the evidence of things not seen." Hebrews 11:1

TIC-TAC-TOE CIPHER

Three tic-tac-toe boards are the basis for this code. Each cipher shape is a picture of the space on the tic-tac-toe board occupied by the corresponding letter of the alphabet. The dots show which board to use. For example, is D, is M, is V, and so on.

A	B	C		J	K	L		S	T	U
D	E	F		M	N	O		V	W	X
G	H	I		P	Q	R		Y	—	!

D. Decode this cipher in the space below it. Then write the message on the lines.

V I D E O T A P E G I V E S E V I
D E N C E T H A T C U R R E N C Y
I N M Y L A O S T E R R I T O R Y
I S C O U N T E R F E I T - S E N
D D E T E C T I V E C O R P S !

VIDEOTAPE GIVES EVIDENCE THAT CURRENCY IN MY LAOS TERRITORY IS COUNTERFEIT- SEND DETECTIVE CORPS!

95

E. Use spelling words to complete the following crossword puzzle.

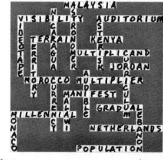

MALAYSIA
VISIBILITY AUDITORIUM
TERRAIN KENYA
MULTIPLICAND JORDAN
MOROCCO MULTIPLIER
MANIFEST
MILLENNIAL GRADUAL
MONACO NETHERLANDS
POPULATION

Down	Across
2. one who studies the stars	1. country of SE Asia—capital: Kuala Lumpur
3. republic of Central America	4. the state or degree of being visible
4. a tape that records a picture	5. a room made for an audience
5. a star-shaped figure	6. the characteristics of the surface of the earth
6. an area of land	7. country of E central Africa
9. the courses of study offered	8. a number that is multiplied by another number
11. able to be heard	10. country of SW Asia, located in NW Arabia
13. a form of money in present use	12. kingdom of NW Africa on the Mediterranean and the Atlantic
15. country of SE Africa	14. a number that tells how many times the multiplicand is multiplied
17. country of SW Asia	15. plainly obvious
18. principality on the Mediterranean Sea	16. happening slowly and steadily
	18. having to do with a period of 1,000 years
	19. kingdom of NW Europe
	20. the total number of people in a place

Words to Master

asterisk	credentials	verdict	Laos
astronomer	audible	manifest	Lebanon
centennial	auditorium	evidence	Malawi
millennial	corps	gradual	Malaysia
terrain	videotape	currency	Monaco
territory	visibility	curriculum	Morocco
multiplier	population	Jordan	Netherlands
multiplicand	solitude	Kenya	Nicaragua

96

Fourth Day

Return last week's journal. Give your student time to correct the misspelled words in his previous journal entry and record them in his Word Bank.

Guide the journal time using the *Journal Entry Idea* on page 97 and the information given in the front of this manual. Talk with your student about a time when you were made fun of or missed out on something because of your Christian faith. Maybe your husband works for less because he is in some kind of Christian service. Even in selecting to home school, you pay for your textbooks, but you still must pay taxes which support the public school system. Ask him if he remembers a time when he suffered somewhat because of his Christian beliefs. After he relates such an experience, tell him to write about it in his journal.

Fifth Day

Guide the study time.

Dictate the word list for the trial test.

Give the following dictation sentences:

1. The jury heard all the **evidence** before giving their **verdict.**
2. What kind of **currency** do the people of **Malawi** use?
3. The speaker's voice was hardly **audible** in the back of the **auditorium.**

Use *The King's English* on page 97. After your student reads this section silently, read it with him orally. Use the Bible verses, discussion, and good comprehension questions to make certain he understands the material. The following questions can be used:

1. Are you glad that Jesus came to earth to be a manifestation of God?
2. What do you think it was like for the apostles to see Jesus after they thought He had died?
3. How can you manifest what Christ has done in your life? (BATs: 2b Servanthood, 2c Faithfulness, 2e Work, 2f Enthusiasm)

Journal Entry Idea

"Mom! Come look at the garage. Somebody wrote bad words all over it!" You couldn't help being hysterical—the garage was almost covered with paint. Most of them were words you wouldn't repeat, but the message was clear: someone in the neighborhood did not like your family's standards. Because you attend a Christian school, they know how important "religion" is to you. As your dad calmly repainted the garage, you asked him if this was what it meant to be persecuted.

Write about a time when something of this sort happened to you or a member of your family. How did you react to it?

The King's English

manifest

Have you ever heard the expression "seeing is believing"? Some people just won't believe a thing exists until they can actually see it. It has to be made **manifest** to them. This word came from the Latin *manifestus*, a compound of two words: *manus* ("hand") and *festus* ("struck.") When something is manifest to you, it becomes so real that it's as if you could strike it or touch it with your hand.

Jesus, when He came to earth in the flesh, was a literal manifestation of God. God can make many truths manifest to us; they don't have to be there physically for us to touch with our hands.

Jesus manifested himself to His disciples after His resurrection by appearing in the flesh. Even though we haven't seen the physical wounds of Jesus, we know that He suffered and died for us.

Today, the evidence of Christ's manifestation in our lives can be seen by others. They see how we live, how we speak, and how we respond to life's problems. In this way, we live our testimony before the world.

John 14:21
I Timothy 3:16
I Peter 1:20

97

Unit 25

Worktext pages 98-101
Dictionary page 168

---------- **Generalization emphasis** ----------

1. **Adding a suffix beginning with a vowel letter to a word ending in silent *e*–**When a suffix beginning with a vowel letter is added to a word ending in a final *e*, the final *e* is dropped before the suffix is added. *examine, examination*

2. **Closed syllable–**When a syllable has a vowel letter followed by one or more consonant letters, the vowel is usually short. This is a *closed syllable*. ex • am • i • na • tion

3. **Open syllable–**When a syllable ends with a vowel letter, the vowel is usually long. This is an *open syllable*. ex • am • i • na • tion

---------- **Materials** ----------

• A world map or atlas
• The *N* and *P* volumes of an encyclopedia
• Prepare the following activity for Day 2.

Rhymealong

Before you purchase, don't be shy;
First __examine__; then you buy.

I met a tall and stately man;
He said his home was __Pakistan__.

A fireman knows his greatest need:
To __terminate__ the fire with speed.

I took a photo when I saw
The great canal at __Panama__.

A watermelon I will carve
And eat it now, before I __starve__.

I had to watch and learn and wait
Before I could __participate__.

Football seems to __fascinate__
The sixth-grade boys; they think it's great!

Jo said, "You'll __narrate__ our big play."
She helped me with my lines today.

First Day

Give the pretest. After you have given the pretest and your student has checked and corrected it, give him time to choose two of the words from his Word Bank and write them as this week's *Word Bank Entries*.

After reading words 1-14 on page 98 to your student, apply generalization number one to the words in the following way, using the suggested questions:

• What do words 1, 3, 5, 7, 9, 11, and 13 have in common? *(They all end in* e.*)*

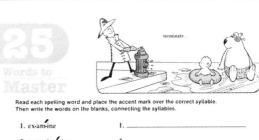

Read each spelling word and place the accent mark over the correct syllable.
Then write the words on the blanks, connecting the syllables.

1. ex·ám·ine   1. _____
2. ex·am·i·ná·tion   2. _____
3. fás·ci·nate   3. _____
4. fas·ci·ná·tion   4. _____
5. tér·mi·nate   5. _____
6. ter·mi·ná·tion   6. _____
7. par·tíc·i·pate   7. _____
8. par·tic·i·pá·tion 8. _____
9. per·spíre   9. _____
10. per·spi·rá·tion   10. _____
11. starve   11. _____
12. star·vá·tion   12. _____
13. nár·rate   13. _____
14. nar·rá·tion   14. _____
15. Ni·gé·ri·a   15. _____
16. Nór·way   16. _____
17. Pák·i·stan   17. _____
18. Pan·á·ma   18. _____
19. Word Bank entry   19. _____
20. Word Bank entry   20. _____

98

• What happened to the final *e* when the ending *-ation* was added? *(It was dropped.)*
• What other pairs of words in the word list is this true of? *(all of them)*
• What can you tell about adding a suffix that begins with a vowel letter to a word that ends in *e*? *(When a suffix beginning with a vowel is added to a word ending in a final* e, *the final* e *is dropped before the suffix is added.)*

Apply generalization number two to the word list in the following manner, using the suggested questions:

• Do you hear a short or long vowel in the second syllable of *examine*? *(short)*
• Why do you think it is short? *(If your student does not know, continue with the following questions.)*
• Ask the same question about the second syllable in the second word and the first syllable in words 3 and 4. *(Each of these syllables has a short vowel.)*
• What follows the vowel letter in each of these syllables? *(a consonant letter)*
• What can you say about a short vowel in a syllable? *(A short vowel is usually followed by a consonant.)*
• Do you know what we call a syllable that has a short vowel followed by one or more consonants? *(a closed syllable)*

Apply generalization number three to the word list in the following manner, using the suggested questions:

- What sound do you hear in the third syllable of *fascination*? *(a long vowel)*
- Ask the same question about the third syllable in words 6 and 10, the fourth syllable in word number 8, and the second syllable in words 12 and 14. *(long vowels)*
- Do consonant letters follow any of these long vowels? *(no)*
- What can you say about a single vowel letter which makes a long vowel (sound) in a syllable? *(no consonant follows it)*
- What do we call a syllable like that? *(an open syllable)*

Introduce words 15-18 on page 98.

- Point out that *Nigeria* is a four-syllable word with a schwa as the last syllable.
- *Panama* is spelled with three *a*'s. The second *a* makes the schwa sound.

Guide a research activity: *Where in the World?* Help your student locate the countries with names in the spelling list on a world atlas or map. Ask him to use the *N* and *P* volumes of an encyclopedia to expand his geographic and general country knowledge according to the ideas and optional activities presented in Unit 1.

Norway is known for its *fjords (fy • ôrds)*. Ask your student to read about this country, study pictures of it, and find out what a fjord is. Provide a time for him to share his knowledge with your family. Ask your student to draw a picture of a fjord.

Use the handwritten list. After your student has written each word on the appropriate line, check his list for spelling and legibility. Instruct him to place an accent mark in each multi-syllable word of the printed list.

Second Day

Use the Bible verse activity on page 99. Make certain that your student understands the meanings of the following difficult words as they are used in this verse: *examine, prove, try, reins*.

Have fun with the *Word for Word* section on page 99.

Use worktext pages 99 and 100 to reinforce word meaning and the skills of the unit. Read the directions and give help, if needed, as your student completes the pages.

Guide a word meaning activity: *Rhymealong*. Provide your student with a copy of the activity found in the *Materials* section. Direct your student to finish the rhymes with spelling words from the unit.

---

name _____

A. Read the verse.
1. Underline the three verbs that describe what the writer is asking God to do.
2. Circle the word in the verse that has the Bible meaning "to test, to try, to prove," but today means "to look at fully; to inspect."

"Examine me, O Lord, and prove me; try my reins and my heart."
Psalm 26:2

B. The incorrect word part in each of these nonsense words contains a clue to help you change it to a correct spelling word.

1. allicipate
2. termoutate
3. potama
4. exayours
5. narmousion
6. examicountry
7. fascoutate
8. persteeple
9. narreat
10. pakaretan

1. participate
2. terminate
3. Panama
4. examine
5. narration
6. examination
7. fascinate
8. perspire
9. narrate
10. Pakistan

C. Find and write a spelling word that is an antonym (the opposite) of each word in italics.

1. My dad told us only yesterday of the *beginning* of his job at the space center.
2. I sat down to *ignore* my new book.
3. My teacher always wants complete *withdrawal* from her class.

1. termination
2. examine
3. participation

D. Arrange the countries in this word list in order according to population size, beginning with the highest population. Use your Spelling Dictionary.

1. Pakistan
2. Nigeria
3. Norway
4. Panama

perspire

Did you know that your skin is full of holes? The next time you perspire after a game of basketball, look at the droplets of moisture on your arm or your face.

The word *perspire* comes from two Latin words: *per*, meaning "through," and *spirare*, meaning "to breathe." The process of perspiration provides your body with a superb cooling system that seems to breathe through the tiny openings, or pores, of your skin.

99

E. Several spelling words are hidden in the design below. Find them by connecting only the lines that are given. (The letters may be used more than once.)

1. participate
2. fascination
3. Nigeria
4. participation
5. Panama
6. termination
7. starvation
8. Pakistan
9. terminate
10. fascinate
11. examine
12. starve
13. examination

F. Write the spelling word that best completes each newspaper advertisement.

Free eye ___1___ . Visit Operation Eye at 290 Reservation Road.

Help fight ___2___ in Africa. Give to the "Fight for Life" fund.

Come to the All-American Auction and ___3___ in the fun by bringing things to sell.

Does your deodorant defeat your ___4___ ? Try "Whip It"—the deodorant for doers!

1. examination
2. starvation
3. participate
4. perspiration

Words to Master			
examine	termination	starve	Norway
examination	participate	starvation	Pakistan
fascinate	participation	narrate	Panama
fascination	perspire	narration	_____
terminate	perspiration	Nigeria	_____

100

Third Day

Give your student time to study the words, using the study method printed on the back cover of the spelling worktext.

Dictate the word list for the trial test.

Give the following dictation sentences:

1. Stories about people in **Norway** always **fascinate** me.
2. We were told to **terminate** the project in **Pakistan** at once.
3. Many people in **Nigeria** will face **starvation** if it doesn't rain.

Dictionary skill: The *part of speech* is given in the dictionary entry in italics. A word's part of speech tells how to use the word in a sentence.

Use page 168 to teach this week's dictionary skill. After you are certain that your student understands the skill, guide him as he completes the exercise.

The <u>part of speech</u> is given in the dictionary entry in italics. In some dictionaries, the parts of speech are abbreviated. If a word can be used as more than one part of speech, that part of speech is also named in italics.

au·to·graph /ô' to grăf/ or /ô' to graf/ —*noun, plural* **autographs** A written name or signature of a famous person. Autographs are saved by fans or collectors. —*verb* **autographed, autographing, autographs** To write one's own name or signature on: *The actor autographed the program of the play for me.*

Look at the excerpt from the dictionary. Find the first part of speech: *noun;* now find the second part of speech: *verb.* For the following exercise, locate each underlined word below in your Spelling Dictionary. Notice the parts of speech that are listed and decide which one applies to the underlined word. Write that part of speech on the blank. The first one is completed for you.

1. Tom's classmates <u>autographed</u> his cast.
2. The <u>moral</u> of the story was "honesty pays."
3. That college graduate is a <u>potential</u> teacher.
4. My brother <u>courted</u> his girl for a long time.
5. We have a <u>direct</u> line to my dad's phone.
6. They <u>named</u> their baby for his grandfather.
7. Our car has an <u>automatic</u> transmission.
8. Uncle George holds a <u>minor</u> office in the state government.
9. Mary's grandfather was a <u>major</u> in the Army.
10. One <u>characteristic</u> of our church is friendliness.
11. Susan and her family attended an <u>aerial</u> show.
12. We could <u>sense</u> the Christmas spirit in our whole family.
13. The young boy offered to be Candy's <u>guide</u>.

1. *verb*
2. noun
3. adjective
4. verb
5. adjective
6. verb
7. adjective
8. adjective
9. noun
10. noun
11. adjective
12. verb
13. noun

168

Use with Unit 25.
Skill: identifying parts of speech

Fourth Day

Return last week's journal. Give your student time to correct the misspelled words in his previous journal entry and record them in his Word Bank.

Guide the journal time using the *Journal Entry Idea* on page 101 and the information given in the front of this manual. Elicit discussion from your student about a place (or places) in the world that he has imagined living in. Start him off by telling about a place in a different country that you have always wanted to visit or have visited. Once you have both talked about favorite places, ask him to write in his journal about the place he would choose to live.

Fifth Day

Guide the study time.

Dictate the word list for the final test.

Give the following dictation sentences.

1. I could feel the **perspiration** on my brow as I took my math **examination.**
2. The child listened in **fascination** to the **narration** on the tape.
3. The man in the white suit began to **perspire** under his **Panama** hat.

Use *The King's English* on page 101. After your student reads this section silently, read it with him orally. Use the Bible verses, discussion, and good comprehension questions to make certain he understands the material. The following questions can be used:

1. What day of the week did God sanctify?
2. What has to happen in your life before God can sanctify you (set you apart)? (BATs: 1a Repentance and faith, 1b Understanding Jesus Christ)
3. When will a Christian's sanctification become complete?

Journal Entry Idea

I live in a little town called Crockleford Heath in southeastern England. My father is a farmer, and we also keep some sheep. The climate here is a lot like it is in some parts of the United States. I find many things to do for fun along the coast, which is not far from where I live. I don't go to school in my town because it is too small; I go to school in Colchester, leaving early Monday morning and staying till school is over on Friday afternoon.

Does this sound interesting to you? Think of a place in another country where you would like to live. Describe life there.

The King's English

sanctification

The Latin word *sanctus*, which means "holy" or "sacred," led to our English word **sanctification.** The Hebrew and Greek terms translated *sanctification* mean "a setting apart" or "separation." Therefore, something that is sanctified is set apart from the world, separated unto God.

In the beginning, when God finished creating the world, He blessed the seventh day and sanctified it, setting it apart for His use.

Every believer belongs to God. Hebrews 10 tells us we are saints, that we are sanctified because we have been saved from the judgment of our sins. When Christ paid the price of our redemption with His own blood, He paid it once and for all. We are His.

Because we are His, we have an obligation to Christ. We continue the process of our sanctification by growing in our Christian life. As we read God's Word, pray, and worship Him, we grow to be more Christ-like. When Christ returns for us, our sanctification will be complete, for we will become like Him.

Exodus 13:2
Hebrews 10:10-14
1 Peter 3:15

101

Unit 26

Worktext pages 102-5
Dictionary page 169

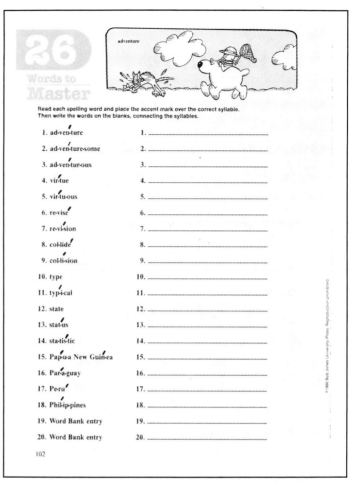

Generalization emphasis

1. **Adding a suffix beginning with a vowel letter to a word ending in e**–When a suffix beginning with a vowel letter is added to a word ending in silent *e*, the *e* is dropped before the suffix is added. *adventure, adventurous*

2. **Adding a suffix beginning with a consonant letter to a word ending in e**–When a suffix beginning with a consonant letter is added to a word that ends in *e*, the spelling of the base word does not change. *adventure, adventuresome*

Materials

- A world atlas or map
- The *P* volume of an encyclopedia
- Prepare the following activity for Day 2.

Think and Replace

1. When we walked up the stairs, we had no idea what *condition* Paul's room would be in. *(state)*
2. Uncle Steve said he hadn't seen the *coming together* of the two trucks. *(collision)*
3. I hope the trip will be an *exciting time. (adventure)*
4. Mother made me *change* the letter before I mailed it. *(revise)*
5. The strongest *good trait* a person can have is truthfulness. *(virtue)*
6. Marvin had a test to see what *kind* of blood he had. *(type)*
7. Sharon screamed a warning when she saw that the cars would *hit each other. (collide)*
8. Grandfather enjoyed the *rewritten version* of his favorite book. *(revision)*
9. The Bible says a *good and godly* woman is precious. *(virtuous)*
10. He seemed to be an *inquisitive and bold* child. *(adventuresome)*
11. Mary Ann's father has reached the highest *rank* that he can attain in the Navy. *(status)*
12. Young Eric's answer was *what you would expect from his type* of little boy. *(typical)*

First Day

Give the pretest. After you have given the pretest and your student has checked and corrected it, give him time to choose two of the words from his Word Bank and write them as this week's *Word Bank Entries*.

After reading words 1-3 on page 102 to your student, apply generalization number one to the words in the following way, using the suggested questions:

- What spelling do these three words have in common? *(adventur)*
- What happened to the spelling of *adventure* when the suffix *-some* was added to make the word *adventuresome? (Nothing; the spelling of the base word stayed the same.)*
- What happened to the spelling of *adventure* when the suffix *-ous* was added to make the word *adventurous? (The final* e *was dropped.)*
- How are the suffixes *-ous* and *-some* different? *(-ous begins with a vowel letter and -some begins with a consonant letter.)*
- What happens to a word that ends in *e* when a suffix that begins with a vowel letter is added, as compared to when a suffix that begins with a consonant letter is added? *(If the suffix begins with a vowel letter, drop the final* e, *and if the suffix begins with a consonant letter, do not drop the final* e.)

After reading words 4-14 to your student, apply generalization number two in the following way, using the suggested questions:

- What do words 4, 6, 10, and 12 have in common? *(All end in* e.)
- In the word pair *virtue, virtuous* what happened to the base word before the suffix *-ous* was added? *(The* e *was dropped.)*

- Ask the same question about the following words: *revise, revision; type, typical; state, status, statistic.*
- Do these words support the generalization: When adding a suffix beginning with a vowel letter to a word ending in *e,* drop the *e* before adding the suffix? *(yes)*

Use questions to lead your student to discover how morphophonemics can be used to help spell the words *collide–collision.*

Introduce words 15-18 on page 102.
- Point out that in the name *New Guinea,* /gĭn/ is spelled *guin,* and /ē/ is spelled *ea.*

Guide a research activity: *Where in the World?* Help your student locate the countries with names in the spelling list on a world atlas or map. Ask him to use the *P* volume of an encyclopedia to expand his geographic and general country knowledge according to the ideas and optional activities presented in Unit 1.

Use the handwritten list. After your student has written each word on the appropriate line, check his list for spelling and legibility. Instruct him to place an accent mark in each multi-syllable word of the printed list.

Second Day

Use the Bible verse activity on page 103. Make certain that your student understands the following words and phrases in the verse: *brethren, true, honest, just, pure, lovely, good report, virtue, praise, think on these things.*

Have fun with the *Word for Word* **section on page 103.**

Use worktext pages 103 and 104 to reinforce word meaning and the skills of the unit. Read the directions and give help, if needed, as your student completes the pages.

Guide a word meaning activity: *Think and Replace.* Provide your student with a copy of the activity found in the *Materials* section. Direct your student to find a spelling word from the unit to replace the italicized word or words in each sentence.

---

name _____

A. Read the verse.
1. Underline the phrase that tells how we should respond to things that are true, honest, just, and so on.
2. Circle the two-syllable word that has the Biblical meaning "force" or "strength," but today means "excellence in moral character."

"Finally, brethren, whatsoever things are true, whatsoever things are honest, whatsoever things are just, whatsoever things are pure, whatsoever things are lovely, whatsoever things are of good report; if there be any virtue and if there be any praise, think on these things."

Philippians 4:8

Look at the words *adventure, adventurous,* and *adventuresome.* What change do you make in the base word when you add a suffix beginning with a consonant (like *-some*) to a word like *adventure* that ends with a vowel? *(none)* What change do you make in the base word when you add a suffix that begins with a vowel (like *-ous*)? *(Drop the final e before adding the suffix.)*

B. Use the three *adventure* words to fill in the missing letters. Then write the correct word on each corresponding blank.

1. adven **t u r e s o m e**   1. _adventuresome_
2. adven **t u r o u s**   2. _adventurous_
3. adven **t u r e**   3. _adventure_

C. The vowels are missing in the following words. Write the words, remembering to capitalize correctly.

1. pr __ __   _Peru_   3. phlppns __   _Philippines_
2. prg __ __   _Paraguay_   4. rvsn __   _revision_

WORD FOR WORD

When three out of four housewives agree that 43 percent of the time two out of every three days would be better spent if forty-two out of sixty-seven products worked 122 percent better, what are they saying? Well, who knows? But we do know that those numbers represent statistics. The word *statistic* comes from the Latin word *status,* which means "manner of standing, or position." When you hear statistics, though, be sure to do some checking before you believe them.

statistics

103

D. Write the spelling word that best fits the context.

Dear Pastor Williams and family,

   I was worried when I heard about the __1__ that involved your small mission plane and a larger one. Did the planes __2__ near Port Moresby, the capital of __3__? I'm sure that you've had to __4__ your plans because of the accident, but when we prayed for you, my dad reminded me that the Lord's timetable is always best.

   Don't be discouraged by this __5__ of affairs! The faithfulness that I see in your life is a __6__ that I'd like to imitate. Please say hello to the family, especially Mary.

Love, Kathy Miller

1. _collision_
2. _collide_
3. _Papua New Guinea_
4. _revise_
5. _state_
6. _virtue_

E. Write the two spelling words in each set that match the given part of speech.

1. **noun:** statistic, revise, status, collide
2. **adjective:** typical, virtue, virtuous, Peru
3. **verb:** type, revise, statistic, collide

1. a. _statistic_   2. a. _typical_
    b. _status_   b. _virtuous_
                    3. a. _revise_
                    b. _collide_
                  Type may also be used.

F. Find these verses in your Bible and write the spelling word that you find in the verse.

1. II Peter 1:3   _virtue_
2. Ruth 3:11   _virtuous_

Words to Master

adventure	revise	typical	Paraguay
adventuresome	revision	state	Peru
adventurous	collide	status	Philippines
virtue	collision	statistic	
virtuous	type	Papua New Guinea	

104

Third Day

Give your student time to study the words, using the study method printed on the back cover of the spelling worktext.

Dictate the word list for the trial test.

Give the following dictation sentences:

1. This **type** of **statistic** is hard to understand.
2. I hope those **adventuresome** race car drivers do not **collide**.
3. Your trip to the **Philippines** should be an **adventure**.

> Dictionary skill: The *etymology* of an entry word, which is the history of the word, is found toward the end of the dictionary entry. The languages are abbreviated, and the most recent language is listed first.

Use page 169 to teach this week's dictionary skill. After you are certain that your student understands the skill, guide him as he completes the exercise.

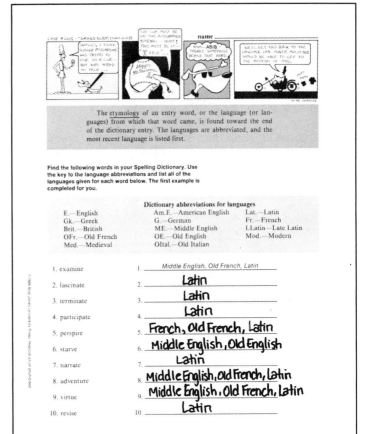

Fourth Day

Return last week's journal. Give your student time to correct the misspelled words in his previous journal entry and record them in his Word Bank.

Guide the journal time using the *Journal Entry Idea* on page 105 and the information given in the front of this manual. Tell your student about a time when you were lost to get him started thinking about how it feels to be lost. You might ask him to name some words that describe the fear one feels when he's lost. As he says some words, list them on a piece of paper. Read the list back to him, using some of the words in sentences to get him excited about writing. Give him the list as he begins to write his journal.

Fifth Day

Guide the study time.

Dictate the word list for the final test.

Give the following dictation sentences.
1. Is rainy weather **typical** in **Peru?**
2. In what **state** was your car after the **collision?**
3. There is great **virtue** in knowing when you need to **revise** your writing.

Use *The King's English* on page 105. After your student reads this section silently, read it with him orally. Use the Bible verses, discussion, and good comprehension questions to make certain he understands the material. The following questions can be used:
1. What does the word *virtue* refer to?
2. What woman in the Bible was a good example of a virtuous woman?
3. What man especially thought Ruth was virtuous?
4. How can you keep your mind virtuous? (BATs: 6a Bible study, 6b Prayer)

Journal Entry Idea

The place? Bogotá, Colombia! The occasion? You have gone there with your dad to visit some missionaries. The setting? The marketplace. The lady you are following has a large basket on her head with delightful-looking fruit piled inside. She is balancing it without even raising a hand. You keep thinking that surely one piece will fall out or the whole thing will tumble, but nothing happens. Giving up, you turn back to find your dad. You search through the sea of faces—no Dad. You retrace your steps—no Dad. Slowly that creepy serpent called "fear" begins to crawl down your back. *Everyone* is speaking Spanish!

Pretend you are lost in a foreign country; describe how you got there, how you got lost, and what you did about it.

The King's English
virtuous

The Latin word *vir* means "man." The word *virtus* was used to indicate manliness, or goodness in a man. Our word *virtue* refers to goodness in either men or women. Proverbs tells us of the **virtuous** woman who managed her household well.

Ruth was an example of a virtuous woman. When she returned to Israel with Naomi, she showed by the way she lived that she was kind and good. She lived above reproach and won the respect of the Israelites. Boaz told Ruth that "all the city of my people doth know that thou art a virtuous woman."

In Philippians 4:8, Paul gives us advice on how to be virtuous. He suggests that we think only about things that are just, pure, lovely, and of a good report. Keeping our minds occupied with things that are good will encourage us to do things that are right, or virtuous.

Ruth 3:11
Proverbs 31:29
Philippians 4:8

105

Unit 27

Worktext pages 106-9
Dictionary page 170

Unit Emphasis

- Difficult spellings and pronunciations

Materials

- A world atlas or map
- The *P*, *R*, and *S* volumes of an encyclopedia

First Day

Give the pretest. After you have given the pretest and your student has checked and corrected it, give him time to choose two of the words from his Word Bank and write them as this week's *Word Bank Entries.*

Introduce the word list. As you read each word in the list, using the pronunciations given below, ask your student to look at the word to discover what the difference is between its pronunciation and its spelling. (Repeat the pronunciation as many times as he needs to see the difference.) Ask him how he is going to remember the spelling of each. If he can't think of a way, give him some tricks to use. All the words are listed below with their pronunciations and suggestions for remembering their spellings.

1. colonel: /kûr′ nəl/–In order to understand the spelling of this word, it helps to know that it is derived from a Latin word *columna,* which means ''pillar.'' It became the Italian word *colonello,* and then *colonna.* It then became the French word *coronel* from which our word is derived. The more practical way to remember the spelling is to think that it is spelled much like *colony* but pronounced like *kernel.*

2. pneumonia: /nŏŏ • mōn′ yə/–The only difficult part of this word is the silent *p* at the beginning. One trick might be to remember that pneumonia makes one very *pale* and *pale* begins with *p.* A more accurate explanation of the spelling is that the Medieval Latin word *pneuma* meant ''breath.''

3. diaphragm: /dī′ ə • frăm/–The difficult part of this word is the silent *g* in the last syllable. Tell your student that one trick to remembering the *g* is to think that when he breathes using his diaphragm, he takes in a big *gust of air,* and *gust* begins with *g.*

4. dungeon: /dŭn′ jən/–If he remembers that *g* is pronounced /j/ before an *e,* he can remember that there is an *e* after the *g* in the second syllable, even though it is not put in when it is pronounced.

5. extraordinary: /ĭk • strôr′ dn • nĕr • ē/–Even though the word is pronounced as if the *a* were not in the word, it will be easy to remember that *extraordinary* is a combination of two words: *ordinary* plus a prefix, *extra.*

6. isthmus: /ĭs′ məs/–Ask your student if he knows what an isthmus is. If he doesn't, tell him that it is ''a narrow strip of land connecting two larger masses of land.'' Show him an isthmus on a world map. One way to remember that there is a silent *th* might be to think of *t* as coming after *s* (the second letter of the word) and *h* as coming after *i* (the first letter of the word).

7. interesting /ĭn′ trĭ • stĭng/–Even though the *e* after the first *t* is not heard in the preferred pronunciation, it is easier to remember the spelling if the word is thought of as *in′ ter • est • ing.*

8. kindergarten /kĭn′ dər • gär • tn/–The last *e* is swallowed up by the *n* that follows it.

9. mortgage: /môr′ gĭj/–Make certain that your student knows what a mortgage is. It will help to remember that though the meaning of this word does not seem to include ''death,'' it actually does. The first part of the word, *mort,* is a Latin word part that means ''death,'' (a meaning that is apparent in the word *mortal*); the *gage* part of the word means ''pledge.''

Worktext page 106

Read each spelling word and place the accent mark over the correct syllable. Then write the words on the blanks, connecting the syllables.

1. col-o-nel
2. pneu-mo-nia
3. di-a-phragm
4. dun-geon
5. ex-traor-di-nar-y
6. isth-mus
7. in-ter-est-ing
8. kin-der-gar-ten
9. mort-gage
10. ma-neu-ver
11. sep-ul-cher
12. ser-geant
13. stom-ach
14. nu-cle-ar
15. Po-land
16. Por-tu-gal
17. Ru-ma-ni-a
18. San Ma-ri-no
19. Word Bank entry
20. Word Bank entry

1. _____
2. _____
3. _____
4. _____
5. _____
6. _____
7. _____
8. _____
9. _____
10. _____
11. _____
12. _____
13. _____
14. _____
15. _____
16. _____
17. _____
18. _____
19. _____
20. _____

106

A good way to explain the word is "I pledge that unless I die, I will pay off this debt." If your student can remember that the word *mort* means death, he can remember that the first part of the word is spelled *mort*.

10. maneuver: /mə • nōō′ vər/–Your student might remember the *eu* spelling for /ōō/ by remembering that /ōō/ in *pneumonia* was spelled the same way.

11. sepulcher: /sĕp′ əl • kər/–Compare this word with word 13, *stomach*, which also has the *ch* spelling for /k/. The word *character* has a beginning /k/ that is spelled *ch*.

12. sergeant: /sär′ jənt/–To understand the spelling of this word, it helps to know that it goes back to an obsolete Italian word, *sergente*, which meant "servant." The practical way to to remember the spelling of this word is to think *sar′ ge • ant*.

13. stomach: /stŭm′ ək/–This word comes from a Latin word, *stomachus*. Ask your student to remember that the spelling for the ending /k/ is *ch*.

14. nuclear: /nōō′ klē • ər/–Pronounce this word several times for your student and ask him to say it after you. Emphasize that the second and third syllables sound like /klē • ər/.

Introduce words 15-18 on page 106.

- The four names of countries in this unit will not be difficult if your student remembers to spell them according to our phonetic rules.

Guide a research activity: *Where in the World?* Help your student locate the countries with names in the spelling list on a world atlas or map. Ask him to use the *P, R,* and *S* volumes of an encyclopedia to expand his geographic and general country knowledge according to the ideas and optional activities presented in Unit 1.

> It may be time to take a fresh look at the activities suggested for this research section in Unit 1. Your student may be ready for a different or additional project. You may want to begin to arrange the projects in some sort of notebook or display.

Use the handwritten list. After your student has written each word on the appropriate line, check his list for spelling and legibility. Instruct him to place an accent mark in each multi-syllable word of the printed list.

Second Day

Use the Bible verse activity on page 107.

Have fun with the *Word for Word* section on page 107.

Use worktext pages 107 and 108 to reinforce word meaning and the skills of the unit. Read the directions and give help, if needed, as your student completes the pages.

Guide a spelling activity: *Alpha and Omega.* Choose a spelling word and write the first and last letters on the chalkboard or on paper, leaving the appropriate number of blanks for the letters in between. Your student is to correctly complete the word. If he spells it correctly, you have several options. You could give him points to be traded for a treat or activity. Or you could give a small token or treat.

Third Day

Give your student time to study the words, using the study method printed on the back cover of the spelling worktext.

Dictate the word list for the trial test.

Give the following dictation sentences:

1. Does **Poland** have **nuclear** power plants?
2. It is **extraordinary** for a child in **kindergarten** to sing so well.
3. It would be **interesting** to hear how the **colonel** escaped from **Rumania**.

A. Read the verse.
 1. Underline the two words that tell what had happened to the stone.
 2. Circle the three-syllable spelling word that means "monument or tomb." (Notice that in this verse, the British spelling is used.)

name _____

 "And they found the stone <u>rolled away</u> from the (sepulchre) *Luke 24:2*

Many of the words on your list this week are tricky to spell because of silent letters or odd pronunciations. The word *colonel* is particularly interesting. It is derived from the Old Italian *colonnello,* "commander of a column of soldiers." The French form, *coronel,* also became popular, however, and for many years both *coronel* and *colonel* were used interchangeably.

About four hundred years ago, *coronel* began to disappear from written accounts, and *colonel* was gradually shortened to two syllables. Today *colonel (ker nul)* sounds very different from the way it looks.

B. The following words are spelled incorrectly, the way they would look if they were spelled the way they sound. Write the correct spelling for each.

| 1. diafram | 3. extrodinary | 5. intristing | 7. numonia | 9. kernul |
| 2. dunjen | 4. ismus | 6. manuver | 8. sarjent | 10. morgaj |

1. diaphragm
2. dungeon
3. extraordinary
4. isthmus
5. interesting
6. maneuver
7. pneumonia
8. sergeant
9. colonel
10. mortgage

WORD FOR WORD

kindergarten

You've probably seen all kinds of gardens, but have you ever seen a garden that grows children? The word *kindergarten* comes from two German words, *kinder* meaning "child," and the word *garten* meaning "garden." Thus, a kindergarten is a "garden of children." You can understand this expression if you think of a garden as a place that provides protection and care, encouraging good, sturdy growth. Did you ever grow in that kind of a garden? Next time you pass a kindergarten class, be kind to the little flowers.

107

C. Complete the following analogies.

1. hotel : motel :: prison : **dungeon**
2. Hawaii : island :: Panama : **isthmus**
3. college : freshman :: elementary school : **kindergarten**
4. stomach : ulcer :: lungs : **pneumonia**
5. cemetery : burial ground :: tomb : **sepulcher**
6. blood circulation : heart :: digestion : **stomach**

D. Complete each of the following expressions. You may discover the answers by rearranging the letters given in italics.

1. as empty as my ____ *(smoatch)*
2. as solemn as a ____ *(scheeplur)*
3. as dark as a ____ *(nodeung)*
4. as strict as a ____ *(rateseng)*
5. as ____ as a mystery novel *(trestingine)*
6. as deadly as a ____ weapon *(carmuel)*

1. stomach
2. sepulcher
3. dungeon
4. sergeant
5. interesting
6. nuclear

E. Solve each riddle with a spelling word that answers the question, "Who am I?" Part of the word you need is underlined.

1. My last syllable is <u>no</u>.
2. I have a <u>mania</u> in me.
3. Part of my name is <u>land</u>.
4. I have a <u>gal</u>.

1. San Marino
2. Rumania
3. Poland
4. Portugal

Words to Master

colonel	isthmus	sepulcher	Portugal
pneumonia	interesting	sergeant	Rumania
diaphragm	kindergarten	stomach	San Marino
dungeon	mortgage	nuclear	
extraordinary	maneuver	Poland	

108

Use page 170 to review etymologies. Your student will need to use the chart on page 169 as well as the Spelling Dictionary at the back of his book to determine the etymology of each word. After you are certain that your student understands the skill, guide him as he completes the exercise.

Fourth Day

Return last week's journal. Give your student time to correct the misspelled words in his previous journal entry and record them in his Word Bank.

Guide the journal time using the *Journal Entry Idea* on page 109 and the information given in the front of this manual. After you and your student read the paragraphs, tell him about a frightening experience that you had as a child and what the outcome was. Elicit ideas from him about what such an experience as told about in the material would be like. The more he verbalizes his ideas, the easier it will be for him to write about them.

Fifth Day

Guide the study time.

Dictate the word list for the final test.

Give the following dictation sentences.

1. The **sergeant** led his troops on a **maneuver** in **Portugal.**
2. The doctor showed me a picture of my **diaphragm** and my **stomach.**
3. The prisoner's **pneumonia** became worse in the cold **dungeon.**

Use *The King's English* on page 109. After your student reads this section silently, read it with him orally. Use the Bible verses, discussion, and good comprehension questions to make certain he understands the material. The following questions can be used:

1. Do you think people could be buried in caves now like they were in the days of Jesus? Why or why not?
2. How was Jesus able to bring Lazarus from the sepulcher? (Bible Promise: I. God as Master)
3. Can you imagine what it was like to be with Jesus the day he raised Lazarus from the dead? Would you have believed that Jesus was God if you had seen Him do that?

Use the key on page 169 to find the original language of these words or word parts. Give only the last language that is mentioned. Remember that the languages are listed from the *most recent* to the earliest or *oldest.*

1. process	Latin	16. tele-	Greek
2. profess	Latin	17. scope	Greek
3. depress	Latin	18. peri-	Greek
4. success	Latin	19. diadem	Greek
5. technical	Greek	20. meter	Greek
6. individual	Latin	21. kilo	Greek
7. drama	Greek	22. assist	Latin
8. habit	Latin	23. annoy	Latin
9. humor	Latin	24. minor	medieval Latin
10. court	Latin	25. major	Latin
11. direct	Latin	26. character	Greek
12. editor	Latin	27. appreciate	Late Latin
13. uni-	Latin	28. caution	Latin
14. biceps	Latin	29. microbe	Greek
15. triune	Latin	30. geo-	Greek

170

Journal Entry Idea
"Attention all passengers for Flight 291: your flight will be delayed for three hours."

You listen to this announcement with interest that turns to panic as you realize, "That was my flight! What should I do now?" As your mind clears, you decide that you ought to call your family. While you're checking your wallet to see how much money you have, an airline employee sits down beside you and asks if 291 was your flight. You nod. With a smile she asks if you would like a free meal at the airport restaurant.

Pretend that something like this has happened to you. Describe the circumstances and what you would do about them.

The King's English
sepulcher

It is not surprising that the word **sepulcher** comes from the Latin word *sepelire,* which means "to bury." A sepulcher is a burial vault.

Most sepulchers had two parts. In the front area was placed the bier, or the platform on which the corpse lay before burial. Below or in the back was the actual burial area. This part held the bodies, which lay in niches carved into the rock wall of the cave. A common sepulcher was about six feet long, nine feet wide, and ten feet high. That provided room for eight niches, three on each side and two opposite the door of the tomb. A heavy stone door, usually round, sealed the opening to the cave.

After the burial of Lazarus, the tomb was sealed. When Jesus came, He ordered the stone moved aside. Then He called Lazarus forth out of the unsealed sepulcher. Lazarus came, risen from the dead, and many believed that Jesus was the Son of God.

Genesis 23:20
John 11:38-39
John 19:41-42

109

Unit 28

Worktext pages 110-13
Dictionary page 171

Generalization emphasis

1. **Difficult pairs of words**

2. **Structural generalizations:**
   a. **Dividing a word with the VCV pattern**—A word with the VCV pattern is often divided after the first vowel. (This is an open syllable.) *cu • rious*
   b. **Dividing a word with the VCV pattern**—A word with the VCV pattern is sometimes divided after the consonant. (This is a closed syllable.) *res • olution*
   c. **Dividing a word with the VCCV pattern**—A word with the VCCV pattern is usually divided between the like or unlike consonants. *sus • pect*
   d. **Dividing a word with the CVVC pattern**—A word with the CVVC pattern is divided between the two vowels, if each vowel letter represents a separate sound. *curi • osity*

Materials

- A world map or atlas
- The *S* volume of an encyclopedia
- Prepare the following activity for Day 2.

Latin Relatives
1. solvere — *solve* — *solution*
2. curiosus — *curious* — *curiosity*
3. revolvere — *revolt* — *revolution*
4. resolvere — *resolve* — *resolution*
5. manutenēre — *maintain* — *maintenance*
6. generosus — *generous* — *generosity*
7. suspectare — *suspect* — *suspicious*

First Day

Give the pretest. After you have given the pretest and your student has checked and corrected it, give him time to choose two of the words from his Word Bank and write them as this week's *Word Bank Entries.*

After reading words 1-4 to your student, discuss their spellings, using the following questions:

- How are the words *curious* and *curiosity* related? (Curious *is the base word for* curiosity.)
- How does the spelling of the base word *curious* change when the suffix -*ity* is added to make *curiosity? (The* u *is dropped before the suffix is added.)*
- How are the words *generous* and *generosity* related? (Generous *is the base word for* generosity.)

Words to Master 28

suspect

Read each spelling word and place the accent mark over the correct syllable. Then write the words on the blanks, connecting the syllables.

1. cu·ri·ous   1. _____
2. cu·ri·os·i·ty   2. _____
3. gen·er·ous   3. _____
4. gen·er·os·i·ty   4. _____
5. sus·pect   5. _____
6. sus·pi·cious   6. _____
7. solve   7. _____
8. so·lu·tion   8. _____
9. re·solve   9. _____
10. res·o·lu·tion   10. _____
11. re·volt   11. _____
12. rev·o·lu·tion   12. _____
13. main·tain   13. _____
14. main·te·nance   14. _____
15. Sa·u·di A·ra·bi·a 15. _____
16. Si·er·ra Le·one   16. _____
17. Sin·ga·pore   17. _____
18. So·vi·et Un·ion   18. _____
19. Word Bank entry   19. _____
20. Word Bank entry   20. _____

110

- How does the spelling of the base word *generous* change when the suffix -*ity* is added to make *generosity? (The* u *is dropped before the suffix is added.)*

After reading words 5 and 6 to your student, discuss their spellings, using the following questions:

- Is the word *suspect* the base word for the word *suspicious? (yes)*
- How does the spelling of the base word change when the suffix -*ious* is added to make the word *suspicious? (The* e *is changed to* i, *and the* ct *is changed to* c.)

After reading words 8-10 to your student, discuss their meanings, using the following questions:

- How are the spellings of *solve* and *resolve* related? (Solve *is the base word for* resolve.)
- How does the spelling of the base word *solve* change when the ending -*tion* is added to make *solution? (The* ve *is changed to* u *before the ending is added.)*
- How does the spelling of the base word *resolve* change when the ending -*tion* is added to make *resolution? (The* ve *is changed to* u *before the ending is added.)*
- How does the spelling of the base word *revolt* change when the ending -*tion* is added to make *revolution? (The* t *is changed to* u *before the* -tion *is added.)*

After reading words 13 and 14 to your student, discuss their spellings, using the following questions:

- How many letters in the words *maintain* and *maintenance* are the same? *(the first five)*
- What happens to the spelling of the base word *maintain* when the suffix *-ance* is added. *(The* ai *is changed to* e *before the suffix is added.)*

Apply the structural generalizations to the word list. Write the four structural generalizations (with letters) that are listed at the top of the page in a place where your student can see them. Encourage him to review them with the following activity:

- Which structural generalization applies to the division between:
    1. the *u* and the *r* in the word *curious? (a)*
    2. the *i* and the *o* in *curiosity? (d)*
    3. the *n* and the *e* in *generous? (b)*
    4. the *s* and the *p* in *suspect? (c)*
    5. the *o* and the *l* in *solution? (a)*
    6. the *n* and the *t* in *maintain? (c)*
    7. the *s* and the *o* in *resolution? (b)*
    8. the *s* and the *p* in *suspicious? (c)*

Introduce words 15-18 on page 110.

- The names *Saudi Arabia, Sierra Leone,* and *Soviet Union* can be used to demonstrate the importance of noticing syllables when trying to spell a word. Give the students this hint: *pronounce each syllable separately as you spell these names.*

Guide a research activity: *Where in the World?* Help your student locate the countries with names in the spelling list on a world atlas or map. Ask him to use the *S* volume of an encyclopedia to expand his geographic and general country knowledge according to the ideas and optional activities presented in Unit 1.

The Soviet Union has been a rival world power for many years. Direct your student to read and talk to several adults about this country and the amazing changes that took place under Gorbachev, especially beginning in 1989.

Use the handwritten list. After your student has written each word on the appropriate line, check his list for spelling and legibility. Instruct him to place an accent mark in each multi-syllable word of the printed list.

Second Day

Use the Bible verse activity on page 111. Make certain that your student understands who is speaking in the psalm and what the following words and phrases mean: *substance, in secret, curiously, wrought, lowest parts of the earth.*

Have fun with the *Word for Word* section on page 111.

Use worktext pages 111 and 112 to reinforce word meaning and the skills of the unit. Read the directions and give help, if needed, as your student completes the pages.

Guide a word meaning activity: *Latin Relatives.* Provide your student with a copy of the activity found in the *Materials* section. Ask your student to determine which of the spelling words are related to the Latin words. Direct him to write these words in the blanks. For an enrichment exercise, have your student look up the spelling words in a dictionary to find the meaning of the Latin words.

---

name _____

A. Read the verse.
1. Underline the words that describe two places where the writer says he was made (or wrought).
2. Circle the word that has the Biblical meaning "done by embroidering," but today means "done with skill or ingenuity."

> *"My substance was not hid from thee, when I was made in secret, and curiously wrought in the lowest parts of the earth."*
>
> *Psalm 139:15*

Certain words change their spelling when a suffix is added. This week's spelling words have *internal* changes that make them tricky to spell unless you remember how each one differs from its base word. Look at *curiosity* and its base word *curious.* Notice how *curious* drops the *u* from its third syllable when the suffix *-ity* is added.

B. From your spelling list, write the other word pair that shows a spelling change in the third syllable when *-ity* is added.

generous, generosity

Count the words that have the letter combination *sol* somewhere in the word. How many did you find? *(four)* Watch out for internal spelling changes in these pairs of words.

C. Read the sentences below carefully and then match a *sol* word with each one.

1. I made my first New Year's _____ today.
2. The teacher asked me to _____ the equation on the chalkboard.
3. If you have a _____ to this problem, please tell us.
4. I hope that you and your friend can _____ the differences that are troubling you.

1. **resolution**
2. **solve**
3. **solution**
4. **resolve**

WORD FOR WORD

Have you ever had a knotty, tangled math problem to solve? At first glance, it looked almost impossible, but if you worked carefully, one step at a time, little by little, you unraveled it until you arrived at a solution. And you hoped that it was the correct solution! The word *solution* comes from the Latin word *solutus,* which means "to loosen." When you work on a math problem, you try to "loosen" the knots in it so that you can solve it.

solution

111

D. Draw a line through each incorrectly used spelling word and write the spelling word that belongs in the sentence.

1. The camp counselors were told to ~~solve~~ good discipline.
2. The grouchy man in the corner house is ~~curious~~ of any kid who rides a bike.
3. We did not ~~resolve~~ that they were planning a surprise party.
4. The students were filled with ~~resolution~~ about what the new principal looked like.
5. In every country there are some people who want to ~~maintain~~ against their government.
6. My father believes in careful ~~curiosity~~, so it is a challenge for him to keep the old church bus running well.
7. My cat is ~~generous~~ about every open drawer that she sees.

1. **maintain**
2. **suspicious**
3. **suspect**
4. **curiosity**
5. **revolt**
6. **maintenance**
7. **curious**

E. Use your Spelling Dictionary to help you match each capital below with a country from the spelling list.

1. Singapore
2. Riyadh
3. Moscow
4. Freetown

1. **Singapore**
2. **Saudi Arabia**
3. **Soviet Union**
4. **Sierra Leone**

F. Write the spelling word that does not belong in each set.
Note: Begin by deciding what part of speech each word is.

1. curious, generous, revolution, suspicious
2. maintenance, solve, solution, curiosity
3. revolve, generosity, revolt, revolved

1. **revolution**
2. **solve**
3. **generosity**

Words to Master

curious	suspicious	revolt	Sierra Leone
curiosity	solve	revolution	Singapore
generous	solution	maintain	Soviet Union
generosity	resolve	maintenance	_____
suspect	resolution	Saudi Arabia	_____

112

Third Day

Give your student time to study the words, using the study method printed on the back cover of the spelling worktext.

Dictate the word list for the trial test.

Give the following dictation sentences:

1. Both spies **maintain** that their people plan to **revolt**.
2. The church gave a **generous** offering to its missionary in **Singapore**.
3. Tom made a New Year's **resolution** to show more **generosity**.

> Dictionary skill: The *label* in the dictionary entry, given in italics, indicates that a definition of a word relates particularly to a certain field of study or interest.

Use page 171 to teach this week's dictionary skill. After you are certain that your student understands the skill, guide him as he completes the exercise.

> The label in the dictionary entry, given in italics, indicates that a definition of a word relates particularly to a certain field of study or interest.

Using the labels and abbreviations given in the box, write the meaning of each label given after the numbered words below. Next, use your Spelling Dictionary to find each word and give the meaning that follows that label. The first example is completed for you.

Anat.-anatomy	Bot.-botany	Biol.-biology
Baseball-baseball	Football-football	Law-law
Mus.-music	Math.-mathematics	Sports-sports
Theol.-theology	Gram.-grammar	Chem.-chemistry

1. monotone (Mus.)
   Music—One tone repeated with different words or in different time.

2. triangle (Mus.) Music – A small musical instrument that is struck to produce a clear tone like that of a bell.

3. aerial (Bot.) Botany – Carried through the air.

4. diagonal (Math.) Mathematics – Joining two points of a many-sided figure that are not adjacent to one another.

5. diagnosis (Biol.) Biology – A special and detailed description of the traits of an organism for the purpose of classification.

6. diagram (Math.) Mathematics – A picture showing an algebraic or geometric relationship.

7. diamond (Baseball) Baseball – The infield.

8. territory (Sports) Sports – The area of a field defended by a team.

Use with Unit 28.
Skill: interpreting subject labels in the dictionary

171

Fourth Day

Return last week's journal. Give your student time to correct the misspelled words in his previous journal entry and record them in his Word Bank.

Guide the journal time using the *Journal Entry Idea* on page 113 of the worktext. Talk again with your student about how the Soviet Union has changed in recent times. Discuss with him how Communism has, for the time being, been discredited. Ask him to recall what you talked about earlier in the week or to share anything he has learned from the news media about life in the Soviet Union today. Ask him to tell you what he thinks it would be like to live there now. After he has verbalized his thoughts, ask him to write them in his journal.

Fifth Day

Guide the study time.

Dictate the word list for the final test.

Give the following dictation sentences.

1. Many people in the **Soviet Union** are **suspicious** of American reporters.
2. They **suspect** us of plotting a **revolution.**
3. His **curiosity** helped him to find a **solution** to the problem.

Use *The King's English* on page 113. After your student reads this section silently, read it with him orally. Use the Bible verses, discussion, and good comprehension questions to make certain he understands the material. The following questions can be used:

1. Who is your "go-between" or the one who makes intercession for you to God? (Bible Promise: F. Christ as Intercessor)
2. Who interprets your prayers to God?
3. Do you remember who interceded for the Israelites when they were wandering in the wilderness?

Journal Entry Idea

"You must come with us!" That's all the explanation we heard the day my father was taken away. He was taken to prison because he was a Christian. Now, since the government has found our little church, we worship only at home or hidden in the woods. My mother is allowed to work on a collective farm, and we are taught daily in school to be loyal only to Lenin and the Communist party. My prayer and hope is that I can be as good a witness for God as my father.

Does this kind of life sound inviting? What if you had been born in the Soviet Union? Write about how you think it might be.

The King's English
intercession

Have you ever tried to explain something your friend did, to keep him out of trouble? If you did, you tried to intercede on your friend's behalf. The word **intercession** comes from a Latin word, *intercedere,* that means "to come between."

In the Bible, *intercession* refers to coming between man and God on behalf of sinful man. Remember Abraham's intercession for Lot when God intended to destroy Sodom? Christians can intercede for each other, pleading each person's need before God through prayer. God has even prepared for those times when Christians are not sure how to pray about a certain matter. The Holy Spirit intervenes in those difficult cases, taking the Christian's burdens before God.

Christ sits at the right hand of God, continually interceding for Christians. Romans 8 promises that nothing can separate Christians from the love of God, nor deny us the privilege of seeking Him. We honor this promise when we pray "in the name of Jesus."
Romans 8:34
    Romans 8:38-39
        Isaiah 53:12

113

Unit 29

Worktext pages 114-17
Dictionary page 172

Generalization emphasis

Adding a suffix that causes an internal change—Sometimes when a suffix is added, the spelling of the base word is changed. *despair, desperate*

Materials

- A world map or atlas
- The *S* volume of an encyclopedia
- Prepare the following activity for Day 2.

Best Choice

1. (explain, explanation) I knew my friend could <u>explain</u> what had happened.
2. (reveal, revelation) This mystery book doesn't <u>reveal</u> Jon's secret until the last chapter.
3. (mischief, mischievous) My cousin is a rascal, and he always looks at me with <u>mischief</u> in his eyes.
4. (abound, abundance) Americans have an <u>abundance</u> of luxuries.
5. (repeat, repetition) Susan's little brother liked to <u>repeat</u> his favorite verses again and again.
6. (despair, desperate) The thin, ragged man had a <u>desperate</u> look on his face.
7. (abound, abundant) Ants and flies <u>abound</u> at that campsite.
8. (desperate, desperation) Arlene had a feeling of <u>desperation</u> as she faced the sheer cliff.
9. (abundant, abundance) I like my pony to graze in a field that has <u>abundant</u> grass.

First Day

Give the pretest. After you have given the pretest and your student has checked and corrected it, give him time to choose two of the words from his Word Bank and write them as this week's *Word Bank Entries*.

After reading words 1-3 to your student, discuss their spellings, using the following questions:

- What spellings do words 1 through 3 have in common? *(the letters* desp*)*
- How does the spelling of the base word *despair* change when the suffix -*ate* is added to make *desperate*? *(The letters* ai *are dropped and an* e *is added.)*
- How does the spelling of the base word change when the ending -*ation* is added to make *desperation*? *(The letters* ai *are changed to* e.*)*

After reading words 4-6 to your student, discuss their spellings, using the following questions:

- Do you think the words *abound, abundant,* and *abundance* are related? *(yes)*
- How do you know? *(Elicit the idea that because the meanings are very similar we can assume they are related.)*
- What happens to the spelling of the base word *abound* when the ending -*ant* is added to make *abundant?* *(The* o *is dropped from the spelling.)*
- What happens to the spelling of the base word *abound* when the ending -*ance* is added to make *abundance?* *(The* o *is dropped.)*

After reading words 7-10 to your student, discuss their spellings, using the following questions:

- What is alike about the spellings of the words *repeat* and *repetition* and the words *reveal* and *revelation*? *(the first four letters in each case)*
- What happens to the spelling of the base words *repeat* and *reveal* when the endings -*ition* and -*ation* are added to make *repetition* and *revelation*? *(The* a*'s are dropped from both words.)*

After reading words 11 and 12 to your student, discuss their spellings, using the following questions:

- What do the spellings of *explain* and *explanation* have in common? *(the first five letters)*

- What happens to the spelling of the base word *explain* when the ending *-ation* is added to make *explanation?* (*The* i *is dropped.*)

After reading words 13 and 14 to your student, discuss their spellings using the following questions:

- What do the spellings of the words *mischief* and *mischievous* have in common? (*the first seven letters*)
- What happens to the spelling of the base word *mischief* when the ending *-ous* is added to make *mischievous?* (*The* f *is changed to* v.)

Introduce words 15-18 on page 114.

- Most of these words can be spelled according to spelling generalizations. Point out the schwa sound at the end of the words *Somalia* and *Africa*.

Guide a research activity: *Where in the World?* Help your student locate the countries with names in the spelling list on a world atlas or map. Ask him to use the *S* volume of an encyclopedia to expand his geographic and general country knowledge according to the ideas and optional activities presented in Unit 1.

Use the handwritten list. After your student has written each word on the appropriate line, check his list for spelling and legibility. Instruct him to place an accent mark in each multi-syllable word of the printed list.

Second Day

Use the Bible verse activity on page 115. Explain the meaning of the verse according to the context in which it appears. Ask such questions as the following:

1. Who wrote this encouragement to the Christians? (*the Apostle Paul*)
2. Whom was he writing to? (*the Christians at Thessalonica*)
3. According to the verse, what does Paul hope that these Christians will abound (or grow larger) in? (*love for each other and toward all men*)
4. Who does he say to use as their example? (*himself and his relationship to them*)
5. Could you tell someone else to use you for an example?

Have fun with the *Word for Word* section on page 115.

Use worktext pages 115 and 116 to reinforce word meaning and the skills of the unit. Read the directions and give help, if needed, as your student completes the pages.

Guide a word meaning activity: *Best Choice.* Provide your student a copy of the activity found in the *Materials* section. Direct your student to choose the correct word from each pair, noticing how the word is used.

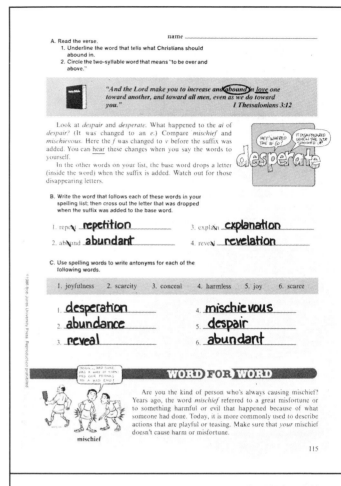

A. Read the verse.
1. Underline the word that tells what Christians should abound in.
2. Circle the two-syllable word that means "to be over and above."

"And the Lord make you to increase and abound in love one toward another, and toward all men, even as we do toward you."
I Thessalonians 3:12

Look at *despair* and *desperate*. What happened to the *ai* of *despair?* (It was changed to an *e*.) Compare *mischief* and *mischievous*. Here the *f* was changed to *v* before the suffix was added. You can hear these changes when you say the words to yourself.

In the other words on your list, the base word drops a letter (inside the word) when the suffix is added. Watch out for those disappearing letters.

B. Write the word that follows each of these words in your spelling list; then cross out the letter that was dropped when the suffix was added to the base word.

1. repeat **repetition**   3. explain **explanation**
2. abound **abundant**   4. reveal **revelation**

C. Use spelling words to write antonyms for each of the following words.

1. joyfulness   2. scarcity   3. conceal   4. harmless   5. joy   6. scarce

1. **desperation**   4. **mischievous**
2. **abundance**   5. **despair**
3. **reveal**   6. **abundant**

WORD FOR WORD

Are you the kind of person who's always causing mischief? Years ago, the word *mischief* referred to a great misfortune or to something harmful or evil that happened because of what someone had done. Today, it is more commonly used to describe actions that are playful or teasing. Make sure that *your* mischief doesn't cause harm or misfortune.

mischief

115

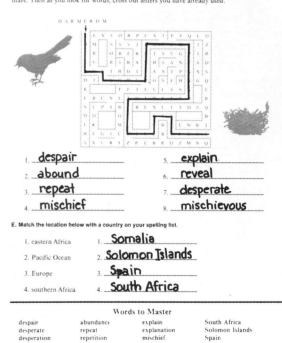

D. Follow the correct path through this maze to find eight spelling words. Use each letter only once. The eight letters at the entrance are the beginning letters of the words. The letters on the maze path are arranged in the order that they occur in the words.

Suggestions: Work in pencil! First draw a line showing the way through the maze. Then as you look for words, cross out letters you have already used.

1. **despair**   5. **explain**
2. **abound**   6. **reveal**
3. **repeat**   7. **desperate**
4. **mischief**   8. **mischievous**

E. Match the location below with a country on your spelling list.

1. eastern Africa   1. **Somalia**
2. Pacific Ocean   2. **Solomon Islands**
3. Europe   3. **Spain**
4. southern Africa   4. **South Africa**

Words to Master

despair	abundance	explain	South Africa
despirate	repeat	explanation	Solomon Islands
desperation	repetition	mischief	Spain
abound	reveal	mischievous	
abundant	revelation	Somalia	

116

Third Day

Give your student time to study the words, using the study method printed on the back cover of the spelling worktext.

Dictate the word list for the trial test.

Give the following dictation sentences:

1. The **desperate** people prayed for **abundant** rainfall.
2. Can you **explain** why people in **South Africa** are fighting?
3. The agent's files **reveal** that she was born in **Somalia**.

> Dictionary skill: One use for the dictionary is to find the meaning of a word, or a word's *definition*.

Use page 172 to teach this week's dictionary skill. After you are certain that your student understands the skill, guide him as he completes the exercise.

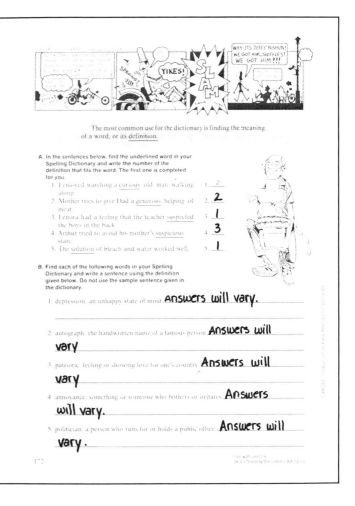

Fourth Day

Return last week's journal. Give your student time to correct the misspelled words in his previous journal entry and record them in his Word Bank.

Guide the journal time using the *Journal Entry Idea* on page 117 and the information given in the front of this manual. Ask your student if he knows what a pen pal is and then elicit discussion from him about what it would be like to have one. If he does have one, encourage him to write about him or her. Talk about the things he could describe to his pal about our country. You may have to suggest some of the interesting and wonderful things to describe. The more your student verbalizes his ideas, the easier it will be for him to write about them.

Fifth Day

Guide the study time.

Dictate the word list for the final test.

Give the following dictation sentences.

1. Please **repeat** your **explanation**.
2. The **mischievous** puppy drove his owner to **desperation**.
3. His writings **abound** in needless **repetition**.

Use *The King's English* on page 117. After your student reads this section silently, read it with him orally. Use the Bible verses, discussion, and good comprehension questions to make certain he understands the material. The following questions can be used:

1. What does the Latin word *revelatio* mean?
2. When will there be an "unveiling of Christ"?
3. What do you think it will be like to know Christ as He knows you? (BAT: 1b Understand Jesus Christ)

Journal Entry Idea

Suppose you had to describe your country to a pen pal. Could you tell about it from the viewpoint of where *you* live? Would you say that the land looks like someone took a rolling pin and flattened it out? Or would you say that where you live, tall buildings that seem to be wearing sunglasses blink at you when you drive past? Or would you tell how bare trees sprout light green cloaks in the spring that spread and spread until the mountains near you are covered with velvety blue-green?

Maybe you would rather describe some interesting sights like national parks or amusement parks. Pretend you are describing your country to a pen pal; say whatever you want, but say it so that he can *see* where you live.

The King's English
revelation

The moment that Jesus died for us, a **revelation** took place. The veil in the temple was torn in half, revealing the holy of holies. The Latin word *revelatio* comes from the root meaning "to take back the veil."

The last book of the Bible is called *Revelation* because it is a special "unveiling" of Christ's final plan for redeemed saints and unrepentant sinners. As a matter of fact, the entire Bible is a revelation from God, for it unveils the truth of God to our clouded minds. Everything that we know about God has been given to us through divine revelation.

There is coming a time when all will be revealed. In I Corinthians, Paul tells us that now we see as in a glass darkly, having only a partial knowledge of Christ. But when Christ comes again and we see Him face to face, then we will know Him as He knows us.

Revelation 1:1
Ephesians 3:3
I Corinthians 13:12

117

Unit 30

Worktext pages 118-21

───── **Generalization emphasis** ─────

Generalization statements can be found in Units 25-29.

───── **Materials** ─────

- Prepare the following activity for Day 2.

Just the Same

1. The little boy's eyes revealed his strong *inquisitiveness*. (curiosity)
2. The *officer* was constantly giving commands to his men. (sergeant)
3. The country has just had a *turnabout* in its government. (revolution)
4. The *kindness of spirit* that the teacher saw in her students pleased her. (generosity)
5. The missionaries stayed with us until the *end* of their furlough. (termination)
6. That corner is where the *accident* between the two cars took place. (collision)
7. The *large number* of baseball cards in Matthew's collection is impressive. (abundance)
8. I felt *distrustful* when I saw the cunning expression on the old man's face. (suspicious)
9. God does not want us to let *hopeless depression* rule our lives. (despair)
10. Mother waited to hear the manager's *reasoning* about the stain on her jacket. (explanation)

First Day

For review, apply the generalizations found in Lessons 25-29 to the word list on page 118.

Use worktext page 118 to reinforce word meaning and the skills of the unit. Read the directions and give help, if needed, as your student completes the page.

Review 30

Words to Master

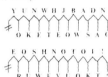

1. fascination	9. diaphragm	17. suspicious	25. New Guinea
2. termination	10. extraordinary	18. revolution	26. Paraguay
3. participation	11. isthmus	19. despair	27. Portugal
4. narration	12. mortgage	20. abundance	28. Rumania
5. adventurous	13. sepulcher	21. explanation	29. Saudi Arabia
6. virtuous	14. sergeant	22. mischievous	30. Singapore
7. revision	15. curiosity	23. Pakistan	31. Somalia
8. collision	16. generosity	24. Nigeria	32. Soviet Union

PICKET FENCE CIPHER

This cipher looks like the top of a picket fence because the message is written on two lines, with every other letter placed on the lower line. No space is left between words. Letters may be arranged in groups of three, four, or five, to make it harder for an outsider to break the code and easier for the cryptographer (you) to decode.

For example, the message *You knew the job was dangerous when you took it!!* is encoded this way:

```
Y  U  N  W  H  J  B  A  D  N
  O  K  E  T  E  O  W  S  A  G

E  O  S  H  N  O  T  O  I  !
  R  U  W  E  Y  U  O  K  T  !
```

It is written like this: YUNWH JBADN EOSHN OTOI! OKETE OWSAG RUWEY UOKT! (The top line of letters on the fence is followed by the bottom line; then they are arranged in groups of five.)

To decode a message written in Picket Fence Cipher, count the letters in the message, divide the total in half, and then arrange the letters, without spaces, on the picket fence. (The first half of the message goes on the points of the pickets, and the second half goes on the lines representing the boards, as in the sample.) Finally, decide where the spaces go between the words. This set of letters is arranged in groups of five.

118

Second Day

Use the Bible verse activity on page 119. Discuss with your student what it usually means to be *troubled, distressed,* and *perplexed.* How can a Christian avoid feeling the despair that normally accompanies problems? Help him to see that as Christians we are to trust in the Lord, resting on His promises to love, protect, and take care of us in each situation we face. As Christians we can experience the "peace that passeth all understanding" if we truly give our problems and our life to Him. (Bible Promises: G. Christ as Friend, H. God as Father)

Use worktext pages 119 and 120 to reinforce word meaning and the skills of the unit. Read the directions and give help, if needed, as your student completes the pages.

Guide a word meaning activity: *Just the Same.* Provide your student with a copy of the activity found in the *Materials* section. Direct your student to replace each italicized word or words with a synonym that is also a spelling word.

Third Day

Give your student time to study the words, using the study method printed on the back cover of the spelling worktext.

Dictate the word list for the trial test.

Give the following dictation sentences:
1. Do you remember the **revolution** in **Rumania**?
2. The **Soviet Union** always has heavy **participation** in the Olympics.
3. The **narration** was about an **adventurous** boy who was visiting **Singapore**.

Guide a spelling activity: *Alike or Not.* Guide your student in completing the following analogies with spelling words. He may do this activity orally or on paper.
1. less : scarcity :: more : *abundance*
2. question : problem :: statement : *explanation*
3. start : beginning :: end : *termination*
4. North America : United States :: Europe : *Portugal or Rumania*
5. wrong : sinful :: right : *virtuous*
6. laughter : happiness :: tears : *despair*
7. Europe : France :: South America : *Paraguay*
8. water : strait :: land : *isthmus*
9. meanness : selfishness :: kindness : *generosity*
10. common : ordinary :: uncommon : *extraordinary*

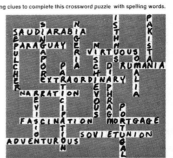

A. Read the verse.
1. Underline the phrase that describes where the writer was troubled.
2. Circle the word that has the Biblical meaning "the condition of having no outlet whatsoever" but today means "lack of all hope."

"We are troubled on every side, yet not distressed; we are perplexed, but not in despair."   II Corinthians 4:8

B. Use the picket fence below to decode this cipher. Then write the message on the blank lines.

Don't forget to divide the message in half before you begin. When starting each new line of pickets, put your first letter on the first point of the picket; follow the sample exactly. Work in pencil, in case you make a mistake.

Cipher: SRENS SIIUO YUMSH EOSAT CPTOI ETARI AYOLS O.EDX

LNTOP OIIGE IINFO RDETR UATVT EOEPC TRIAI NFOIS NAOEE

GATUP COSFO RICIV UPRII AINNX RODNR CLIIN SNEPA AINRM

SNRVS OOYUA VNUOS CIIIS RXETE MNTOO JBNIG PR.

sergeant suspicious of your mischievous participation in extraordinary collision. Send explanation promising revision of your adventurous activities or expect termination of job in Singapore.

119

C. Use the following clues to complete this crossword puzzle with spelling words.

Down
1. a narrow strip of land
2. country of southern Asia
3. country of Southeast Asia
4. republic of West Africa
5. a burial place
7. playful, teasing
9. country of extreme East Africa
10. the act of taking part
11. a part of the body
15. the act of changing
16. country of southwestern Europe

Across
5. kingdom comprising most of the Arabian Peninsula
6. country of South America
8. of good moral character
12. country of southeastern Europe
13. unusual
14. the act of telling
17. the condition of being spellbound
18. a temporary pledge to a debtor
19. country of eastern Europe and northern Asia
20. risky; exciting

D. Fill in vowels among the consonants to form spelling words.
1. dspr
2. gnrst
3. bndnc
4. crst

1. *despair*   3. *abundance*
2. *generosity*   4. *curiosity*

Words to Master

fascination	diaphragm	suspicious	New Guinea
termination	extraordinary	revolution	Paraguay
participation	isthmus	despair	Portugal
narration	mortgage	abundance	Rumania
adventurous	sepulcher	explanation	Saudi Arabia
virtuous	sergeant	mischievous	Singapore
revision	curiosity	Pakistan	Somalia
collision	generosity	Nigeria	Soviet Union

120

Fourth Day

Return last week's journal. Give your student time to correct the misspelled words in his previous journal entry and record them in his Word Bank.

Guide the journal time using the *Journal Entry Idea* on page 121 and the information given in the front of this manual. Talk with your student, eliciting from him the feelings he has about himself. Ask your student to describe himself to you, as if you were someone who has never seen him. If he falters, tell him some ways that you would describe him to others, making only positive comments. When you feel the subject is thoroughly talked-out, ask him to write these things in his journal.

Fifth Day

Guide the study time.

Dictate the word list for the final test.

Give the following dictation sentences:

1. **New Guinea** has an **abundance** of wild life.
2. The **sergeant** told about his **participation** in the **revolution.**
3. Was it **curiosity** that sent those **adventurous** divers to the bottom of the ocean?

Use *The King's English* on page 121. After your student reads this section silently, read it with him orally. Use the Bible verses, discussion, and good comprehension questions to make certain he understands the material. The following questions can be used:

1. Why do you think God led Elisha to this particular woman? (BAT: 7b Faith in the power of the Word of God; Bible Promise: I. God as Master)
2. Did God give the woman only what she needed for that day? (Bible Promise: H. God as Father)
3. According to *The King's English* on page 121, what does God want us to do and what will He do for us?

Journal Entry Idea

"Me? You want to hear about me?" You're writing a pen pal whom you've never seen, and he (or she) wants you to describe yourself. Where would you begin? You might start by saying, "I have short brown hair and brown eyes. I'm five feet tall, and I'm so skinny that clothes just about fall off me."

Then you would need to tell him (or her) what you like to do, where you like to go, all about your family, your school, your church—things like that. You might want to mention your standards in certain areas, such as music, friends, or activities.

Describe yourself to your pen pal. Be honest! Be yourself!

The King's English
abundance

In the days when people lived on what the land produced, life was not always easy. Years of **abundance** could be followed by years of famine. Most knew, as Joseph did, to lay up stores of food against the lean years.

In Latin, *abundare* means "to overflow." Of course, not everyone produced his own food or had enough "overflow" to store. When the widow in II Kings 4 was in danger of losing her sons because of debt, Elisha told her to bring out empty jars. Following his instructions, she poured the oil into the jars and had such an abundance that she was able to sell some. This miracle shows us that even though we might have only a little, the Lord can supply our needs out of His abundance.

In Luke 6:38, the Lord Jesus said, "Give, and it shall be given unto you; good measure, pressed down, and shaken together, and running over." If a Christian gives of himself and his possessions, God will supply him with rich spiritual blessings that no one else can give.

Luke 6:38
II Kings 4
II Kings 2:9

121

Unit 31

Worktext pages 122-25
Dictionary page 173

Generalization emphasis

1. **/nā/ or /nə/ spelled *na* at the beginning of a word**–/nā/ or /nə/ at the beginning of a word is spelled *na*, if the meaning of the word is related to "to be born." *native*

2. **/nā/ or /năt/ spelled *na* or *nat* at the beginning of a word**–/nā/ or /năt/ at the beginning of a word is spelled *na* or *nat*, if the meaning of the word is related to "nature." *nature, natural*

3. **/grā/ or /grăt/ spelled *gra* or *grat* at the beginning of a word**–/grā/ or /grăt/ at the beginning of a word is spelled *gra* or *grat*, if the meaning of the word is related to "good will" and "pleasing." *gracious, gratitude*

4. **/sûr/ or /sər/ spelled *cir* at the beginning of a word**–/sûr/ or /sər/ at the beginning of a word is spelled *cir*, if the meaning of the word is related to "circle" or "around." *circular, circumference*

Materials

- A world map or atlas
- The *S* volume of an encyclopedia
- Prepare the following activity for Day 2.

Which Word?

1. Kenneth is a ___native___ of western Pennsylvania.
2. The baseball coach remarked that Ronnie has a ___natural___ pitching arm.
3. Cindy wants to be a ___gracious___ hostess in the art museum, like her mother.
4. To reach the church belfry, Mr. Crump must climb a ___circular___ stairway.
5. Mother measured the ___circumference___ of the table to make a tablecloth.
6. Bethany caused a short ___circuit___ by plugging in her blow dryer.
7. Mrs. Clapper showed the class her ___gratitude___ by letting us out early.
8. Carrie will need to ___circulate___ among her guests at her birthday party.

First Day

Give the pretest. After you have given the pretest and your student has checked and corrected it, give him time to choose two of the words from his Word Bank and write them as this week's *Word Bank Entries*.

31
Words to Master

Read each spelling word and place the accent mark over the correct syllable. Then write the words on the blanks, connecting the syllables.

1. ná-tive
2. na-tív-i-ty
3. ná-ture
4. nát-u-ral
5. gráce
6. grá-cious
7. grát-i-tude
8. cír-cle
9. cír-cu-lar
10. cír-cu-late
11. cir-cúm-fer-ence
12. cir-cúm-stance
13. cír-cus
14. cír-cuit
15. Su-dán
16. Sú-ri-nam
17. Swé-den
18. Swít-zer-land
19. Word Bank entry
20. Word Bank entry

122

After reading words 1 and 2 on page 122 to your student, apply the first generalization, following the steps given below, using the suggested questions or statements:

- How are words 1 and 2 related? (Native *is the base word for* nativity.)
- Do you know what either of these words means? Using discussion, during which your student gives some kind of answer to each question you ask, bring out the meanings of the words. Ask him how *native* relates to *nativity*. Relate the meaning of the word *nativity* to the way that word is used at Christmas, in songs and to the set of figures used to create the *nativity* scene.
- Use a college dictionary (or one that contains information about word origins) to guide a research activity, during which your student looks up both words. Work with him as he traces the origin of each word all the way back to the Latin root *nasci* which means "to be born."
- Show him how the two words relate to that Latin beginning.

- Ask your student how /nā′ tĭv/ or /nə • tĭv′/ is spelled if it comes at the beginning of a word with a meaning related to "to be born." *(nativ)*

Any answer your student gives that shows that he is thinking is better than a memorized or "parroted" statement that he does not understand. (This is also true with Bible verses.) Accept any answer, not by saying it is correct, but by using it to lead him to the correct one. He knows more than he realizes he knows, but he must be made to **think** if what he has learned is to be permanent.

After reading words 3 and 4 to your student, follow exactly the same steps to apply generalization number two as you did with number one, using the same kind of questions. End with the following question:

- What is the spelling of /nāt/ if it comes at the beginning of a word with a meaning related to "nature"? *(nat)*

After reading words 5-7 to your student, follow the same steps to apply generalization number three that you did to apply generalization number one. Add the following variations:

- Discuss, by asking questions and waiting for his answers, what the word *grace* means. He should arrive at the idea only, not state a memorized catechism. *(God's grace is God's undeserved favor; it is divine good will.)*
- Take this time to explain how God showed us His grace by providing for the forgiveness of our sins through His own Son's death. (BATs: 1a Understanding Jesus Christ, 1b Repentance and faith, 7a Grace)
- Bring out the fact that the Latin word *gratia* means "good will" and the Latin word *gratus* means "pleasing." He will find that they are both at the heart of these three words when he follows one of the words to its origin.
- Ask him to offer a definition for any one of words 5 through 7, leading him from his idea to the actual meaning of each word. The following definitions will help:

  gracious: "characterized by kindness or warm courtesy"
  gratitude: "thankfulness"

- Ask your student how /grăt/ and /grā/ are spelled if either comes at the beginning of a word with a meaning that is related to "good will" or "pleasing." *(grat and gra)*

After reading words 8-14 to your student, follow exactly the same steps you did when you applied the first two generalizations, using the suggested questions. Add the following variations:

- Which of words 8 through 14 do you know a meaning of? *(If your student offers an idea on any of these words, lead him from that to the actual meaning and show him how each relates to the Latin word part* circul *which means "around.")* The following definitions will be helpful:

  circle, circular: "of or pertaining to a plane curve equidistant from a certain point (forming a circle)"
  circulate: "to move through a circuit or circle; to move around"
  circumference: "the boundary line of a circle"
  circumstance: "conditions or situations that surround"
  circus: "a show that takes place in a circular area"
  circuit: "the region enclosed by a curved line"

- Ask your student how /sûr/ or /sər/ is spelled if either comes at the beginning of a word that has a meaning related to "circle." *(cir)*

Introduce words 15-18 on page 122.

- Compare /ōo/ in the word *Sudan* with /oo/ in the word *Surinam*. They are both spelled with a *u*.

Guide a research activity: *Where in the World?* Help your student locate the countries with names in the spelling list on a world atlas or map. Ask him to use the *S* volume of an encyclopedia to expand his geographic and general country knowledge according to the ideas and optional activities presented in Unit 1.

Use the handwritten list. After your student has written each word on the appropriate line, check his list for spelling and legibility. Instruct him to place an accent mark in each multi-syllable word of the printed list.

Second Day

Use the Bible verse activity on page 123. Discuss the verse with your student, using the following questions:
1. What is a *hearer of the Word*?
2. What is a *doer of the Word*?
3. What does *beholding himself in a glass* mean?
4. What does the word *straightway* mean?
5. What would you be doing if you straightway forgot what manner of man you were?
6. What is God telling us in this verse?
7. What can we learn from this verse? (BATs: 6a Bible study, 6b Prayer)

Have fun with the *Word for Word* section on page 123.

Use worktext pages 123 and 124 to reinforce word meaning and the skills of the unit. Read the directions and give help, if needed, as your student completes the pages.

Guide a word meaning activity: *Which Word?* Provide your student with a copy of the activity found in the *Materials* section. Direct your student to use the context of each sentence and choose a spelling word that best fits each blank.

Third Day

Give your student time to study the words, using the study method printed on the back cover of the spelling worktext.

Dictate the word list for the trial test.

Give the following dictation sentences:

1. We should show **gratitude** for the land of our **nativity.**
2. How do you find the **circumference** of a **circle?**
3. It is her **nature** to be **gracious** to everyone she meets.

> Dictionary skill: The dictionary is used more to check *spelling* than for any other purpose. You may want to find the spelling of an *entry word* or a particular *form of that entry word.*

Use page 173 to teach this week's dictionary skill. After you are certain that your student understands the skill, guide him as he completes the exercise.

Spelling is another of the primary uses for the dictionary. Sometimes you need to know the spelling of a form of the entry word. The word forms are given in bold print. Other word forms are given at the end of the entry. In the excerpt from the dictionary given below, the words *graciously* and *graciousness* are forms of the word *gracious.*

gra·cious \ grā'shǝs \ *adjective* Courteous and kind, warm-hearted. *graciousness* *noun* **graciously**

Using the first example as your guide, find each word listed below in your Spelling Dictionary. Choose the form of the entry word that best fits into the sentence that follows the word.

1. gracious: Mary accepted the gift ____.
2. nativity: In the book of Luke we read of the ____ of John the Baptist and Jesus.
3. circulate: The paper kept ____ around the room.
4. circumstance: The witness revealed the ____ that led to the accident.
5. circuit: They told us that the electricity had short-____ and that was why our air conditioner wasn't working.
6. revise: The teacher said that we would be ____ our compositions.
7. virtuous: Christians should love God and live ____.
8. mortgage: The family had two ____ on houses in our town.
9. narrate: The best reader in the class ____ the Christmas program.
10. liberty: We enjoy many ____ in the United States.
11. liberal: The Bible says to give to others with ____.
12. century: Through the ____ many have given their lives for Christ.

1. ____ *graciously*
2. **nativities**
3. **circulating**
4. **circumstances**
5. **circuited**
6. **revising**
7. **virtuously**
8. **mortgages**
9. **narrated**
10. **liberties**
11. **liberality**
12. **centuries**

Use with Unit 31
Skill: spelling word forms correctly

173

Fourth Day

Return last week's journal. Give your student time to correct the misspelled words in his previous journal entry and record them in his Word Bank.

Guide the journal time using the *Journal Entry Idea* on page 125 and the information given in the front of this manual. Talk with your student about his grandparents. Ask him to tell you what traits of each grandparent he likes best. After a thorough discussion, ask him to write about one of his grandparents in his journal.

Fifth Day

Guide the study time.

Dictate the word list for the final test.

Give the following dictation sentences.

1. I admired the **natural grace** of the swans on the lake.
2. My grandmother is a **native** of **Switzerland.**
3. Under no **circumstance** may you go to the **circus** tonight.

Use *The King's English* on page 125. After your student reads this section silently, read it with him orally. Use the Bible verses, discussion, and good comprehension questions to make certain he understands the material. The following questions can be used:

1. How does one become "born again"?
2. Whose family will you be in when you are born a second time? (Bible Promise: H. God as Father)
3. Do you become one of God's family by doing anything?

Journal Entry Idea

My grandma! She is super! One thing she does is to save all of the greeting cards she receives. She cuts off the signatures and uses the pictures for all kinds of things. She needs a lot of cards because she sends me a card *every* week, and there is always a stick of gum and a dollar inside. Besides that, I like her soft, squishy arms and her poems about each of us grandkids. Grandpa is a different kind of super. I know how much he loves me when he smiles at me; his eyes crinkle at the corners and almost close, and I can see the love shining out.

Describe your grandparents or some other older person and tell why you love them.

The King's English
regeneration

Regeneration is God's act of giving spiritual life. The word comes from the Latin *regenerare*, which means "to reproduce." From your human parents, you received a sinful nature as well as human life. Because sin separates you from God, you need to be "born again," thereby receiving spiritual life.

To be born the second time, you must realize that you are a sinner, repent of your sin, and accept Jesus as your Saviour. Then you are a child of God and a joint-heir with Jesus Christ. When you are born again, God removes your sins so that He looks on you as righteous.

Some people think their parents' faith will save them. Nicodemus thought that his religious deeds would save him. Ephesians 2:8-9 says that spiritual birth is through an act of God, lest any man boast of achieving it himself.

Have you had a second "birthday"? Have you been born again?
Titus 3:5
John 3:3
Ephesians 2:8-9

125

Unit 32

Worktext pages 126-29
Dictionary page 174

Generalization emphasis
---

1. **/dĭk/ spelled _dict_ at the beginning of a word**–/dĭk/ at the beginning of a word is spelled _dict_, if the meaning of the word is related to the definition "to say." _dictate_

2. **/pôrt/ spelled _port_**–/pôrt/ is spelled _port_, if the meaning of the word is related to the definition "to carry." _portable_

3. **/spē/, /spĕsh/, or /spə/ spelled _spec_**–/spē/, /spĕsh/, or /spə/ is spelled _spec_, if the meaning of the word is related to "kind" or "appearance." _species_

Materials

- A world map or atlas
- The _S_ and _T_ volumes of an encyclopedia
- Prepare the following activity for Day 2.

Definition Delight

1. Ralph was _precious and dear_ to his grandfather. _(special)_
2. On our canoe trip we had to _carry_ our canoe each time we came to a fallen tree. _(portage)_
3. The pastor would not _give us a command as to_ how we should vote. _(dictate)_
4. The secretary got the job because she is so good at _writing on paper what her boss says. (dictation)_
5. It is good that the United States can _sell_ steel _to other countries. (export)_
6. Our class studied every _kind_ of that particular animal family. _(species)_
7. Frank took speech lessons to improve his _way of speaking. (diction)_
8. The United States continues to _buy_ textiles _from other countries. (import)_
9. When you want to know a correct spelling, use your _book filled with words and definitions. (dictionary)_
10. Molly's grandmother gave her a typewriter that was _able to be carried from place to place. (portable)_
11. Our whole family was _exceptionally_ excited about the party. _(especially)_
12. The leader of the revolution went on to become the _supreme ruler_ of the small country. _(dictator)_
13. Uncle Stephen carried all his money in his _carrying case. (portfolio)_
14. Lucille had a _particular_ book in mind when she went shopping. _(specific)_

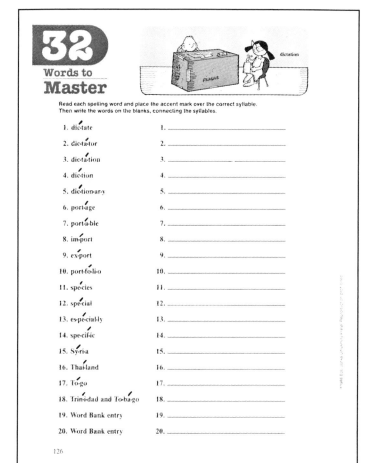

Read each spelling word and place the accent mark over the correct syllable. Then write the words on the blanks, connecting the syllables.

1. díc·tate   1. _____
2. dic·tá·tor   2. _____
3. dic·tá·tion   3. _____
4. díc·tion   4. _____
5. díc·tion·ar·y   5. _____
6. pórt·age   6. _____
7. pórt·a·ble   7. _____
8. im·pórt   8. _____
9. éx·port   9. _____
10. port·fó·li·o   10. _____
11. spé·cies   11. _____
12. spé·cial   12. _____
13. es·pé·cial·ly   13. _____
14. spe·cíf·ic   14. _____
15. Sý·ri·a   15. _____
16. Thái·land   16. _____
17. Tó·go   17. _____
18. Trin·i·dad and To·bá·go 18. _____
19. Word Bank entry 19. _____
20. Word Bank entry 20. _____

126

First Day

Give the pretest. After you have given the pretest and your student has checked and corrected it, give him time to choose two of the words from his Word Bank and write them as this week's _Word Bank Entries_.

After reading words 1-5 on page 126 to your student, apply generalization number one in the following way, using the suggested questions or statements:

- Look at the first five words. Do you know what any of them mean? _(Your student will recognize the word_ dictionary _and, hopefully, know what_ dictate _means.)_ Begin with your student's answer as to what one of the words means and lead him to the fact that the word part _dict_ comes from a Latin word that means "to say."
- Tie each of the first five words into the definition "to say," by asking questions such as the following:
  > What does it mean when someone says you have good _diction?_
  > If your teacher _dictates_ words, what is she doing?
- The following definitions will be helpful:
  > dictate, dictation: "having to do with saying something aloud"
  > dictator: "a ruler having absolute authority"

diction: "choice of words in speaking"

dictionary: "a reference book containing an explanatory alphabetical list of words"

- Ask your student how /dĭk/ is spelled if it comes at the beginning of a word and has a meaning related to the definition "to say." *(dict)*

After reading words 6-10 to your student, apply generalization number two to these words in exactly the same way that you applied generalization number one. The following definitions will be helpful:

portage: "the carrying of boats and supplies between two waterways"

portable: "capable of being carried"

import: "to bring or carry in from an outside source"

export: "to send or carry something abroad"

portfolio: "a portable case for holding loose papers"

- Ask your student how /pôrt/ is spelled if it is part of a word that has a meaning related to the definition "to carry." *(port)*

After reading words 11-14 to your student, apply generalization number three to these words in exactly the same way that you did when you applied generalization number one. The following definitions will be helpful:

species: "a kind, variety, or type"

special: "distinct among others of a kind"

especially: "pertaining to something that stands apart from others"

specific: "intended for, applying to, or acting upon a particular thing"

- Ask your student how /spē/, /spĕsh/, or /spə/ is spelled if either sound is part of a word that has a meaning related to the definition "kind" or "appearance." *(spec)*

Introduce words 15-18 on page 126.

- Point out that the *i* in *Syria* is /ē/.
- The *h* and *a* in the first syllable of *Thailand* do not make any sound at all.

Guide a research activity: *Where in the World?* Help your student locate the countries with names in the spelling list on a world atlas or map. Ask him to use the *S* and *T* volumes of an encyclopedia to expand his geographic and general country knowledge according to the ideas and optional activities presented in Unit 1.

Use the handwritten list. After your student has written each word on the appropriate line, check his list for spelling and legibility. Instruct him to place an accent mark in each multi-syllable word of the printed list.

Second Day

Use the Bible verse activity on page 127. Make certain that your student understands the verse by asking the following questions:

1. What does it mean to *do good unto all men?*
2. Who would those be who are *of the household of faith?*
3. What is the main point of this verse?

Have fun with the *Word for Word* section on page 127.

Use worktext pages 127 and 128 to reinforce word meaning and the skills of the unit. Read the directions and give help, if needed, as your student completes the pages.

Guide a word meaning activity: *Definition Delight.* Provide your student with a copy of the activity found in the *Materials* section. Tell your student that each sentence contains an italicized word or phrase that is the definition for one of the spelling words. Direct him to choose the correct word that matches each definition.

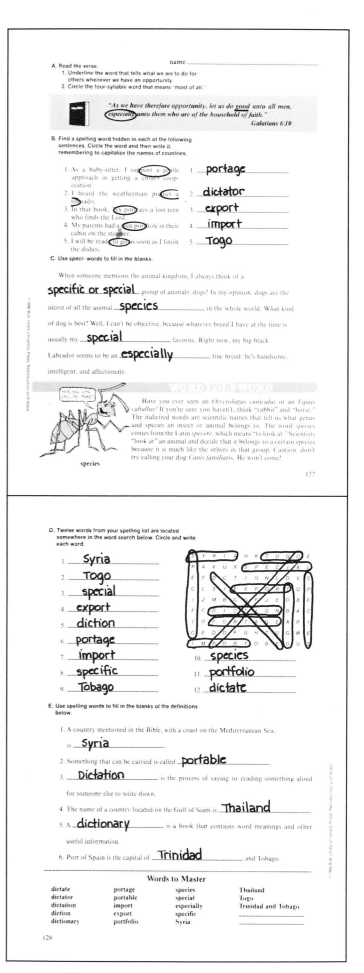

Third Day

Give your student time to study the words, using the study method printed on the back cover of the spelling worktext.

Dictate the word list for the trial test.

Give the following dictation sentences:

1. The country of **Togo imports** many things from France.
2. The island of **Tobago** is the home of many **species** of beautiful birds.
3. The young artist had an **especially** good **portfolio** of paintings.

> Dictionary skill: Use the dictionary to find the spelling of a word after a suffix is added.

Use page 174 to teach this week's dictionary skill. After you are certain that your student understands the skill, guide him as he completes the exercise.

Adding a suffix to a base word often changes its spelling. A good reason for using your dictionary is to check the spelling of a word that has a suffix.

Each of the numbered words is an incorrect form of another word. If you don't know the correct spelling, look for the word in a dictionary and then write it correctly.

The game of baseball develope from a game original called *Cricket* (1) (2) and from one called *Rounders*. Boston children played a street game they unofficial called *Townball*. In New York, children played a game that (3) (4) (5) resemble it. Both used four base and a batter's box. In 1839, Abner Doubleday lined a diamond-shaped field with four bases and specify that (6) the game be label *Baseball*. (7)

Baseball is the nation game of the United States. Its popular (8) (9) stem from its variety and from the numerous skill it employs. The game (10) (11) combine both individual and team play. It is enjoy by young and old and, (12) (13) although slow-move, is excite. (14) (15)

1. developed
2. originally
3. unofficially
4. resembled
5. bases
6. specified
7. labeled
8. national
9. popularity
10. stems
11. skills
12. combines
13. enjoyed
14. moving
15. exciting

174

Use with Unit 32.
Skill: using the dictionary to add suffixes

Fourth Day

Return last week's journal. Give your student time to correct the misspelled words in his previous journal entry and record them in his Word Bank.

Guide the journal time using the *Journal Entry Idea* on page 129 and the information given in the front of this manual. Begin by telling your student all about your salvation experience: how old you were, where you were, who was with you, and any other interesting facts about it. Ask your student, then, to tell you about his salvation experience, even if you were the one who led him to Christ. After he has talked about it, ask him to write what he just said in his journal.

Fifth Day

Guide the study time.

Dictate the word list for the final test.

Give the following dictation sentences.
1. Check your **dictionary** for **specific** help in spelling that word.
2. What **special** products does **Thailand export?**
3. My boss tries to use good **diction** when he gives **dictation.**

Use *The King's English* on page 129. After your student reads this section silently, read it with him orally. Use the Bible verses, discussion, and good comprehension questions to make certain he understands the material. The following questions can be used:
1. Why do you suppose God wanted His children to rest from work on the seventh day?
2. What could they do on the Sabbath? (BATs: 6b Prayer, 7c Praise)
3. What do we, as Christians, need to do on our day of rest, Sunday? (BATs: 7b Exaltation of Christ, 7c Praise)

Journal Entry Idea
One night after I had crawled into bed, my sister said from the hall, "Shannon, are you asleep?"

"Yes," I mumbled.

"I have to talk to you, Shannon," she said, perching on the the edge of my bed. I told her to talk away, that it's a free country. Then I saw the serious look on her face.

"Shannon," she said slowly, "I'm afraid that you might die unsaved. Don't you want to put your trust in Jesus and ask God to save you?" After we talked about it for a while, I prayed and asked God to save me through the blood of Jesus. I'll never forget that night.

Tell about when you got saved or another unforgettable experience you have had.

The King's English
sabbath
Our word **sabbath** comes from the Hebrew word *shābath*, which means "he rested." Genesis 2 tells us that God finished His creation in six days. On the seventh day He rested.

When God gave manna to the children of Israel, He instructed them to gather enough for the Sabbath, for no manna fell on that day. If they gathered too much, the remainder rotted; if they gathered too little, they did without. Later, God included the Sabbath in the Ten Commandments, instructing the Israelites to keep the day holy. The Jews worship God in their synagogues on Saturday.

After His resurrection, Christ met with the apostles and disciples on the first day of the week, Sunday. This practice was continued by the early church. The "Lord's Day" then became our day of rest and worship.
Genesis 2:2-3
Exodus 16:23
Matthew 28:1

129

Unit 33

Worktext pages 130-33
Dictionary page 175

─────── **Generalization emphasis** ───────

/trănz/ spelled *trans* at the beginning of a word–/trănz/ at the beginning of a word is spelled *trans*, if the meaning of the word is related to "across" or "through." *transfer*

─────────── **Materials** ───────────

• A world map or atlas
• The *T* and *U* volumes of an encyclopedia

First Day

Give the pretest. After you have given the pretest and your student has checked and corrected it, give him time to choose two of the words from his Word Bank and write them as this week's *Word Bank Entries.*

After reading words 1-14 on page 130 to your student, apply the generalization to the words in the following way:

• Read each word and then ask the following questions about it:
  1. Do you know what _____ means?
  2. What makes you think it means that?
  3. Can you use it in a sentence?
  4. Listen as I use it in a sentence: *Daddy's boss is going to _____ him to another city.* Now what do you think it means?

  (Whatever your student gives for the meaning of the word, use that to lead him to the more correct meaning.) The following definitions will help:

  transfer: "to shift from one person or place to another"
  transfusion: "to transfer liquid from one vessel to another"
  transect: "to divide by cutting transversely"
  transistor: "a device that operates so that the current between one pair of terminals controls the current between another pair"
  transition: "changing or passing from one form, state, activity, or place to another"
  translate: "to convey from one form, style, or language to another"
  transmitter: "the portion of the telephone that converts sounds into electrical impulses"
  transparent: "able to transmit light so that objects can be seen as if there were no intervening material"
  transpire: "give off; to become known; to happen"

Words to Master

Read each spelling word and place the accent mark over the correct syllable. Then write the words on the blanks, connecting the syllables.

1. trans·fer′   1. _____
2. trans·fu·sion   2. _____
3. tran·sect′   3. _____
4. tran·sis·tor   4. _____
5. tran·si·tion   5. _____
6. trans·late′   6. _____
7. trans·mit·ter   7. _____
8. trans·par·ent   8. _____
9. tran·spire′   9. _____
10. trans·plant′   10. _____
11. trans·port′   11. _____
12. trans·pose′   12. _____
13. trans·mis·sion   13. _____
14. trans·fig·u·ra·tion 14. _____
15. Tur·key   15. _____
16. U·gan·da   16. _____
17. U·nit·ed Ar·ab E·mir·ates 17. _____
18. U·nit·ed King·dom 18. _____
19. Word Bank entry   19. _____
20. Word Bank entry   20. _____

130

transplant: "to uproot and replant"
transport: "to carry from one place to another"
transpose: "to reverse the order or place of; to change a song from one key to another"
transmission: "the assembly of gears in an automobile that enables power to be carried from the engine to a driving axle"
transfiguration: "to alter radically one's appearance; the sudden emanation of radiance from Jesus' person that happened on the mountain"

• Ask your student how /trănz/ is spelled if it comes at the beginning of a word that has a meaning related to the definition "to carry." *(trans)*

Introduce words 15-18 on page 130.

• Point out that *Emirates* begins with *emir,* a word that refers to a Middle Eastern prince or chieftain.
• Three of the names begin with /ū/.

Guide a research activity: *Where in the World?* Help your student locate the countries with names in the spelling list on a world atlas or map. Ask him to use the *T* and *U* volume of an encyclopedia to expand his geographic and general country knowledge according to the ideas and optional activities presented in Unit 1.

Ask your student to find out the four major areas that comprise the *United Kingdom* and locate them on a map. Ask him to read to determine the unique characteristics that set each area apart from the others. Provide a time for him to share his findings with your family. *(These areas are England, Scotland, Wales, and Northern Ireland.)*

Use the handwritten list. After your student has written each word on the appropriate line, check his list for spelling and legibility. Instruct him to place an accent mark in each multi-syllable word of the printed list.

Second Day

Use the Bible verse activity on page 131. After reading the verse, talk with your student about whom he thinks this verse is referring to. Why would he know that it is about Jesus? Have him describe what Jesus must have looked like.

Have fun with the *Word for Word* section on page 131.

Use worktext pages 131 and 132 to reinforce word meaning and the skills of the unit. Read the directions and give help, if needed, as your student completes the pages.

Guide a spelling activity: *Words Within.* Ask your student to find within each spelling word as many different words as he can. He must keep the basic spelling order; sometimes the letters will immediately follow each other, and sometimes he will skip letters. Examples: *transfer: ran, tan; transistor: ant, sis.*

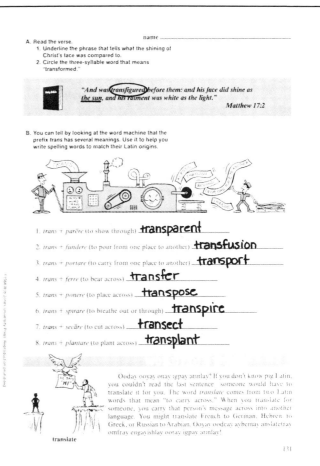

A. Read the verse.
1. Underline the phrase that tells what the shining of Christ's face was compared to.
2. Circle the three-syllable word that means "transformed."

"And was (transfigured) before them: and his face did shine as the sun, and his raiment was white as the light."
Matthew 17:2

B. You can tell by looking at the word machine that the prefix *trans* has several meanings. Use it to help you write spelling words to match their Latin origins.

1. *trans* + *parēre* (to show through) **transparent**
2. *trans* + *fundere* (to pour from one place to another) **transfusion**
3. *trans* + *portare* (to carry from one place to another) **transport**
4. *trans* + *ferre* (to bear across) **transfer**
5. *trans* + *ponere* (to place across) **transpose**
6. *trans* + *spirare* (to breathe out or through) **transpire**
7. *trans* + *secāre* (to cut across) **transect**
8. *trans* + *plantare* (to plant across) **transplant**

translate

Ooday ooyay onay igpay atinlay? If you don't know pig Latin, you couldn't read the last sentence someone would have to translate it for you. The word *translate* comes from two Latin words that mean "to carry across." When you translate for someone, you carry that person's message across into another language. You might translate French to German, Hebrew to Greek, or Russian to Arabian. Ooyay oodcay aybemay anslatetray omfray engayishlay ootay igpay atinlay!

131

C. Use spelling words to complete the following statements.
1. If you were a musician, you might ____ music.
2. If you were a gardener, you might ____ flowers.
3. If you wrote a report on England, Scotland, Wales, and Northern Ireland, you could entitle it "The ____."
4. If you were an interpreter, you could ____ languages.
5. If you were an automobile mechanic, you might fix the ____ of a car.
6. If you were a radio operator, you would know how to use a ____.
7. If you visited the country on the Persian Gulf that is a federation of seven Arab sheikdoms, you could say you had been to the ____ ____ ____.
8. If you were a radio repairman, you would know a lot about a ____.

1. **transpose**
2. **transplant**
3. **United Kingdom**
4. **translate**
5. **transmission**
6. **transmitter**
7. **United Arab Emirates**
8. **transistor**

D. Using the vertical message below as a guide, arrange spelling words on the blanks.

TRANSFI☐URATION
TRANSP☐SE
UGAN☐A

☐RANSLATE
T☐ANSITION
TRANSP☐RENT
TRA☐SISTOR
TRAN☐FUSION
TRANS☐ER
TRANSP☐RT
TU☐KEY
TRANS☐ITTER
TRAN☐PIRE
TRANS☐ISSION
TRANS☐CT

Words to Master

transfer	translate	transport	Uganda
transfusion	transmitter	transpose	United Arab Emirates
transect	transparent	transmission	United Kingdom
transistor	transpire	transfiguration	
transition	transplant	Turkey	

132

Third Day

Give your student time to study the words, using the study method printed on the back cover of the spelling worktext.

Dictate the word list for the trial test.

Give the following dictation sentences:

1. Please **transplant** this flower into a **transparent** pot so we can see some of the roots.
2. The mechanic listened to a **transistor** radio while he worked on the **transmission** of our car.
3. The **transition** from living in the **United Kingdom** to living in the **United States** was not easy.

> Dictionary skill: The dictionary is the best resource to use for *checking the spelling* of a word.

Use page 175 to teach this week's dictionary skill. After you are certain that your student understands the skill, guide him as he completes the exercise.

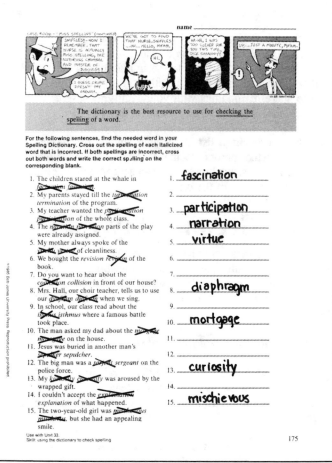

Fourth Day

Return last week's journal. Give your student time to correct the misspelled words in his previous journal entry and record them in his Word Bank.

Guide the journal time using the *Journal Entry Idea* on page 133 and the information given in the front of this manual. Hold a discussion about the differences between a teen-ager and a grade schooler and the reasons for those differences. Lead students to mention the additional responsibilities that they think their teen-age years will bring and the new goals that they could set as they enter their teens. (BAT: 2d Goal setting)

Fifth Day

Guide the study time.

Dictate the word list for the final test.

Give the following dictation sentences.

1. **Transpose** the music to a lower key when you **translate** this Spanish song.
2. **Transfer** the **transmitter** to **Turkey**.
3. We must **transport** this blood to **Uganda** for the king's **transfusion**.

Use *The King's English* on page 133. After your student reads this section silently, read it with him orally. Use the Bible verses, discussion, and good comprehension questions to make certain he understands the material. The following questions can be used:

1. What is *husbandry?*
2. What do we call people today who work the soil for a living?
3. What is a parable and why would Jesus use parables when he spoke to his listeners?

Journal Entry Idea

Oh, to be more than twelve! Thirteen sounds so much older! There really is a big difference between *grade school* and *high school*. Being a teen means Mom and Dad will give me more responsibility, like letting me baby-sit for them and other people or even allowing me to get a paper route. I'll also be able to work in junior church and on a bus route, and I can join in activities at church like youth visitation.

Are you looking forward to being a teen? Tell about some of the reasons.

The King's English
husbandman

Our word **husbandman** comes from two Old Norse words that mean "house" and "dwelling." Long ago, when a person or group of persons stopped wandering in search of game, they settled in dwellings. A permanent location meant time to plant, grow crops, and care for the land.

Husbandry, or taking care of the land, has long been an honorable occupation. All Hebrews, except those in religious service, were *'ish ha'damah,* Hebrew for "man of the soil." They cleared land, sowed and cared for the crops, and reaped the harvest.

Jesus' parables were often about husbandmen and the land, for they were subjects the Jewish people understood. One of the parables told of a man who let husbandmen care for his vineyard. When he sent his servants to collect the harvest, they were beaten, stoned, or killed. Finally, the man sent his son, thinking people would respect the heir. Instead, they killed him also. Do you know what the Lord meant in this parable? Who were the husbandmen? Who was the heir?
Matthew 21:33-40
1 Corinthians 3:9
Matthew 13

133

Unit 34

Worktext pages 134-37
Dictionary page 176

Generalization emphasis

1. **/sǐm/ or /sǐn/ spelled *sym* or *syn* at the beginning of a word**–/sǐm/ or /sǐn/ at the beginning of a word is spelled *sym* or *syn*, if the meaning of the word is related to "together," "same," or "at the same time." *symphony, synopsis*

2. **/krŏn/ spelled *chron* at the beginning of a word**–/krŏn/ at the beginning of a word is spelled *chron*, if the meaning of the word is related to "time." *chronological*

3. **/ĭks/ spelled *ex* at the beginning of a word**–/ĭks/ at the beginning of a word is spelled *ex*, if the meaning of the word is related to "to reach" or "outward." *external*

Materials

- A world map or atlas
- The *U, V,* and *W* volumes of an encyclopedia
- Prepare the following activity for Day 2.

Fillerup

1. "I've been coughing all winter," wheezed Uncle Josh. "The doctor says I have a case of *chronic* bronchitis."
2. The *exterior* of the old house was dingy and weather-beaten.
3. The evening twittering of the birds has a lovely *symphonic* sound.
4. I was amazed at the ___*extent*___ of Aunt Sally's ranch in Wyoming.
5. Cousin Mazie warned Tom that his aching back was a *symptom* of old age.
6. *Uruguay* is a South American country with a coast on the Atlantic Ocean.
7. Try to smile and ___*extend*___ your hand politely when Uncle George roars, "Shake, my boy!"
8. We visited *Venezuela* because it is on the Caribbean Sea.
9. Mark sent us an outline, or ___*synopsis*___, of his latest book.
10. My older brother is a veteran of the war in *Vietnam* .
11. Frank needs an *extension* ladder to paint the upper story of our house.
12. The old diary that Maria found turned out to be an exciting *chronicle* of events during the Civil War.

First Day

Give the pretest. After you have given the pretest and your student has checked and corrected it, give him time

34 Words to Master

Read each spelling word and place the accent mark over the correct syllable. Then write the words on the blanks, connecting the syllables.

1. sym-pho-ny   1. _____
2. sym-phon-ic   2. _____
3. symp-tom   3. _____
4. syn-on-y-mous 4. _____
5. syn-op-sis   5. _____
6. syn-a-gogue   6. _____
7. chron-ic   7. _____
8. chron-i-cle   8. _____
9. chron-o-log-i-cal 9. _____
10. ex-tent   10. _____
11. ex-tend   11. _____
12. ex-ten-sion   12. _____
13. ex-ter-nal   13. _____
14. ex-te-ri-or   14. _____
15. U-ru-guay   15. _____
16. Ven-e-zue-la 16. _____
17. Viet-nam   17. _____
18. West-ern Sa-mo-a 18. _____
19. Word Bank entry 19. _____
20. Word Bank entry 20. _____

134

to choose two of the words from his Word Bank and write them as this week's *Word Bank Entries*.

After you have read words 1-6 on page 134 to your student, apply generalization number one to the words in the following way, using the suggested questions and statements:

- Look at the first six words. Do you know what any of them mean? *(Your student will probably know* symphony *and* symptom. *Begin with your student's answer as to what one of the words means and lead him to the fact that the word parts* sym *and* syn *mean "together," "same," or "at the same time." Tie each of the first six words into these meanings.)*

- The following definitions will help:
  symphony: "a usually long sonata for orchestra, consisting of four related movements; a symphony orchestra"
  symphonic: "pertaining to or having the character or form of a symphony; harmonious in sound"
  symptom: "something which becomes an indication or characteristic of a condition or event"
  synonymous: "expressing a similar meaning"

synopsis: "a brief statement or outline of a subject"

synagogue: "a building or place of meeting for Jewish worship and religious instruction"

Apply generalization number two to words 7-9, using the following direction:

- Ask if your student knows the meanings of these words. The following definitions will help you lead your student to the understanding that *chron* is related to the Greek word that means "time," *khronos*.

  chronic: "of long duration; continuing; constant"

  chronicle: "a chronological record of historical events"

  chronological: "arranged in order of time of occurence"

Apply generalization number three to words 10-14, using the following questions and statements:

- Again talk with your student about the meanings of these words. Begin with one he knows and guide his definition to include the meanings "to reach or stretch out" and "outward." These come from two Latin words *extendere* and *exterus*.
- The following definitions will help:

  extent: "the range, magnitude, or distance over which a thing extends"

  extend: "to open or straighten out; to stretch or spread out to fullest length"

extension: "the act or condition of being extended"

external: "pertaining to the outside or an outer part"

exterior: "outer; external"

Introduce words 15-18 on page 134.

- Point out that the last syllable of *Uruguay* sounds like /gwī/, and *Venezuela* has two schwas.

Guide a research activity: *Where in the World?* Use a world map or an atlas to determine the location of the four countries in the spelling list. Use the *U, V,* and *W* volumes of an encyclopedia to expand your student's geographic and general country knowledge according to the ideas and optional activities presented in Unit 1.

- Ask your student to read about America's involvement in the *Vietnam* War. Provide opportunities for him to talk with men who served our country there. Direct him to find out about the Washington, D.C. memorial to the soldiers who died in this war. Ask him to find out if your community has a memorial to the Vietnam soldiers or to other soldiers who served in other wars. Visit the memorials in your area.

Use the handwritten list. After your student has written each word on the appropriate line, check his list for spelling and legibility. Instruct him to place an accent mark in each multi-syllable word of the printed list.

Second Day

Use the Bible verse activity on page 135. Make sure your student understands that a *chronicle* is a chronological record of historical events. Explain that chronological means "arranged in order of time of occurrence."

Have fun with the *Word for Word* section on page 135.

Use worktext pages 135 and 136 to reinforce word meaning and the skills of the unit. Read the directions and give help, if needed, as your student completes the pages.

Guide a word meaning activity: *Fillerup*. Provide your student with a copy of the activity found in the *Materials* section. Direct your student to use what he has learned about his spelling words to help him fill in the blanks.

---

name _____

A. Read the verse.
1. Underline the word that tells who ordered the book of records to be read.
2. Circle the three-syllable word that means "historical events."

"On that night could not the <u>king</u> sleep, and he commanded to bring the book of records of the (chronicles) and they were read before the king."   Esther 6:1

B. Find eleven spelling words in the following word search and write them on the blanks. Be sure to capitalize correctly.

order may vary.

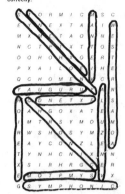

1. Vietnam
2. Uruguay
3. Western Samoa
4. Venezuela
5. chronic
6. exterior
7. symptom
8. symphony
9. extent
10. extend
11. symphonic

© 1986 Bob Jones University Press. Reproduction prohibited.

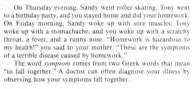

WORD FOR WORD

symptom

WELL, DOC, WHAT'S THE DIAGNOSIS?

On Thursday evening, Sandy went roller skating, Tony went to a birthday party, and you stayed home and did your homework. On Friday morning, Sandy woke up with sore muscles; Tony woke up with a stomachache; and you woke up with a scratchy throat, a fever, and a runny nose. "Homework is hazardous to my health!" you said to your mother. "These are the symptoms of a terrible disease caused by homework."

The word *symptom* comes from two Greek words that mean "to fall together." A doctor can often diagnose your illness by observing how your symptoms fall together.

135

The spelling words beginning with *syn-* and *sym-* come from the Greek *sun-* and all of them refer to some form of togetherness.

C. Choose a spelling word to go with these Greek origins.

1. *sun-* (same) + *onoma* (name)   1. synonymous
2. *sun-* (together) + *agein* (to lead)   2. synagogue
3. *sun-* (together) + *phone* (sound)   3. symphony
4. *sun-* (together) + *opsis* (view)   4. synopsis

The spelling words beginning with *chron-* are derived from a Greek word meaning "time."

D. Choose a *chron-* word from your spelling list to match each of these definitions.

1. arranged in the order of time   1. chronological
2. continuing or lasting for a long time   2. chronic
3. a record of historical events, usually in chronological order   3. chronicle

E. Choose spelling words to answer the questions below.

Which word
1. has an *a* following the prefix *syn-* instead of an *o* or a *p*?
2. contains the word *phony* but has nothing to do with being a fake?
3. contains the word *tent*?
4. contains the word *synonym*?
5. contains the word *end*?
6. begins with *c* and contains two schwa sounds (second and last syllable)?
7. begins with *e* and has an *s* and a schwa sound in the last syllable?
8. begins with *ex-* and ends with *-al*?

1. synagogue
2. symphony
3. extent
4. synonymous
5. extend
6. chronlogical
7. extension
8. external

© 1986 Bob Jones University Press. Reproduction prohibited.

Words to Master

symphony	synagogue	extend	Venezuela
symphonic	chronic	extension	Vietnam
symptom	chronicle	external	Western Samoa
synonymous	chronological	exterior	_____
synopsis	extent	Uruguay	_____

136

Third Day

Give your student time to study the words, using the study method printed on the back cover of the spelling worktext.

Dictate the word list for the trial test.

Give the following dictation sentences:

1. This **synopsis** of the play lists the events in **chronological** order.
2. The newly built **extension** to the old **symphony** hall will be ready for the next concert.
3. **External** forces have helped to shape the history of Vietnam.

> The best tool for checking the correct spelling of a word is the dictionary.

Use page 176 to teach this week's dictionary skill(s). After you are certain that your student understands the skill, guide him as he completes the exercise.

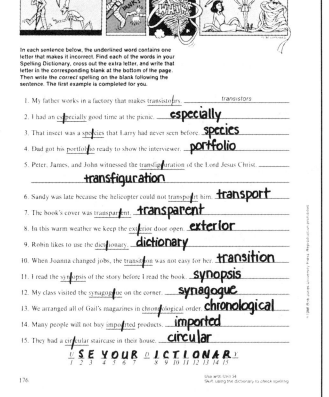

In each sentence below, the underlined word contains one letter that makes it incorrect. Find each of the words in your Spelling Dictionary, cross out the extra letter, and write that letter in the corresponding blank at the bottom of the page. Then write the *correct* spelling on the blank following the sentence. The first example is completed for you.

1. My father works in a factory that makes transistoars. _____ transistors
2. I had an especially good time at the picnic. **especially**
3. That insect was a species that Larry had never seen before. **species**
4. Dad got his portfolio ready to show the interviewer. **portfolio**
5. Peter, James, and John witnessed the transfiguration of the Lord Jesus Christ. _____
   transfiguration
6. Sandy was late because the helicopter could not transport him. **transport**
7. The book's cover was transparent. **transparent**
8. In this warm weather we keep the exterior door open. **exterior**
9. Robin likes to use the dictionary. **dictionary**
10. When Joanna changed jobs, the transition was not easy for her. **transition**
11. I read the synopsis of the story before I read the book. **synopsis**
12. My class visited the synagogue on the corner. **synagogue**
13. We arranged all of Gail's magazines in chronological order. **chronological**
14. Many people will not buy imported products. **imported**
15. They had a circular staircase in their house. **circular**

U S E   Y O U R   D I C T I O N A R Y
1 2   3   4 5 6 7   8 9 10 11 12 13 14 15

176
Use with Unit 34
Skill: using the dictionary to check spelling

Fourth Day

Return last week's journal. Give your student time to correct the misspelled words in his previous journal entry and record them in his Word Bank.

Guide the journal time using the *Journal Entry Idea* on page 137 and the information given in the front of this manual. Ask your student to suggest some promise verses such as Philippians 4:6–"in every thing by prayer and supplication with thanksgiving let your requests be made known unto God." Remind him that we are to thank God for His answers to prayer. (BATs: 6b Prayer, 8a Faith in God's promises; Bible Promise: C. Basis for prayer)

Fifth Day

Guide the study time.

Dictate the word list for the final test.

Give the following dictation sentences.

1. The **exterior** of that **synagogue** looks almost like our church building.
2. She showed every **symptom** of a **chronic** illness.
3. How far back does this **chronicle** of our town **extend?**

Use *The King's English* on page 137. After your student reads this section silently, read it with him orally. Use the Bible verses, discussion, and good comprehension questions to make certain he understands the material. The following questions can be used:

1. Why did the Jews form *synagogues?*
2. How many men were needed to form a synagogue?
3. What are the differences and similarities between a synagogue and a church?
4. What were the synagogues of the New Testament like?
5. Have you ever visited a synagogue? Can you describe it?

Journal Entry Idea

"They're back? The children are back with their parents?"

I couldn't believe it. "The kidnapers just returned them? No ransom? No injury?" An old friend had called only two days before, and we had started to pray for two little kids who had been kidnaped by men whom the police believed to be "real pros." They had asked for half a million dollars ransom!

Then we had prayed, and now I could hardly believe it when my parents told me that the kidnapers had returned the children unharmed.

Have you ever had such little faith about something you had prayed for? Tell about an answer to prayer.

The King's English

synagogue

Before King Nebuchadnezzar carried the Jews to captivity in Babylon, he destroyed the temple in Jerusalem. When the Jews returned to their land, they no longer had a place to assemble for public worship and religious instruction. Undeterred, the Jews soon formed the habit of meeting locally in small groups on Sabbath days. They called their meeting places **synagogues**. Since ten or more Jewish men could start a synagogue, the small meeting places flourished.

The synagogues of the New Testament were the centers of religious and public education for the Jews. Jesus regularly attended the synagogue as He grew up. He taught in several synagogues during His public ministry. After Paul's conversion, the apostle preached the gospel in synagogues. Even today, many Jews still meet in synagogues on the Sabbath.

Luke 4:16-22
Acts 9:20

137

Unit 35

Worktext pages 138-41
Dictionary page 177

Emphasis

Words of French origin—Many interesting words in the English language are derived from the French language. *amateur*

Materials

- A world map or atlas
- The *Y* and *Z* volumes of an encyclopedia
- Prepare the following activity for Day 2.

Match-Up

1. a small cake of minced food (*croquette*)
2. an outdoor game involving wooden balls and long-handled mallets (*croquet*)
3. a person who engages in an occupation as a pastime, not as a profession (*amateur*)
4. the man that a girl is engaged to marry (*fiancé*)
5. a castle or manor house (*chateau*)
6. a hoofed mammal or the soft material made from its hide (*chamois*)
7. to make a piece of needlework by looping thread with a hooked needle (*crochet*)
8. a chest of drawers (*bureau*)
9. a bunch of flowers (*bouquet*)
10. a feast (*banquet*)
11. a cook (*chef*)

First Day

Give the pretest. After you have given the pretest and your student has checked and corrected it, give him time to choose two of the words from his Word Bank and write them as this week's *Word Bank Entries*.

Apply the generalization to words 1-14 on page 138, using the following directions:

- Direct attention to the first paragraph under the verse at the top of worktext page 139. Ask your student to read it aloud. Mention that the English language has been adopting words from the French for almost a thousand years, ever since 1066 when the French Normans invaded and conquered England.
- Turn back to the spelling list on page 138, and slowly pronounce the words while your student listens and follows the list in his book. Point out silent letters and unusual-sounding vowel combinations. Have your student read the words orally. The following pronunciations will help.

Read each spelling word and place the accent mark over the correct syllable. Then write the words on the blanks, connecting the syllables.

1. am·a·teur
2. an·tique´
3. ban·quet´
4. bou·quet´
5. bu·reau
6. cham·ois
7. cha·teau´
8. chauf·feur
9. chef
10. cro·quette´
11. cro·quet´
12. cro·chet´
13. res·tau·rant
14. fi·an·cé´
15. Yu·go·sla·vi·a
16. Zaire
17. Zam·bi·a
18. Zim·bab·we
19. Word Bank entry
20. Word Bank entry

138

1. amateur /ăm′ ə • tûr′/
2. antique /ăn • tēk′/
3. banquet /băng′ kwĭt/
4. bouquet /bō • kā′/
5. bureau /byŏŏr′ ō/
6. chamois /shăm′ ē/
7. chateau /shă • tō′/
8. chauffeur /shō′ fər/
9. chef /shĕf/
10. croquette /krō • kĕt′/
11. croquet /krō • kā′/
12. crochet /krō • shā′/
13. restaurant /rĕs′ tər • ənt/
14. fiancé /fē • än • sā′/

- Mention the similarity in spelling between *banquet* and *bouquet*. Take time to see that your student is familiar with all the words.
- When you are talking about *fiancé*, you may want to explain that the spelling of this word changes slightly (*fiancée*) when it is used to refer to an engaged woman, but it is still pronounced in the same way.

Introduce words 15-18 on page 138.

- Note the unusual pronunciation of *Zaire* (/zī′ îr/) and the /ā/ in the last syllable of *Zimbabwe*.

Guide a research activity: *Where in the World?* Help your student locate the countries with names in the spelling list on a world atlas or map. Ask him to use the *Y* and *Z* volumes of an encyclopedia to expand his geographic and general country knowledge according to the ideas and optional activities presented in Unit 1.

- If your student has been drawing maps, writing reports, or making pictures that represent the different countries, direct him to create a book of all his materials.

Use the handwritten list. After your student has written each word on the appropriate line, check his list for spelling and legibility. Instruct him to place an accent mark in each multi-syllable word of the printed list.

Second Day

Use the Bible verse activity on page 139. Ask your student about the meaning of the expression *antiquity is of ancient days.* Also look up the meaning of the word *sojourn* and discuss what is being said in this verse. *(The general idea is that the people of this very old, ''joyous city'' will end up living far away from their homeland as part of their judgment.)*

Have fun with the *Word for Word* section on page 139.

Use worktext pages 139 and 140 to reinforce word meaning and the skills of the unit. Read the directions and give help, if needed, as your student completes the pages.

Guide word meaning activity: *Match-Up.*
Provide your student with a copy of the activity found in the *Materials* section. You could present the definitions to your student orally. Ask him to write the spelling word that matches each definition.

---

name _____

A. Read the verse.
1. Underline the word that describes the city.
2. Circle the noun that means "quality of being old."

 "Is this your joyous city, whose antiquity is of ancient days? her own feet shall carry her afar off to sojourn."   Isaiah 23:7

Pronounce each of the first fourteen spelling words in this week's list to yourself. Can you guess which language we borrowed these words from? *(French)* You will notice that many of them have silent letters at the end of the word *(bouquet, chamois)* or interesting vowel combinations that sound different from the way they are spelled.

Now read the respellings below and see if you pronounced the words correctly.

B. Write the spelling words for these respellings.

1. ăn tēk′/
2. /ăm′ ə tûr
3. /bō kā′/
4. /byŏŏr′ ō/
5. /shăm′ ē/
6. /shä tō′/
7. /shō′ fər/
8. /krō shā′/
9. /krō kā′/
10. /krō kĕt′/
11. /fē än sā′/

1. antique
2. amateur
3. bouquet
4. bureau
5. chamois
6. chateau
7. chauffeur
8. crochet
9. croquet
10. croquette
11. fiancé

WORD FOR WORD

bouquet

At some time you have probably given your mother a bouquet of flowers for her birthday or for Mother's Day. The word *bouquet* comes from a French word that means "little forest," so you could say that a bouquet of flowers is a little forest of flowers.

Have you ever watched a fireworks display that ended in a beautiful, noisy climax of several rockets all going off at once? That final great burst of fireworks is also called a bouquet: a bouquet of rockets. So be careful what kind of bouquet you hand out!

139

C. Find the misspelled words in the following paragraphs and write them correctly on the blanks below.

For lunch on Friday, Mom served tuna crokets instead of a big meal because we were going to a banqwit for amatur athletes that night. To celebrate the occasion, I bought Mom a bokay of daffodils and pretended to be her shofer as we drove into town.

They had hired a famous shef to cook the meal, but all we had was creamed chicken, peas, and some sort of gooey pudding. Then the speaker, a tall, broad-shouldered athlete, spent half of his time describing how to croshay a dresser scarf. He even advised us to trim it with anteek lace. I found out later that he's the feansay of a girl who runs a craft shop. I was pretty bored, because I don't much care what my byuro is covered with. The rest of his speech was dull too, so we were pretty disappointed when we left that fancy resterunt. Now I'm happy to stay at home and enjoy Mom's super hamburgers—any time.

1. croquettes
2. banquet
3. amateur
4. bouquet
5. chauffeur
6. chef
7. crochet
8. antique
9. fiancé
10. bureau
11. restaurant

D. Match the capital cities below with the countries on your spelling list. Your Spelling Dictionary will help.

1. Zambia
2. Zimbabwe
3. Yugoslavia
4. Zaire

1. Lusaka
2. Salisbury
3. Belgrade
4. Kinshasa

Words to Master

amateur	chamois	croquet	Zaire
antique	chateau	crochet	Zambia
banquet	chauffeur	restaurant	Zimbabwe
bouquet	chef	fiancé	
bureau	croquette	Yugoslavia	_____

140

Third Day

Give your student time to study the words, using the study method printed on the back cover of the spelling worktext.

Dictate the word list for the trial test.

Give the following dictation sentences:

1. My aunt is going to **crochet** a lace scarf for my **bureau.**
2. The prince gave a huge **banquet** at his **chateau** in **Yugoslavia.**
3. I am still only an **amateur** at the game of **croquet.**

> Dictionary skill: The dictionary is a useful proofreading tool because it can help to ensure correct spelling.

Use page 177 to teach this week's dictionary skill(s). After you are certain that your student understands the skill, guide him as he completes the exercise.

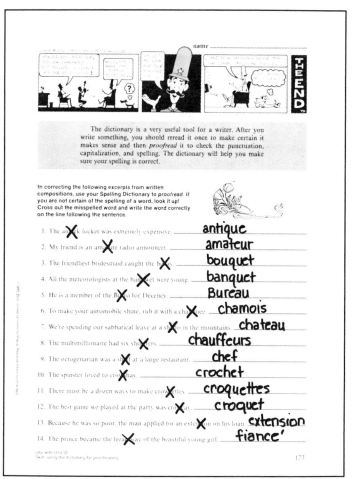

Fourth Day

Return last week's journal. Give your student time to correct the misspelled words in his previous journal entry and record them in his spelling dictionary.

Guide the journal time using the *Journal Entry Idea* on page 141 and the information given in the front of this manual. Motivate your student by encouraging him to describe some of his own funny or exciting experiences. Talk about some that you have had in your lifetime. When you have shared some laughter and funny moments and you feel your student is ready to express himself on paper, begin the writing time.

Fifth Day

Guide the study time.

Dictate the word list for the final test.

Give the following dictation sentences.
1. The **chauffeur** used a **chamois** to give the car a quick shine.
2. The **chef** in that **restaurant** makes a good tuna **croquette**.
3. My sister's **fiancé** gave her a **bouquet** of flowers for her birthday.

Use *The King's English* on page 141. After your student reads this section silently, read it with him orally. Use the Bible verses, discussion, and good comprehension questions to make certain he understands the material. The following questions can be used:
1. What does it mean to *endure* something?
2. What things have you had to endure?
3. What will endure all things according to I Corinthians?
4. Why would *love* endure all things?
5. Why is Christ "the perfect example of love"? (BAT: 1a Understanding Jesus Christ)

Journal Entry Idea

At 5:30 in the morning, as you're finishing up your paper route, you realize that you're at the home of Pouncer, the paper-boy chaser, a huge hound who hates you. Just as you stealthily lay a paper in the spot pinpointed by Mrs. Picky-about-her-paper, the familiar roar resounds through the neighborhood. You begin to run; then you notice that Pouncer is still hulking behind the fence. He's locked up! But his howl has not gone unnoticed, and like clockwork, the whole neighborhood is alive with dogs' protests. You decide to make a fast exit. Have *you* ever had an exciting or funny experience while doing a job? Tell about it.

The King's English

endure

In Latin, the word *duran* meant "hard." One who **endures** hardens himself against difficulties, determined not to be weakened by them. In II Timothy, Paul reminded the young preacher that a good soldier will endure hardship because he is made strong through the Lord Jesus.

In I Corinthians, we are told that love will endure all things. Other gifts, such as faith, knowledge, and hope, are good, but they will not endure as love will. That passage says that even when we are persecuted and endure suffering for Christ's sake, it is only profitable if we do it in love. We see, therefore, that love will enable us to endure whatever comes into our lives.

Jesus was the perfect example of love, and because of His love for us, He hardened Himself against pain and humiliation so that He could endure. We read in Hebrews 12 that Jesus endured the cross, though despising the shame, to become the author and finisher of our faith.

II Timothy 2:3
I Corinthians 13:7
Hebrews 12:2

141

Unit 36

Worktext pages 142-45

Generalization emphasis

Generalization statements can be found in Units 31-35.

Materials

- Prepare the following activity for Day 2.

The Clue Review

1. longer *(extension)*
2. Hanoi *(Vietnam)*
3. athlete *(amateur)*
4. thankfulness *(gratitude)*
5. radio *(transmitter)*
6. Kinshasa *(Zaire)*
7. disease *(symptom)*
8. Christmas *(nativity)*
9. needle *(crochet)*
10. ruler *(dictator)*
11. around *(circumference)*
12. food *(restaurant)*
13. Bern *(Switzerland)*
14. driver *(chauffeur)*
15. time *(chronological)*
16. short form *(synopsis)*

First Day

For review, apply the generalizations found in Lessons 31-35 to the word list on page 142.

Use worktext page 142 to reinforce word meaning and the skills of the unit. Read the directions and give help, if needed, as your student completes the page.

Second Day

Use the Bible verse activity on page 143. This verse refers to the beginnings (the nativity) of Israel. Read Genesis 11:31–12:5 where it tells that Abram and his wife Sarai left ''Ur of the Chaldees to go into the land of Canaan.''

Use worktext pages 143 and 144 to reinforce word meaning and the skills of the unit. Read the directions and give help, if needed, as your student completes the pages.

Guide word meaning activity: *The Clue Review.* Provide your student with a copy of the activity found in the *Materials* section. For each clue, he is to write a spelling word from this unit. Remind him to capitalize proper nouns.

B. Read the verse.
  1. Underline the name of the land that the Lord says is the land of Jerusalem's nativity.
  2. Circle the four-syllable word that has the Bible meaning "birth" or "kindred," but today means "of or pertaining to birth."

name _____

"And say, Thus saith the Lord God unto Jerusalem; Thy birth and thy nativity *is of the land of* Canaan; *thy father was an Amorite, and thy mother an Hittite."* Ezekiel 16:3

THE ANCIENT OGHAM CIPHER

This cipher was invented hundreds of years ago by the ancient Irish people. Some of their messages were carved on stone monuments in Britain that you can still visit today.

The Ogham Cipher is a substitution cipher in which straight lines, called oghams, represent certain letters of the alphabet. Below is a modernized form.

C. Decipher this message; then write it on the lines below.

NEWTRANSMITTER INCIRCULARS
HIELDFROMUGANDA;BEGINTRANSM
ISSION WHENCHAUFFEUR ENTE
RSRESTAURANT.

NEW TRANSMITTER IN CIRCULAR SHIELD FROM UGANDA;
begin transmission when chauffeur enters restaurant

143

D. Complete the following crossword puzzle with spelling words.

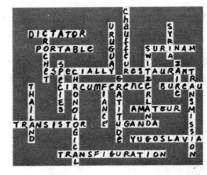

Down   **Across**

1. a person hired to drive
2. country of southeastern South America
3. country of southwestern Asia, on the Mediterranean coast
5. needlepoint done by looping thread
7. republic of west central Europe
8. a certain category or kind
9. republic of west central Africa
11. arranged according to time
13. the act of sending something
14. the state of being thankful
15. country of Southeast Asia
17. a man to whom a lady is engaged

4. a person whose rule is supreme
6. movable
7. country of northeastern South America
10. above what is common or ordinary
12. public eating place
16. the distance around a circle
18. a chest of drawers
19. the opposite of professional
20. something that carries power
21. country of east central Africa
22. republic of southeastern Europe
23. a change from one form to another

Words to Master

nativity	transistor	amateur	Syria
gratitude	transmission	bureau	Thailand
circular	transmitter	chauffeur	Turkey
circumference	transfiguration	crochet	Uganda
dictator	symptom	restaurant	Uruguay
portable	synopsis	fiancé	Vietnam
species	chronological	Surinam	Yugoslavia
especially	extension	Switzerland	Zaire

144

Third Day

Give your student time to study the words, using the study method printed on the back cover of the spelling worktext.

Dictate the word list for the trial test.

Give the following dictation sentences:
1. The young lady expressed **gratitude** to her **fiancé** for the lovely ring.
2. We ate at a very unusual **restaurant** when we were in **Switzerland.**
3. I measured the **circumference** of the circle.

Guide a spelling activity: *Country Haiku.* Use the following information to describe a haiku to your student: A haiku is a Japanese poem form with a unique pattern. There are three lines to the poem, with each line containing a specific number of syllables. Line one has five syllables, line two has seven syllables, and line three has five syllables. Direct your student to choose one of the countries that he has studied this year and write a haiku describing a distinguishing feature(s) of that country.

> Egypt, ancient land,
> The river Nile snaking past
> Pharaoh's solemn tomb.

Assist your student in mounting his final copy on colored paper, and display it for your family to see.

Fourth Day

Return last week's journal. Give your student time to correct the misspelled words in his previous journal entry and record them in his Word Bank.

Guide the journal time using the *Journal Entry Idea* on page 145 and the information given in the front of this manual. Discuss the activities, educational trips, and subjects that have been a special part of sixth grade. Remember projects, stories, books, artwork, or anything that stands out as a highlight in this past year. Share the memories until you feel your student is ready to write about them.

Fifth Day

Guide the study time.

Dictate the word list for the final test.

Journal Entry Idea

"Patrol! I liked being a patrol person!"
"What I liked was being one of the *seniors* of the elementary school!"
"Sixth-graders get the best program parts!"
"Sixth-graders get the best field trips!"
"The best part about sixth grade is knowing it's your last year in elementary school. But you sort of hate to leave, too. You have mixed feelings! It feels kind of weird."
What did you like about sixth grade? Write about it.

The King's English
transfiguration
The Latin word *transfigurare* comes from two parts: *trans*, which means "beyond," and *figura*, which means "figure." The Greek term *metamorphō* means "to change into another form."
When we speak of the **transfiguration,** we mean the historical event attended by three of Christ's disciples. Jesus took Peter, John, and James up on a high mountain to pray, but the disciples fell asleep. When the three men awoke, they saw Jesus standing with two figures: Moses and Elijah. Luke 9:29 tells us that as Jesus prayed, "the fashion of his countenance was altered, and his raiment was white and glistering."
Do you remember that when God passed before Moses, Moses' face glowed? That was the reflected brilliance of God's presence. The brightness of Jesus' transfiguration was different. This glow was not reflected. It came from Jesus Himself. As He prayed, His glory shone out from His human form. He was transformed, or changed.
Luke 9:28-36
II Peter 1:16-18
Romans 12:2

145

Give the following dictation sentences:
1. On the way to the **restaurant,** the **chauffeur** discovered that something was wrong with the **transmission** of the car.
2. This **portable transistor** radio can also be used with an **extension** cord.
3. The **dictator** of the small country spent a holiday in **Switzerland.**

Use *The King's English* on page 145. After your student reads this section silently, read it with him orally. Use the Bible verses, discussion, and good comprehension questions to make certain he understands the material. The following questions can be used:
1. What is the *transfiguration?*
2. Why do you think Jesus took the three disciples with him to the transfiguration? (BAT: 8a Faith in God's promises)
3. How was Moses' glowing face different from the brightness of Christ's transfiguration?

Spelling Generalizations

Broad Generalizations

Closed-syllable generalization–*When a short vowel is heard in a word or syllable, it is usually followed by one or more consonant letters. This is called a* closed syllable.

Silent *e* generalization–*When a long vowel is heard in a word or syllable, it is sometimes followed by a consonant letter and an* e.

Two-vowel generalization–*When a long vowel is heard in a word or syllable, it is sometimes spelled with two vowel letters. The letters* w *and* y *sometimes act as vowels in these two vowel combinations.*

Open-syllable generalization–*When a long vowel is heard in a word or syllable, it is often the last letter in the word or syllable. This is called an* open syllable.

R-influenced vowel generalization–*When /r/ is heard in a word or syllable, it is usually preceded by a vowel letter and it often influences that letter's sound.*

Specific Generalizations

Short vowel generalizations

1. /ă/

   /ă/ is usually spelled *a* in a closed syllable. *(man, last)*

2. /ĕ/
   a. /ĕ/ is usually spelled *e* in a closed syllable. *(red, mend)*
   b. /ĕ/ can be spelled *ea*. *(head)*

3. /ĭ/
   a. /ĭ/ is usually spelled *i* in a closed syllable. *(it, list)*
   b. /ĭ/ can be spelled *y*. *(myth, hymn)*

4. /ŏ/
   a. /ŏ/ is usually spelled *o* in a closed syllable. *(ox, pond)*
   b. /ŏ/ can be spelled *a* after *w*. *(watch, swat)*

5. /ŭ/
   a. /ŭ/ is usually spelled *u* in a closed syllable. *(up, budget)*
   b. /ŭ/ can be spelled *ou*. *(touch, young, rough)*

Long vowel generalizations

1. /ā/
   a. /ā/ is sometimes spelled *a + consonant + e*. *(ate, game)*
   b. /ā/ is sometimes spelled *ay* or *ey* at the end of a word or syllable. *(pay, obey)*
   c. /ā/ is sometimes spelled *ai* or *ei* before a consonant. *(paid, veil)*

2. /ē/
   a. /ē/ is sometimes spelled *e + consonant + e*. *(Pete)*
   b. /ē/ is sometimes spelled *e* at the end of a word or in an open syllable. *(me, detail)*
   c. /ē/ is sometimes spelled *i* at the end of a syllable. *(radio, serial)*
   d. /ē/ is sometimes spelled *ee* or *ea*. *(seem, tree, bead, tea)*
   e. /ē/ is sometimes spelled *ie* before a consonant *(field)*, except after *c*, when it is spelled *ei* *(receive)*.
   f. /ē/ in an unstressed syllable at the end of a word is usually spelled *y*. *(baby, happy)* It can be spelled *ey*. *(turkey)*

3. /ī/
   a. /ī/ is often spelled *i + consonant + e*. *(mice)*
   b. /ī/ in a stressed syllable at the end of a word can be spelled *y* or *ie*. *(try, supply, pie, tie)*
   c. /ī/ is sometimes spelled *y* before a consonant and an *e*. *(type)*
   d. /ī/ is sometimes spelled *i* before the consonants *ld (wild)*, *nd (find)*, and *gh (night)*.
   e. /ī/ is often spelled *igh*. *(nigh)*

4. /ō/
   a. /ō/ is often spelled *o + consonant + e*. *(hope)*
   b. /ō/ is sometimes spelled *o* at the end of a word or at the end of a stressed syllable. *(go, hotel)*
   c. /ō/ is sometimes spelled *oe* or *ow* at the end of a word or syllable *(toe, snow)* and *oa* before a consonant *(goat)*.
   d. /ō/ is sometimes spelled *o* before the consonants *ld (gold)*, *lt (colt)*, final *st (most)*, and final *th (both)*.

5. /o͞o/ **and** /yo͞o/ (**ū**)
   a. /o͞o/ and /yo͞o/ can be spelled *u + consonant + e*. *(mule, flute)*
   b. /o͞o/ and /yo͞o/ can be spelled *u* at the end of a stressed syllable. *(pupil, frugal)*
   c. /o͞o/ and /yo͞o/ is sometimes spelled *ew (newt, few, blew)* and sometimes *ue (cue, blue)*.
   d. /o͞o/ is sometimes spelled *oo*. *(boot)*

R-influenced vowel generalizations

1. /ar/

    /ar/ is usually spelled *ar*. *(shark, car)*

2. /âr/

    /âr/ is sometimes spelled *are (care)*, *air (hair)*, *ere (there)*, *ear (bear)*, and *eir (their)*.

3. /îr/

    /îr/ is sometimes spelled *ear (hear)*, *eer (deer)*, *ere (here)*, *ier (pier)*, and *eir (weird)*.

4. /īr/

    /īr/ is sometimes spelled *ire*. *(fire)*

5. /or/

    /or/ can be spelled *or (corn, horse)*, *ore (sore)*, *oar (boar, hoarse)*, *our (mourn, source)*, *oor (door)*, and *ar* after *w (dwarf)*.

6. /ûr/

    /ûr/ can be spelled *ur (survey)*, *er (eternity)*, *ear (pearl)*, *ir (thirsty)*, *our (journal)*, and *or* after *w (worthy)*.

7. /yûr/

    /yûr/ can be spelled *ure*. *(pure)*

Schwa generalizations

1. /əl/

    a. /əl/ is usually spelled *le*. *(tattle)*

    b. /əl/ can be spelled *el, al, il, ol, ul*, or *ile*. *(rebel, total, council, capitol, consul, futile)*

2. /ər/

    a. /ər/ is usually spelled *er*. *(butter)*

    b. /ər/ can be spelled *ar, ir*, or *or*. *(polar, tapir, doctor)*

3. /əs/

    /əs/ can be spelled *ace* or *ous*. *(menace, nervous)*

4. /ən/

    /ən/ can be spelled *en*. *(golden)*

5. /əns/

    /əns/ can be spelled *ence* or *ance*. *(independence, allowance)*

Special vowel generalizations

1. /o͝o/

    /o͝o/ is usually spelled *oo*. *(foot)*

2. /oi/

    a. /oi/ is usually spelled *oi* before a consonant. *(boil)*

    b. /oi/ is usually spelled *oy* at the end of a word or syllable. *(joy, royal)*

3. /ou/

    a. /ou/ is usually spelled *ou* before most consonants. *(cloud)*

    b. /ou/ is sometimes spelled *ow* before final *l* or *n* *(howl, clown)* and at the end of a word or syllable *(how, tower)*.

4. /ô/

    a. /ô/ is usually spelled *a, o*, and *au* before most consonants. *(already, cost, sauce)*

    b. /ô/ is sometimes spelled *augh* or *ough* before *t*. *(taught, bought)*

    c. /ô/ is sometimes spelled *aw* before final *k, l*, and *n (hawk, crawl, lawn)* and at the end of a word *(law)*.

Consonant generalizations

1. /b/

    /b/ is usually spelled *b* or *bb*. *(bed, tab, ebb, ribbon)*

2. /ch/

    a. /ch/ is usually spelled *ch*. *(church)*

    b. /ch/ is spelled *tch* after a short vowel at the end of a word or syllable. *(catch, crutches)*

3. /d/

    a. /d/ is usually spelled *d* or *dd*. *(dog, had, add, hidden)*

    b. /d/ is sometimes spelled *ed* when it is added to a word as a suffix. *(shared)*

4. /f/

    a. /f/ is usually spelled *f (fox, wife)* or *ff* after a short vowel at the end of a word *(gruff)*.

    b. /f/ is sometimes spelled *ph (phone)* or *gh (rough)*.

5. /g/

    a. /g/ is spelled *g* or *gg*. *(beg, egg, beggar)*

    b. /g/ is sometimes spelled *gu* at the beginning of a word. *(guess, guilt)*

    c. /gz/ is sometimes spelled *x*. *(exact)*

6. /h/

    /h/ is usually spelled *h*. *(hat)*

7. /hw/

    /hw/ is spelled *wh*. *(where, whistle)*

8. /j/

    a. /j/ at the beginning of a word is usually spelled *j* before the vowels *a, o*, and *u*. *(jack, joke, jump)*

    b. /j/ at the beginning of a word or syllable is usually spelled *g* before the vowels *e, i*, and *y*. *(gentle, giant, gym)*

    c. /j/ at the end of a word or syllable with a short vowel is usually spelled *dge*. *(budge)*

    d. /j/ at the end of a word or syllable with a long vowel is usually spelled *ge*. *(range)*

9. /k/

    a. /k/ at the beginning of a word or syllable (or after an initial *s*) is usually spelled *k* before the vowels *e, i*, and *y*. *(keep, kind, sky)*

    b. /k/ at the beginning of a word or syllable (or after an initial *s*) is usually spelled *c* before the vowels *a, o*, and *u*. *(cap, cold, cut, scare)*

    c. /k/ at the end of a one-syllable word can be spelled *k + silent e, k* after two vowels, and *k* after a consonant. *(lake, beak, bask)*

d. /k/ at the end of a word or syllable is usually spelled *ck* after a short vowel. *(pack)* It can be spelled *c*. *(picnic)*

e. /k/ is sometimes spelled *lk* at the end of a word. *(walk)*

f. /ks/ is sometimes spelled *x*. *(fox)*

g. /kw/ is sometimes spelled *qu*. *(quid)*

10. /l/

/l/ is usually spelled *l* or *ll*. *(lion, pal, will)*

11. /m/

a. /m/ is usually spelled *m* or *mm*. *(monkey, ham, mommy)*

b. /m/ is sometimes spelled *mb* at the end of a word. *(lamb, tomb)*

12. /n/

a. /n/ is usually spelled *n*. *(not, gun)*

b. /n/ is sometimes spelled *kn* or *gn*. *(know, gnat, sign)*

13. /ng/

a. /ng/ is usually spelled *ng*. *(ring, hanger)*

b. /ngk/ is spelled *nk*. *(sink)*

14. /p/

/p/ can be spelled *p* or *pp*. *(pick, tap, puppy, happy)*

15. /r/

a. /r/ can be spelled *r* or *rr*. *(red, bar, purr, furry)*

b. /r/ is often spelled *wr* at the beginning of a word. *(write)*

16. /s/

a. /s/ is usually spelled *s*. *(soap)*

b. /s/ can be spelled *c* or *sc* before *e*, *i*, and *y*. *(cent, city, cycle, scent, scythe)*

c. /s/ at the end of a final stressed syllable is usually spelled *ss* after a short vowel *(class, discuss)* or *ce* or *se* after other vowels and consonants *(nice, loose, fence, sense)*.

d. /s/ can be spelled *sc* at the beginning of a word. *(scent)*

17. /sh/

a. /sh/ is usually spelled *sh*. *(shell, crash)*

b. /sh/ can be spelled *ch*, *c*, *ci*, *ss*, or *ti*. *(machine, ocean, racial, mission, motion)*

18. /t/

/t/ can be spelled *t* or *tt*. *(tent, sit, putt, little)*

19. /th/

/th/ is spelled *th*. *(thin, three, breath)*

20. /TH/

/TH/ is usually spelled *th*. *(then, feather)*

21. /v/

a. /v/ is usually spelled *v*. *(van, cave)*

b. /v/ can be spelled *ph*. *(Stephen)*

22. /w/

/w/ is usually spelled *w*. *(wind)*

23. /y/

/y/ is usually spelled *y*. *(yes, yellow)*

24. /z/

/z/ can be spelled *zz* and *z*. *(buzz, daze)*

25. /zh/

/zh/ can be spelled *si* before final *on*. *(television)*

Double consonants

1. Consonant letters are often doubled after short vowels: *bb (robber), dd (riddle), ff (sniffle), gg (egg, beggar), ll (filly), mm (mommy), nn (funny), pp (happy), rr (furry), ss (dress, messy), tt (little, mitt), zz (fuzzy, buzz)*.

2. The letter *c* is sometimes doubled to make one sound *(occur, occasion)* and is sometimes doubled to make two sounds *(success)*.

Structural Generalizations

Broad Generalizations

1. **Recognizing Syllables**
   a. A syllable is a short word or part of a word that has a single *vowel (sound).*
   b. Every vowel (sound) in a word is in a separate syllable.
   c. Almost every syllable has a vowel (sound).

2. **Adding Suffixes**
   a. Most nouns are made plural by adding *-s.*
   b. Nouns ending in *ch, sh, s, x,* or *z* are made plural by adding *-es.*
   c. When a common noun ends in a consonant letter plus *y,* the plural is made by changing the *y* to *i* and adding *-es. (babies, skies)*
   d. Most nouns ending in *o* are made plural by adding *-es. (tomatoes)*
   e. Most nouns ending in /f/ are made plural by adding *-s. (staffs, chiefs, fifes)*
   f. Some nouns ending in /f/ are made plural by changing the *f* or *fe* to *v* and adding *-es. (leaves, knives)*
   g. Some nouns have irregular plurals. *(men, deer, mice)*
   h. When a final stressed syllable has a short vowel plus a single consonant letter, the consonant letter should be doubled before a suffix that begins with a vowel is added. *(hopped, beginning)*
   i. When a word ends in *e,* the *e* is usually dropped before a suffix beginning with a vowel. *(coming)*
   j. The final *e* before a consonant letter is not usually dropped. *(nicely)*
   k. When a word ends in a consonant letter plus *y,* change the *y* to *i* before adding a suffix that begins with any vowel other than *i. (tried, copies, glorious, flying)*
   l. When a word ends in a consonant letter plus *y,* change the *y* to *i* also before *-fy, -ful, -ness,* and sometimes other suffixes. *(glorify, beautify, beautiful, dutiful, heaviness, sleepiness, iciness, likelihood, penniless, thirtyfold, babyhood)*

3. **Dividing Words into Syllables**
   a. Dividing compound words
      1) Compound words are always divided between the main parts of compound words. *(green • house)* There may be other divisions as well. *(bas • ket • ball)*
   b. Dividing words with affixes
      1) Prefixes are usually separate syllables. *(un • do, dis • agree)*
      2) Some suffixes are separate syllables. *(go • ing, need • less, nice • ly, peach • es)*
         a) A suffix spelled *-ed* is not always a separate syllable. *(loved)*
         b) A suffix spelled *-s* is not usually a separate syllable. *(cats)*
   c. Dividing words that end with a consonant letter plus *le*
      1) When a word ends in a consonant letter plus *le,* the consonant letter usually goes with the last syllable. *(ca • ble)*
      2) When a word ends with a consonant digraph plus *le,* the digraph stays with the first syllable. *(pick • le)*
   d. Dividing words with a specific word pattern
      1) The V/V pattern–In division of words with two vowel letters together:
         a) The two vowels may represent two separate sounds that will be in two separate syllables. *(vi • o • let, cre • a • tion, pi • a • no)*
         b) Words cannot be divided between vowel letters that work together to make one sound. *(beaver)*
      2) The V/CV and VC/V patterns–In division of words with a single consonant letter between two vowels:
         a) The consonant letter often goes with the second syllable if the first vowel is long. *(fa • mous)*
         b) The consonant letter sometimes goes with the first syllable if the first vowel is short. *(fam • ish)*
      3) The VC/CV, VCC/V, and V/CCV patterns–In division of words with two consonant letters between two vowels:
         a) Words are usually divided between two identical consonant letters *(lad • der)* and between two different consonant letters *(al • ter).*
         b) Words cannot be divided between letters that form a consonant digraph. When the two consonant letters form a blend or a digraph, they will sometimes go with the first syllable *(buck • et),* and sometimes with the second *(se • cret).*
      4) The VC/CCV and VCC/CV patterns–In division of words with three consonant letters together:
         The syllable division usually occurs after the first consonant letter. *(sim • pli • fy, mon • grel)*

Bible Action Truths

The quality and consistency of a man's decisions reflect his character. Christian character begins with justification, but it grows throughout the lifelong process of sanctification. God's grace is sufficient for the task, and a major part of God's gracious provision is His Word. The Bible provides the very "words of life" that instruct us in salvation and Christian living. By obeying God's commands and making godly decisions based on His Word, Christians can strengthen their character.

Too often Christians live only by vague guidance–for instance, that we should "do good" to all men. While doing good is desirable, more specific guidance will lead to more consistent decisions.

Consistent decisions are made when man acts on Bible principles–or Bible Action Truths. The thirty-seven Bible Action Truths (listed under eight general principles) provide Christians with specific goals for their actions and attitudes. Study the Scriptures indicated for a fuller understanding of the principles in Bible Action Truths.

Thousands have found this format helpful in identifying and applying principles of behavior. Yet, there is no "magic" in this formula. As you study the Word, you likely will find other truths that speak to you. The key is for you to study the Scriptures, to look for Bible Action Truths, and to be sensitive to the leading of the Holy Spirit.

1. **Salvation–Separation Principle**
   Salvation results from God's direct action. Although man is unable to work for this "gift of God," the Christian's reaction to salvation should be to separate himself from the world unto God.
   a. **Understanding Jesus Christ** (Matthew 3:17; 16:16; I Corinthians 15:3-4; Philippians 2:9-11) Jesus is the Son of God. He was sent to earth to die on the cross for our sins. He was buried but rose from the dead after three days.
   b. **Repentance and faith** (Luke 13:3; Isaiah 55:7; Acts 5:30-31; Hebrews 11:6; Acts 16:31) If we believe that Jesus died for our sins, we can accept Him as our Saviour. We must be sorry for our sins, turn from them, confess them to God, and believe that He will forgive us.
   c. **Separation from the world** (John 17:6, 11, 14, 18; II Corinthians 6:14-18; I John 2:15-16; James 4:4; Romans 16:17-18; II John:10-11) After we are saved, we should live a different life. We should try to be like Christ and not live like those who are unsaved.

2. **Sonship–Servant Principle**
   Only by an act of God the Father could sinful man become a son of God. As a son of God, however, the Christian must realize that he has been "bought with a price"; he is now Christ's servant.
   a. **Authority** (Romans 13:1-7; I Peter 2:13-19; I Timothy 6:1-5; Hebrews 13:17; Matthew 22:21; I Thessalonians 5:12-13) We should respect, honor, and obey those in authority over us.
   b. **Servanthood** (Philippians 2:7-8; Ephesians 6:5-8) Just as Christ was a humble servant while He was on earth, we should also be humble and obedient.
   c. **Faithfulness** (I Corinthians 4:2; Matthew 25:23; Luke 9:62) We should do our work so that God and others can depend on us.
   d. **Goal setting** (Proverbs 13:12, 19; Philippians 3:13; Colossians 3:2; I Corinthians 9:24) To be faithful servants, we must set goals for our work. We should look forward to finishing a job and going on to something more.
   e. **Work** (Ephesians 4:28; II Thessalonians 3:10-12) God never honors a lazy servant. He wants us to be busy and dependable workers.
   f. **Enthusiasm** (Colossians 3:23; Romans 12:11) We should do *all* tasks with energy and with a happy, willing spirit.

3. **Uniqueness–Unity Principle**
   No one is a mere person; God has created each individual a unique being. But because God has an overall plan for His creation, each unique member must contribute to the unity of the entire body.
   a. **Self-concept** (Psalm 8:3-8; 139; II Corinthians 5:17; Ephesians 2:10; 4:1-3, 11-13; II Peter 1:10) We are special creatures in God's plan. He has given each of us special abilities to use in our lives for Him.
   b. **Mind** (Philippians 2:5; 4:8; II Corinthians 10:5; Proverbs 23:7; Luke 6:45; Proverbs 4:23; Romans 7:23, 25; Daniel 1:8; James 1:8) We should give our hearts and minds to God. What we do and say really begins in our minds. We should try to think of ourselves humbly as Christ did when He lived on earth.
   c. **Emotional control** (Galatians 5:24; Proverbs 16:32; 25:28; II Timothy 1:7; Acts 20:24) With the help of God and the power of the Holy Spirit, we should have control over our feelings. We must be careful not to act out of anger.
   d. **Body as a temple** (I Corinthians 3:16-17; 6:19-20) We should remember that our bodies are the dwelling place of God's Holy Spirit. We should keep ourselves pure, honest, and dedicated to God's will.
   e. **Unity of Christ and the church** (John 17:21; Ephesians 2:19-22; 5:23-32; II Thessalonians 3:6, 14-15) Since we are saved, we are now part of God's family and should unite ourselves with others to worship and grow as Christians. Christ is the head of His Church, which includes all believers. He wants us to work together as His church in carrying out His plans, but He forbids us to work in fellowship with disobedient brethren.

4. Holiness–Habit Principle

Believers are declared holy as a result of Christ's finished action on the cross. Daily holiness of life, however, comes from forming godly habits. A Christian must consciously establish godly patterns of action; he must develop habits of holiness.

   a. **Sowing and reaping** (Galatians 6:7-8; Hosea 8:7; Matthew 6:1-8) We must remember that we will be rewarded according to the kind of work we have done. If we are faithful, we will be rewarded. If we are unfaithful, we will not be rewarded. We cannot fool God.

   b. **Purity** (I Thessalonians 4:1-7; I Peter 1:22) We should try to live lives that are free from sin. We should keep our minds, words, and deeds clean and pure.

   c. **Honesty** (II Corinthians 8:21; Romans 12:17; Proverbs 16:8; Ephesians 4:25) We should not lie. We should be honest in every way. Even if we could gain more by being dishonest, we should still be honest. God sees all things.

   d. **Victory** (I Corinthians 10:13; Romans 8:37; I John 5:4; John 16:33; I Corinthians 15:57-58) If we constantly try to be pure, honest, and Christ-like, with God's help we will be able to overcome temptations.

5. Love–Life Principle

We love God because He first loved us. God's action of manifesting His love to us through His Son demonstrates the truth that love must be exercised. Since God acted in love toward us, believers must act likewise by showing godly love to others.

   a. **Love** (I John 3:11, 16-18; 4:7-21; Ephesians 5:2; I Corinthians 13; John 15:17) God's love to us was the greatest love possible. We should, in turn, show our love for others by our words and actions.

   b. **Giving** (II Corinthians 9:6-8; Proverbs 3:9-10; Luke 6:38) We should give cheerfully to God the first part of all we earn. We should also give to others unselfishly.

   c. **Evangelism and missions** (Psalm 126:5-6; Matthew 28:18-20; Romans 1:16-17; II Corinthians 5:11-21) We should be busy telling others about the love of God and His plan of salvation. We should share in the work of foreign missionaries by our giving and prayers.

   d. **Communication** (Ephesians 4:22-29; Colossians 4:6; James 3:2-13; Isaiah 50:4) We should have control of our tongues so that we will not say things displeasing to God. We should encourage others and be kind and helpful in what we say.

   e. **Friendliness** (Proverbs 18:24; 17:17; Psalm 119:63) We should be friendly to others, and we should be loyal to those who love and serve God.

6. Communion–Consecration Principle

Because sin separates man from God, any communion between man and God must be achieved by God's direct action of removing sin. Once communion is established, the believer's reaction should be to maintain a consciousness of this fellowship by living a consecrated life.

   a. **Bible study** (I Peter 2:2-3; II Timothy 2:15; Psalm 119) To grow as Christians we must spend time with God daily by reading His Word.

   b. **Prayer** (I Chronicles 16:11; I Thessalonians 5:17; John 15:7, 16; 16:24; Psalm 145:18; Romans 8:26-27) We should bring all our requests to God, trusting Him to answer them in His own way.

   c. **Spirit-filled** (Ephesians 5:18-19; Galatians 5:16, 22-23; Romans 8:13-14; I John 1:7-9) We should let the Holy Spirit rule in our hearts and show us what to say and do. We should not say and do just what we want to do, for those things are often wrong and harmful to others.

   d. **Clear conscience** (I Timothy 1:19; Acts 24:16) To be good Christians, we cannot have wrong acts or thoughts or words bothering our consciences. We must confess them to God and to those people against whom we have sinned. We cannot live lives close to God if we have guilty consciences.

   e. **Forgiveness** (Ephesians 4:30-32; Luke 17:3-4; Colossians 3:13; Matthew 18:15-17; Mark 11:25-26) We must ask forgiveness of God when we have done wrong. Just as God forgives our sins freely, we should forgive others when they do wrong things to us.

7. Grace–Gratitude Principle

Grace is unmerited favor. Man does not deserve God's grace. However, after God bestows His grace, believers should react with an overflow of gratitude.

   a. **Grace** (I Corinthians 15:10; Ephesians 2:8-9) Without God's grace we would be sinners on our way to hell. He loved us when we did not deserve His love and provided for us a way to escape sin's punishment by the death of His Son on the cross.

   b. **Exaltation of Christ** (Colossians 1:12-21; Ephesians 1:17-23; Philippians 2:9-11; Galatians 6:14; Hebrews 1:2-3; John 1:1-4, 14; 5:23) We should realize and remember at all times the power, holiness, majesty, and perfection of Christ, and we should give Him the praise and glory for everything that is accomplished through us.

   c. **Praise** (Psalm 107:8; Hebrews 13:15; I Peter 2:9; Ephesians 1:6; I Chronicles 16:23-36; 29:11-13) Remembering God's great love and goodness toward us, we should continually praise His name.

d. **Contentment** (Philippians 4:11; I Timothy 6:6-8; Psalm 77:3; Proverbs 15:16; Hebrews 13:5) Money, houses, cars, and all things on earth will last only for a little while. God has given us just what He meant for us to have. We should be happy and content with what we have, knowing that God will provide for us all that we need. We should also be happy wherever God places us.

e. **Humility** (I Peter 5:5-6; Philippians 2:3-4) We should not be proud and boastful but should be willing to be quiet and in the background. Our reward will come from God on Judgment Day, and men's praise to us here on earth will not matter at all. Christ was humble when He lived on earth, and we should be like Him.

8. **Power—Prevailing Principle**

Believers can prevail only as God gives the power. "I can do all things through Christ." God is the source of our power used in fighting the good fight of faith.

a. **Faith in God's promises** (II Peter 1:4; Philippians 4:6; Romans 4:16-21; I Thessalonians 5:18; Romans 8:28; I Peter 5:7; Hebrews 3:18-4:11) God always remains true to His promises. Believing that He will keep all the promises in His Word, we should be determined fighters for Him.

b. **Faith in the power of the Word of God** (Hebrews 4:12; Jeremiah 23:29; Psalm 119; I Peter 1:23-25) God's Word is powerful and endures forever. All other things will pass away, but God's Word shall never pass away because it is written to us from God, and God is eternal.

c. **Fight** (Ephesians 6:11-17; II Timothy 4:7-8; I Timothy 6:12; I Peter 5:8-9) God does not have any use for lazy or cowardly fighters. We must work and fight against sin, using the Word of God as our weapon against the Devil. What we do for God now will determine how much He will reward us in heaven.

d. **Courage** (I Chronicles 28:20; Joshua 1:9; Hebrews 13:6; Ephesians 3:11-12; Acts 4:13, 31) God has promised us that He will not forsake us; therefore, we should not be afraid to speak out against sin. We should remember that we are armed with God's strength.

Bible Promises

A. **Liberty from Sin**—Born into God's spiritual kingdom, a Christian is enabled to live right and gain victory over sin through faith in Christ. (Romans 8:3-4—"For what the law could not do, in that it was weak through the flesh, God sending his own Son in the likeness of sinful flesh, and for sin, condemned sin in the flesh: that the righteousness of the law might be fulfilled in us, who walk not after the flesh, but after the Spirit.'')

B. **Guiltless by the Blood**—Cleansed by the blood of Christ, the Christian is pardoned from the guilt of his sins. He does not have to brood or fret over his past because the Lord has declared him righteous. (Romans 8:33—"Who shall lay any thing to the charge of God's elect? It is God that justifieth." Isaiah 45:24—"Surely, shall one say, in the Lord have I righteousness and strength: even to him shall men come; and all that are incensed against him shall be ashamed.'')

C. **Basis for Prayer**—Knowing that his righteousness comes entirely from Christ and not from himself, the Christian is free to plead the blood of Christ and to come before God in prayer at any time. (Romans 5:1-2—"Therefore being justified by faith, we have peace with God through our Lord Jesus Christ: by whom also we have access by faith into this grace wherein we stand, and rejoice in hope of the glory of God.'')

D. **Identified in Christ**—The Christian has the assurance that God sees him as a son of God, perfectly united with Christ. He also knows that he has access to the strength and the grace of Christ in his daily living. (Galatians 2:20—"I am crucified with Christ: nevertheless, I live; yet not I, but Christ liveth in me: and the life which I now live in the flesh I live by the faith of the Son of God, who loved me, and gave himself for me." Ephesians 1:3—"Blessed be the God and Father of our Lord Jesus Christ, who hath blessed us with all spiritual blessings in heavenly places in Christ.'')

E. **Christ as Sacrifice**—Christ was a willing sacrifice for the sins of the world. His blood covers every sin of the believer and pardons the Christian for eternity. The purpose of His death and resurrection was to redeem a people to Himself. (Isaiah 53:4-5—"Surely he hath borne our griefs, and carried our sorrows: yet we did esteem him stricken, smitten of God, and afflicted. But he was wounded for our transgressions, he was bruised for our iniquities: the chastisement of our peace was upon him; and with his stripes we are healed." John 10:27-28—"My sheep hear my voice, and I know them, and they follow me: and I give unto them eternal life; and they shall never perish, neither shall any man pluck them out of my hand.'')

F. **Christ as Intercessor**–Having pardoned them through His blood, Christ performs the office of High Priest in praying for His people. (Hebrews 7:25–"Wherefore he is able also to save them to the uttermost that come unto God by him, seeing he ever liveth to make intercession for them." John 17:20–"Neither pray I for these alone, but for them also which shall believe on me through their word.")

G. **Christ as Friend**–In giving salvation to the believer, Christ enters a personal, loving relationship with the Christian that cannot be ended. This relationship is understood and enjoyed on the believer's part through fellowship with the Lord through Bible reading and prayer. (Isaiah 54:5–"For thy Maker is thine husband; the Lord of hosts is his name; and thy Redeemer the Holy One of Israel; The God of the whole earth shall he be called." Romans 8:38-39–"For I am persuaded, that neither death, nor life, nor angels, nor principalities, nor powers, nor things present, nor things to come, nor height, nor depth, nor any other creature, shall be able to separate us from the love of God, which is in Christ Jesus our Lord.")

H. **God as Father**–God has appointed Himself to be responsible for the well-being of the Christian. He both protects and nourishes the believer, and it was from Him that salvation originated. (Isaiah 54:17–"No weapon that is formed against thee shall prosper; and every tongue that shall rise against thee in judgment thou shalt condemn. This is the heritage of the servants of the Lord, and their righteousness is of me, saith the Lord." Psalm 103:13–"Like as a father pitieth his children, so the Lord pitieth them that fear him.")

I. **God as Master**–God is sovereign over all creation. He orders the lives of His people for His glory and their good. (Romans 8:28–"And we know that all things work together for good to them that love God, to them who are the called according to his purpose.")

Glossary

accent mark   A small dark line slanting toward the stressed syllable as shown in the respelling of a dictionary entry word. *beaver, /bē′ vər/*

Note: Sometimes a word with multiple syllables has both a dark and a light mark representing a primary (dark) and a secondary (light) accent. *backbone, băk′ bōn; Deuteronomy, /doo′ tə • rŏn′ ə • mē/*

affix   A word element (prefix or suffix) put at the beginning or end of a base word, changing the meaning of the base word. *un-, unhappy*

base word   The basic word to which a prefix or a suffix can be added. *sing, singing*

blend   A cluster of two or more consonant letters that are pronounced together as a blend one after the other at the beginning or end of a syllable, as *br* in *brown* or *nd* in *send.*

breve   The small, half-circle mark found above a short vowel to show its pronunciation. */kăt/, cat*

Note: The universal pronunciation of a vowel *is* its short sound; therefore, in most dictionaries, when a vowel appears in a word without a diacritical marking, it should be pronounced as a short vowel.

circumflex   The small carat marking found above a vowel to show its pronunciation. */kâr/, care*

closed syllable   A syllable that has one vowel letter and ends with a consonant. */băn′ dĭt/*

compound word   A word made up of two independent words–base words–that lend their meanings to create a new, related meaning. *sunset; sun, set*

consonant   A speech sound that is made when two parts of the mouth touch each other or come close together to slow the flow of air. *c* and *t* in *cat*

consonant letters and vowel letters   Categories that all letters of the alphabet fall into. *vowel letters (a, e, i, o, u), consonant letters (all the other letters).*

diacritical marking   The marking over a letter that tells how to pronounce it.

dieresis   The small set of double dots placed over a vowel to show its pronunciation. /chär ′ kōl/, charcoal

digraph   A combination of letters representing a single sound, as the vowel digraph *ea* in the word *sea* and the consonant digraph *ch* in the word *church*.

diphthong   A combination of vowels in which the sound begins on one vowel and moves to the other. *oy* in *boy*

generalization   A general statement about a particular phonetic or structural spelling pattern.

inductive teaching   A method of teaching whereby a student is stimulated through observation, questions, and discussion to apply logical reasoning and form a general principle.

macron   The short horizontal bar located over a long vowel to show how it is pronounced. /līk/, like

multisyllable word   A word containing several syllables.

open syllable   A syllable that ends with a long vowel, as the first syllable in Bible, /Bī′ bəl/.

phonogram   A group of letters representing the sound a vowel and the consonant(s) following it make in a syllable, as *at* in *cat*, *oon* in *moon*, and *old* in *cold*.

prefix   An affix added to the beginning of a base word which changes the meaning of the word. *un-, unjust*

pretest   A test given prior to the introduction of new material, serving as the initial contact with the information and providing a base of relevancy for the information gained.

pronunciation key   The box found on a dictionary page that shows how individual vowels and consonants are pronounced.

ă	pat	ĕ	pet
ā	pay	ē	be
â	care	ĭ	pit
ä	father	ī	pie
î	fierce	oi	**oil**
ŏ	pot	o͝o	book
ō	go	o͞o	boot
ô	paw,	yo͞o	abuse
	for	ou	**out**
ŭ	cut	zh	vision
û	fur	ə	ago, item,
th	the		pencil, atom,
th	thin		circus
hw	which	ər	butter

r-influenced vowel   A vowel that is followed by an *r*, thereby having its sound influenced by the *r*. *cart, fort, bird, hurt, term*

respelling   The phonetic spelling following an entry word in the dictionary that gives only the sounds heard in the word and using symbols identified in the pronunciation key. *refill, /rē • fĭl′/*

schwa   A sound in an unstressed syllable that is pronounced *uh* no matter how it is spelled, as *a* in *ago*, *e* in *item*, *i* in *pencil*, *o* in *atom*, and *u* in *circus*.
Note: Sometimes an unstressed syllable has the sound of a short *i. quiet, /kwī ′ ĭt/*

semivowel letters: Those letters that are sometimes used as vowels and sometimes as consonants: *y* and *w*.

short vowel The following are examples of short vowels: /ă/ (as in *pat*), /ĕ/ (as in *pet*), /ĭ/ (as in *pit*), /ŏ/ (as in *pot*), /ŭ/ (as in *cut*).

stressed syllable   The syllable in a word that receives more voice stress or emphasis than the others and is followed by an accent mark, as the first syllable in *salad*, /săl′ əd/.

suffix   An affix put at the end of word to form a new word or show a grammatical function. *-er, sweeter; -ing, running*

syllable   Each part of a word that contains a vowel. /dy • nam′ ic/

VCCV   Stands for a pattern within a word–*Vowel, Consonant, Consonant, Vowel. happy, collar*
Note: Other such representations used are *VCV, VV.*

vowel   A speech sound made by the breath passing through the mouth freely without being cut off or blocked and determined by the shape of the mouth. /ō/

word family   A group of words that all end with the same phonogram, as in *night, light,* and *fight.*